Bergson

Also Available from Bloomsbury

Nietzsche's Search for Philosophy, Keith Ansell-Pearson
Nietzsche and Political Thought, edited by Keith Ansell-Pearson
Key Writings, Henri Bergson

Bergson

Thinking Beyond the Human Condition

By Keith Ansell-Pearson

Bloomsbury Academic
An imprint of Bloomsbury Publishing Plc

B L O O M S B U R Y
LONDON · OXFORD · NEW YORK · NEW DELHI · SYDNEY

Bloomsbury Academic

An imprint of Bloomsbury Publishing Plc

50 Bedford Square	1385 Broadway
London	New York
WC1B 3DP	NY 10018
UK	USA

www.bloomsbury.com

BLOOMSBURY and the Diana logo are trademarks of Bloomsbury Publishing Plc

First published 2018

© Keith Ansell-Pearson, 2018

Keith Ansell-Pearson has asserted his right under the Copyright, Designs and
Patents Act, 1988, to be identified as Author of this work.

British Library Cataloguing-in-Publication Data
A catalogue record for this book is available from the British Library.

ISBN: HB: 978-1-3500-4394-7
PB: 978-1-3500-4395-4
ePDF: 978-1-3500-4396-1
ePub: 978-1-3500-4397-8

Library of Congress Cataloguing-in-Publication Data
Names: Ansell-Pearson, Keith, 1960- author.
Title: Bergson: thinking beyond the human condition / by Keith Ansell-Pearson.
Description: New York: Bloomsbury Academic, 2018. |
Includes bibliographical references and index.
Identifiers: LCCN 2017042660 (print) | LCCN 2017051819 (ebook) |
ISBN 9781350043961 (PDF eBook) | ISBN 9781350043978 (EPUB eBook) |
ISBN 9781350043947 (hardback: alk. paper) | ISBN 9781350043954 (pbk.: alk. paper)
Subjects: LCSH: Bergson, Henri, 1859-1941.
Classification: LCC B2430.B43 (ebook) | LCC B2430.B43 A568 2018 (print) | DDC 194–dc23
LC record available at https://lccn.loc.gov/2017042660

Cover image © Andrew Wyeth, *Soaring*, 1942-1950. Tempera on masonite, 48 x 87 in.
Collection of Shelburne Museum, museum purchase, acquired from Maxim Karolik.
1961-186.6. Photography by J. David Bohl. / ARS, NY and DACS, London 2017

Typeset by Deanta Global Publishing Services, Chennai, India
Printed and bound in Great Britain

To pierce the mystery of the deep, it is sometimes necessary to regard the heights. It is earth's hidden fire which appears at the summit of the volcano.

—(Bergson 'Life and Consciousness', the Huxley lecture delivered in the University of Birmingham, May 24, 1911).

Contents

Acknowledgements

This book derives from work I have been doing over the past two decades on Bergson's writings in the form of lecture courses, workshop contributions, public lectures, and publications. I have been helped and inspired in my appreciation and understanding of Bergson by readers and scholars working in Australia, France, Japan, the United Kingdom, and the United States, including Alia Al-Saji, Hisashi Fujita, Elisabeth Grosz, Pete Gunter, Suzanne Guerlac, Tatsuya Higaki, Michael R. Kelly, Wahida Khandker, Michael Kolkman, David Lapoujade, Leonard Lawlor, Alexandre Lefebvre, Paul-Antoine Miquel, John O. Maoilearca, Jim Urpeth, Michael Vaughan, and Frederic Worms. For the academic year 2013–14 I had the good fortune of being a Visiting Senior Research Fellow in the Humanities Research Centre at Rice University. This fellowship enabled me to enrich my understanding of the history of materialism and vitalism, and provided me with the time needed to carry out much of the research that has gone into the writing of this book. For instruction and inspiration I wish to extend my heartfelt thanks to the members of the Rice Seminar, where I participated in a seminar on old and new materialisms, especially to my hosts Sarah Ellenzweig and Jack Zammito. My University, Warwick, generously provided me with sabbatical leave in 2017, and this enabled me to complete this study. Thanks are also due to my editors at Bloomsbury, Liza Thompson and Frankie Mace, for their unwavering support and enthusiasm. Finally, thanks are due to my colleagues at Warwick, especially Miguel Beistegui and Stephen Houlgate, for their friendship, to my brother Trevor and my sister Diane for love and support, and last, and most important of all, to my wife, Nicky, and to Jasmine and Rick, for their tremendous love.

Chapter 1 is a modified version of an essay that first appeared in *The Routledge Companion to Nineteenth Century Philosophy* (Routledge, 2010), edited by Dean Moyar. Chapter 2 first appeared in *Pli: The Warwick Journal of Philosophy*, volume 27, 2015, edited by Dino Jakusic. Chapter 3 has been especially written for this study, though for some sections I draw on material first presented in chapter 1 of my book, *Bergson and the Time of Life* (Routledge, 2002). Chapter 4 was first published in Susannah Radstone and Bill Schwarz (eds.), *Memory: Histories,*

Theories, Debates (New York: Fordham University Press, 2010). Chapter 5 was first published in the *Journal of French and Francophone Philosophy*, volume XXIV: 2, 2016, guest edited by Mark Westmoreland. Chapter 6 is a modified version of an essay that first appeared in *Continental Philosophy Review*, 47:1, 2014. Chapter 7, co-authored with Jim Urpeth, was first published in Alexandre Lefebvre and Melanie White (eds.), *Bergson, Politics, and Religion* (Duke University Press, 2012). Chapter 8 was first published in Adam Bartlett, Justin Clemens, Jessica Whyte (eds.), *What is Education?* (Edinburgh University Press, 2017). I express my thanks to the editors and publishers of these publications for permission to republish material in this study. Each chapter has been edited and finessed for the purposes of this study. I wish to apologize to the reader for some repetition that characterizes the book. I have sought to keep this to a minimum and trust it does not spoil the reader's pleasure in encountering the book.

List of Abbreviations and Editions Used

BKW   *Bergson Key Writings*, ed. Keith Ansell-Pearson and John Mullarkey (London: Bloomsbury Press, 2014, second edition).

CE   *Creative Evolution*, trans. Arthur Mitchell (Lanham, MD: University Press of America, 1983).

CM   *Creative Mind*, trans. M. L. Andison (Totowa, NJ: Littlefield, Adams & Co., 1965).

DS   *Duration and Simultaneity*, ed. Robin Durie (Manchester: Clinamen Press, 2000).

IM   *Introduction to Metaphysics*, trans. T. E. Hulme (Basingstoke: Palgrave Macmillan, 2007).

M   *Mélanges* (Paris, Presses Universitaires de France, 1972).

ME   *Mind Energy*, trans. H. Wildon Carr (Basingstoke: Palgrave Macmillan, 2007).

MM   *Matter and Memory*, trans. N. M. Paul and W. S. Palmer (New York: Zone Books, 1991).

O   *Oeuvres* (Paris, Presses Universitaires de France, 1959).

TFW   *Time and Free Will*, trans. F. L. Pogson (New York: Dover, 2001).

TSMR   *The Two Sources of Morality and Religion*, trans. R. Ashley Audra and Cloudesley Brereton with the assistance of W. Horsfall Carter (Notre Dame, IN: University of Notre Dame Press, 1977).

Introduction: Thinking Beyond the Human Condition

This book seeks to make a contribution that will aid the teaching of, and research into, Bergson's texts in the English-speaking world. These are texts that have exerted an influence on several generations of French thinkers, including some of the most important philosophers of the twentieth century, such as Vladimir Jankélévitch, Jean-Paul Sartre, Simone de Beauvoir, Maurice Merleau-Ponty, Emmanuel Levinas, Paul Ricoeur, and Gilles Deleuze. In contrast to Nietzsche who accurately predicted that he would be born posthumously, Bergson was the most celebrated philosopher of his time with an influence on intellectual life that extended far beyond the academic world. However, his reputation fell into serious decline after his death and the end of the Second World War, when existentialism quickly established itself as the new intellectual fashion. Today, however, we are witnessing a serious renaissance of interest in Bergson's writings, and his contributions figure in new research in the philosophy of mind, the philosophy of time, and the philosophy of biology, such as complexity theory. In addition, he is now granted a place of crucial significance in histories of twentieth-century thought. Gary Gutting, for example, locates Bergson's enduring greatness as a philosopher in the combination of descriptive concreteness and systematic scope and metaphysical ambition that characterizes his work.[1] Although Bergson possessed tremendous knowledge of the history of philosophy – he was in his lifetime a professor of both ancient philosophy and modern philosophy – he was primarily interested in problems and in ascertaining whether our problems are well posed or badly posed, whether our problems are ones to be resolved or to be *dissolved*. Merleau-Ponty notes that for Bergson many traditional questions of philosophy, such as 'Why have I been born?' 'Why is there something rather than nothing?' and 'How can I know anything?' can be held to be pathological in the sense that they presuppose a subject already installed in being, that is, they are the questions of a doubter who no longer knows whether he has closed the window.[2] All of Bergson's major concerns closely correspond to today's practice in philosophy, and there is nothing that is peculiarly 'continental' about his interests that range from inquiry into the nature of freedom and time to consideration of questions about life and evolution.

A number of important thinkers have found liberation in Bergson's attempt to reform philosophy, and in considering afresh the nature of his reformation of philosophy it is helpful to bear in mind this previous impact so we can continue to draw inspiration from it. These thinkers include William James, who said that it was Bergson who liberated him from intellectualism. For James, this consists in a critique of the view that 'mere conceptual logic can tell us what is impossible or possible in the world of being or fact'.[3] James notes that for Bergson the function of the intellect is practical, not theoretical (on this point Bergson follows in the footsteps of thinkers such as Schopenhauer and Nietzsche). James also offered astute appreciation of the texts. He compared what Bergson accomplished in *Matter and Memory* to a Copernican revolution and considered it with some justification a work to be ranked alongside Berkeley's *Principles of Human Knowledge* and Kant's *Critique of Pure Reason*. He hailed the publication of *Creative Evolution* as marking a new era in thought and considered it to be 'a real wonder in the history of philosophy'.[4] Gilles Deleuze locates in Bergson's writings a 'superior empiricism' that can prove its contemporary worth and relevance.[5] Emmanuel Levinas argues that against our pan-logical civilization Bergsonism brings to bear an inestimable message, namely its perception of a mode of change which does not stop at any identity and teaches that time is something other than a mobile image of an immobile eternity, which is what it has been in the history of Western thought, signifying the forfeiture of the permanence of being and the privation of eternity. Levinas thus wishes to underline the importance of Bergsonism 'for the entire problematic of contemporary philosophy' on account of the fact that it is no longer a thought of a 'rationality revealing a reality which keeps to the very measure of a thought'. In effecting a reversal of traditional philosophy by contending the priority of duration over permanence, Bergson has provided thought with 'access to novelty, an access independent of the ontology of the same'.[6]

At the centre of Bergson's intellectual endeavour is an attempt to reform philosophy so as to steer it in a novel direction, one that brings it into close rapport with positive science and so as to give us, with renewed vigour, access to the absolute. It is, however, a modest enterprise of philosophy driven by empiricism in as much as it is contra abstract ideas (Kant) and geometrical reasoning (Spinoza). For Bergson, the idea that we need a critique of the faculty of knowledge before we go in search of knowledge – that is, analysing the mechanism of thought before seeking knowledge– is sterile and will never take us to where we want to go. He also considers the idea that we can anticipate experience by the force of reasoning alone, and by constructing an iron-bound system of thought, to be a failure of empirical thought and mental attentiveness. Instead of imposing on reality a rigid and diagrammatic idea we should instead aim to follow 'the sinuous and mobile contours' of reality (ME 3). We can then better deal with the questions that inspire our minds: Whence are we? What we are? And whither do we tend? The aim is not to have immediate certainty, as this could only be ephemeral, but to educate the mind by showing the value of taking one's time: 'Borne along in an experience growing ever wider and wider, rising to ever higher and higher probabilities, it would strive towards final certainty as to a limit' (ME 3). The philosopher, as Bergson understands him, is not after a mathematical deduction of reality or out to discover a decisive fact that would clinch the matter and dissolve all problems. Rather, as philosophers, we need to acknowledge that there are different regions of experience and in them there is to be found different groups of facts. Philosophy exists to do justice to these different regions and groups. Bergson, then, wants to establish a new philosophy on the model of positive science and insists that it be a work of collaboration. If we accept that there are different regions of experience that merit our attention, then philosophy is not simply a work of construction, say by an individual genius, or the systematic work of a single thinker. Bergson produces a method of thought that is open to correction, revision, and transformation.

Bergson posits lofty goals for philosophy, but these goals can be seen to be part of philosophy's traditional aspirations, including the effort to enhance our power to act and to live. 'Good sense' should teach us the unity of thought and action. At the same time as pursuing these ventures Bergson restores philosophy's ancient commitment to attaining a cosmic perspective and expanding our perception of the universe. My own experience of encountering Bergson is similar to the one described by Pierre Hadot, who noted that for him as a young student of philosophy at the Sorbonne, 'Bergsonism was not an abstract, conceptual philosophy, but rather took the form of a new way of seeing the world.'[7] For Bergson, there is a need to break with sedimented habits of thoughts, including and especially spatializing habits, that prevent the adequate conception of ourselves as beings of time (duration). In seeking to disclose the world to us afresh I see Bergson as a philosopher akin to Nietzsche's description of the ancient Greek philosophers: each cultivated a singular vision and dedication to a new way of looking at the world and creating a new perspective on it. As he memorably puts it: 'Each one of these philosophers simply saw the world come into being!'[8] This is echoed in Merleau-Ponty's insight into Bergson's philosophy: in unveiling the perceived world 'along with nascent duration, Bergson rediscovers in the heart of man a pre-Socratic and "prehuman" sense of the world'.[9]

Bergson seeks to reorient metaphysics, to bring science and philosophy into a new rapport, with the ultimate aim of reconnecting human thought and existence to, as Gilles Deleuze puts it, the 'universal consciousness' of the whole (*le Tout*).[10] Indeed, in *Creative Evolution* Bergson conceives philosophy as an effort to dissolve again into the whole (CE 191). The whole for Bergson is, in essence, universal mobility and universal interaction. As such, the whole is never, and can never be, given. Of course, this fact presents an extraordinary challenge to our ingrained habits of thinking. Deleuze stresses that the whole enjoys neither interiority nor totality; individuated forms of life have a tendency towards closure but this is never accomplished. As Deleuze emphasizes, that the whole is not given should meet with our delight – it is only our habitual confusion of time with space, and the assimilation of time into space, that makes us think the whole is given, if only in the eyes of God.[11]

That Bergson's thinking orients itself around a philosophy of life is not an incidental feature but an absolutely fundamental aspect. It is from the primacy that is to be accorded to life that adequate conceptions of the rest of philosophy can be developed such as metaphysics, epistemology, and ethics. 'Intelligence reabsorbed into its principle, may thus live back again in its genesis' (CE 123). Such a method of thinking has to work against the most inveterate habits of the mind and consists in an interchange of insights that correct and add to each other. For Bergson, as Deleuze notes, such an enterprise ends by expanding the humanity within us and so allows humanity to surpass itself by reinserting itself in the whole. This is accomplished through philosophy, for it is philosophy that provides us with the means (methods) for reversing the normal directions of the mind (instrumental, utilitarian), so upsetting its habits. Bergson conceives the going beyond or surpassing of the human condition, namely the ambition to restore the absolute and the whole, as the legitimate object of philosophy's quest. Why should we feel motivated by this endeavour to think beyond our human condition? Deleuze provides, I believe, the essential insight that is required here: we find ourselves born or thrown into a world that is ready-made and that we have not made our own.[12] For Bergson, there is also the joy of perception or vision: this is the joy of seeing the world come into being as if for the first time and always afresh. There is also the joy to be had from cultivating a superior human nature and through engaging in the creation of the self by the self.[13]

There is a Bergsonian revolution and it amounts to an upheaval in philosophy comparable in significance to the ones we are more familiar with, from Kant to Nietzsche and Heidegger, and that make up our intellectual modernity. If this book goes some way towards convincing the reader of this, it will have succeeded. I present Bergson's revolution in thought in terms of the goal he lays down for the philosophy of thinking beyond the human condition. On an initial encounter this may strike the reader as an odd and paradoxical task for philosophical activity: Will it not deny what is characteristically human about the human being? How can we, as human beings, think beyond our own condition? Bergson is well aware of these concerns on the part of his reader and I show in several of the chapters that follow that he is attentive to the complexities and difficulties involved in the task. The way forward is to seek to demonstrate the need for new methods and modes of thinking. There is also the need to indicate that the human intellect has evolved and as an instrument of evolution it has developed specific habits of representation that prevent the full comprehension of ourselves as creatures of novelty, creativity, and freedom. It is not so much that we are caught up in an existential predicament when the appeal is made to think beyond the human condition; it is rather that the restriction of philosophy to the human condition fails to appreciate the extent to which we are not simply creatures of habit and automatism but are also creatures involved in a creative evolution of becoming. The task is not to leave the human behind but rather to broaden the horizon of our experience of life. As noted by one commentator, for Bergson the fate of philosophy is not bound up with either arbitrary construction or criticism; there is, rather, a different method and a different future to be hoped for.[14] We can cite Bergson on this:

> Such is, in truth, the ordinary course of philosophical thought: we start from what we take to be experience, we attempt various possible arrangements of the fragments which apparently compose it, and when at last we feel bound to acknowledge the fragility of every edifice that we have built, we end by giving up all effort to build. But there is a last enterprise to be undertaken. It would be to seek experience at its source, or rather above that decisive *turn* where, taking a bias in the direction of utility, it becomes properly *human* experience. (MM 184)

In seeking the 'source' above the decisive turn at which experience becomes human, Bergson's philosophy of experience shows its departure from a straightforward philosophy of the subject and of subjectivity: 'It is neither a humanistic or existential philosophy, nor a transcendental philosophy'.[15] Deleuze thus rightly notes that 'Bergson is not one of those philosophers who ascribes a properly human wisdom and equilibrium to philosophy'.[16]

We need to ask, though: Why should we make the effort to dissolve into the whole as Bergson invites us to do? (CE 191) Bergson argues that we are carried within the ocean of life and our failure to fully appreciate this fact explains in large part why we are so alienated from life and from our full conditions of existence. Today, Bergson's lesson contains a valuable ecological lesson. He articulates what we might call, with some hesitation, a 'post-human' mode of perception. This consists in the attempt to think from the perspective of life itself and to do so in a way that challenges anthropocentrism and necessitates what Rosi Braidotti has called an 'eco-philosophy of becoming'.[17] The 'post-human' has a number of senses and I intend it in the sense of denoting, as Bradotti puts it, a 'sensibility that aims at overcoming anthropocentrism'.[18]

Bergson insists that although it is the case that nature itself has made separable the living body of life, evolution involves 'sympathetic communication' and the activity of 'reciprocal implication and interpenetration' between the parts (CE 189). Bergson opens *Creative Evolution* by reflecting on the incompleteness of the history of the evolution of life and seeks to draw attention to the evolution of the human intellect. He wants to indicate that it is the result of an uninterrupted progress, 'along a line which ascends through the vertebrate series up to man'. It is, for him, closely bound up with action in the world, hence his description of the 'faculty of understanding' as an appendage of the 'faculty of acting', and to be conceived as a more precise, complex, and supple adaptation of the consciousness of living beings to their conditions of existence. Bergson extends and refines Schopenhauer's understanding of the intellect, in which it is construed as a tool of struggling existence and not as a faculty for solving metaphysical riddles. The intellect has evolved for Bergson 'to think matter', that is, to secure the fitting of our body to its environment and to represent the relations of external things among themselves (CE ix). This specific evolution of the intellect explains, Bergson thinks, why the intellect feels most at home in the presence of inanimate objects. Moreover, our concepts have been formed on the model of solids and our logic is primarily the logic of solids, and this means that the human intellect 'triumphs in geometry', showing the kinship between logical thought and unorganized matter (CE ix). Bergson's contention is that human thinking, at least in its logical form, is unable to appreciate the 'true nature of life' and 'the full meaning of the evolutionary movement' (CE ix–x). If the intellect has been created in definite circumstances so as to act on definite things, how can it embrace the whole of life since it is only one aspect of it? It is to evolution itself that Bergson appeals to both demonstrate the nature of the intellect and its limits. None of the categories of our thinking do justice to the nature of evolution: notions of unity, multiplicity, mechanical causality, and intelligent finality all fall short when it comes to thinking the evolution of life. Evolution challenges many of our cherished beliefs and ideas: when we examine evolution can we say with certainty where individuality begins and ends? Or, whether the living being is one or many? Or whether it is the cells that associate themselves into the organism or the organism that dissociates itself into cells? We are in the habit of forcing the living into our moulds of thinking but life makes them crack since they prove themselves to be too narrow and rigid. No biological discovery is due to pure reasoning; even when we appeal to experience we find that biology is full of surprises: the logic of life challenges the way human logic works and thinks (CE x).

One of Bergson's main contentions, then, is: '*The intellect is characterized by a natural inability to comprehend life*' (CE 165). We need, as I have noted, new modes and methods of thinking, and this is what is signified in the appeal to think beyond the human condition. This effort is highly relevant to our post-human situation: it has ecological resonances and it contains the prospect of extending human perception beyond its normal frame of reference. *Creative Evolution* has yet to receive the attention it deserves in the intellectual community. More than any other work in the philosophy of life, this text is predominantly understood in light of what came after it. This is not to say merely that we interpret it in retrospect, but that the philosophical community has had a century to acclimatize itself to the scientific world view that Bergson recognized at its inception. It stands as a lesson in how philosophy can accompany rather than follow science, and how both disciplines gain from this partnership. Dynamic theories of biology and evolution both can only operate through the recognition of the temporal character of living systems, and ecological theories can only operate through the recognition of sympathy between organisms; and Bergson developed both these approaches at a time when biological science on the whole operated by treating organisms as raw material. Our thinking of life today is moving away from control and towards participation, away from exploitation and towards sustainability, and only now is scientific thought embarking on the path that Bergson pointed out a century ago, a path that he had seen indicated in the evolutionary biology of the late nineteenth and early twentieth centuries.

Bergson's ideas are not of course the only resource for this project, but they surely merit being placed at the centre of any serious philosophical response to questions about life and evolution, human and post-human.

In what follows, I seek to illuminate Bergson's treatment of key philosophical problems and cover all his major texts as well as some lesser-known materials. The first chapter offers an introduction to Bergson and is then followed by treatments of Bergson on time and freedom, on memory, on life and evolution, on ethics, on religion, and finally on education and the art of life. The one text I have not provided a treatment of is the essay on *Laughter*. There has been a long history of commentary on, and analysis of, this piece and at this stage of my writing I have nothing to add to the existing literature on it. For insight into it, the reader is directed to the references I provide in Chapter 8.

1

An Introduction to Bergson

Introduction

Henri Bergson (1859–1941) is widely recognized to be France's greatest philosophical thinker of the modern period. He was the author of four classic texts of philosophy, three of them characterized by a combination of exceptional philosophical gifts and impressive mastery of extensive scientific literature. Each text offers readers a number of theoretical innovations. *Time and Free Will* (1889) provides a novel account of free will by showing that time is not space and that psychic states do not lend themselves to treatment as magnitudes. *Matter and Memory* (1896) provides a non-orthodox (non-Cartesian) dualism of matter and mind, seeking to show that while the difference between matter and perception is one of degree (unless we construe it in these terms the emergence of perception out of matter becomes something mysterious and inexplicable), that between perception and memory is one of kind (unless we construe it in these terms memory is deprived of any autonomous character and is reduced to being a merely diluted form of perception, a secondary perception as we find in Locke). *Matter and Memory* offers an extremely rich and novel account of different types of memory that philosophical psychology is still catching up with today. In *Creative Evolution* (1907) Bergson endeavours to demonstrate the need for a philosophy of life in which the theory of knowledge and a theory of life are viewed as inseparably bound up with one another. In the text Bergson seeks to establish what philosophy must learn from the new biology (the neo-Darwinism established by August Weismann) and what philosophy can offer the new theory of the evolution of life. It is a tour de force, a work of truly extraordinary philosophical ambition. In *The Two Sources of Morality and Religion* (1932), his final text, and where the engagement with scientific literature is not as extensive, Bergson outlines a novel approach to the study of society (sociology) with his categories of the 'closed' and the 'open' and the 'static' and the 'dynamic'.

He advances a criticism of the rationalist approach to ethics that merits being taken as seriously as Nietzsche's critique of attempts to establish ethics on a rational foundation.[1] Finally, there are two important collections of essays: *Mind Energy* and *Creative Mind*.

Bergson's philosophy has a number of unique features to it. He has an impressive grasp of the history of science and of new scientific developments such as thermodynamics and neo-Darwinism. His ambition was to restore the absolute as the legitimate object of philosophy and to accomplish this by showing how it is possible to think beyond the human condition. Although he contests Kant's stress on the relativity of knowledge to the human standpoint in a manner similar to Hegel, his conception of the absolute is not the same. This is the surprise of Bergson, and perhaps explains why he appears as such an unfamiliar figure to us today: he seeks to demonstrate the absolute through placing man back into nature and the evolution of life. That is, he uses the resources of naturalism and empiricism to support an apparently Idealist philosophical programme. Indeed, Bergson argues that 'true empiricism' is 'the real metaphysics' and is of the opinion that the more the sciences of life develop the more they will feel the need to reintegrate thought into the very heart of nature (IM 22). In his own day he was read primarily as an empiricist whose thinking amounted, in the words of his former pupil and later harsh critic, Jacques Maritain, to a 'wild experimentalism'. Maritain accused Bergson of realizing in metaphysics 'the very soul of empiricism', of producing an ontology of becoming not 'after the fashion of Hegel's panlogism' but rather 'after the fashion of an integral empiricism'.[2] Julien Benda vigorously protested against Bergson's demand for new ways of thinking and new methods in philosophy and called for a return to the hyper-rationalism of Spinoza.[3] Bergson does not readily fit into the two main camps that define the contemporary academic institution of philosophy: neither the continental one which insists on keeping apart philosophy and science and regards any interest in science as philosophically suspect, nor the analytic one which cheerfully subsumes philosophy within the ambit of the natural sciences and renders metaphysics otiose.

In histories of modern philosophy it is standard to place Bergson alongside Friedrich Nietzsche (1844–1900) and Wilhelm Dilthey (1833–1911) as a philosopher of life and to portray him, along with Nietzsche, as an irrationalist.[4] This standard criticism of Bergson amounts to a caricature. Bergson promotes reason; what is subjected to critique is a self-sufficient reason and intellectualism. Bergson is not anti-rationalist but anti-intellectualist.[5] Bergson wants a philosophy that can do justice to contingency, to particularity, to individuality, to spontaneous forces and energies, to the creation of the new, and so on. Nietzsche famously advocates translating the human back into nature;[6] we find this echoed in Bergson when he argues in favour of a genetic approach to questions of morality and religion that places 'man back in nature as a whole' (TSMR 208). Those phenomena that have been denied a history and a nature must be given them back.

What stands in the way of our intellectual development and growth? Bergson's answer is the same as Nietzsche's: the prejudices of philosophers with their trust in immediate certainties and penchant for philosophical dogmatizing (IM 40).[7] Both accuse Schopenhauer's will to life of being an empty generalization that proves disastrous for science. For Nietzsche, Schopenhauer's doctrine can only result in a 'false reification' since it leads to the view that that all that exists empirically is the manifestation of one will.[8] For Bergson, the 'will to life' is an empty concept supported by a barren theory of metaphysics (TSMR 115). It is impossible, he argues, to cite a biological discovery due to pure reasoning while all the moulds in which we seek to force the living crack, being too narrow and too rigid for what we try to put into them. Both thinkers practise historical philosophizing and identify this with the intellectual virtue of modesty. Both insist on the need to provide a genesis of the intellect as a way of ascertaining the evolutionary reasons as to why we have the intellectual habits we do. What really unites Nietzsche and Bergson is their rejection of a two-world theory and the attempt to do justice to the world as becoming. At certain points in his development Nietzsche is willing to sacrifice metaphysics to history and hands over to science the task of deciding over the history of the genesis of thought and concepts.[9] For Bergson this is a task that can only be adequately be performed by a reformed metaphysics that proceeds via a new method of intuition. This is, in essence, Bergson's response to Kant's Copernican revolution. Nietzsche only came to allow himself this path in 1886 with the doctrine of the will to power, which is posited in terms of a 'morality of method' that works against Platonic metaphysics and Kantian morality, such as the metaphysical need for the beyond that satisfies the 'heart's desire' for a realm of being that is pure, eternal, and unconditional. In 1878 he insists that there is only representation (*Vorstellung*) and that no hunch can take us any further.[10] By 1886, however, Nietzsche commits himself to the view that there is, in fact, a dimension of the world outside of representation – the will to power as a pre-form (*Vorform*) of life – but insists that this is to be approached through the 'conscience of method',[11] a critical project which, like all others in Nietzsche, denotes the method of the 'intellectual conscience' that seeks to replace what Nietzsche takes to be the fundamentally theological motivations of Kant's critical project with properly scientific ones.[12] Perhaps taking his cue from Kant's confession that he found it necessary to deny knowledge in order to make room for faith, Nietzsche holds that Kant's project is compromised by its positing of an intelligible realm of postulates of pure practical reason – God, the immortality of the soul, absolute freedom of the will – which we have to conceive as *unintelligible* (this realm does not lend itself to knowledge, Kant insists). Bergson's response to Kant is equally critical and focuses attention on the soundness of the decisions Kant has made about the nature and extent of theoretical knowledge.[13]

There are two main criticisms that have traditionally been advanced against the kind of project undertaken by Bergson. One is that naturalism cannot account for differences in kind insofar as it reduces modes of existence to differences of degree, especially between the human and the rest of nature. The other is that Bergson's thinking is guilty of the error of biologism (a criticism also levelled at Nietzsche's work), that is, of making an illegitimate extension of the biological to all spheres of existence such as the moral and the social.[14] This criticism is, in effect, implied in the first concern. In the course of this chapter I shall suggest that neither point has purchase when applied to Bergson.

Bergson's Reception of Kant

Bergson does not accept two key theses of Kant's Copernican revolution: (1) the claim that knowledge is relative to our faculties of knowing, and (2) the claim that metaphysics is impossible on the grounds that there can be no knowledge outside of science (Newtonian mechanism) or that science has correctly determined the bounds of metaphysics.[15] For Bergson a new relation between philosophy and science is called for and knowledge of the absolute is to be restored:

> If we now inquire why Kant did not believe that the matter of our knowledge extends beyond its form, this is what we find. The criticism of our knowledge of nature that was instituted by Kant consisted in ascertaining what our mind must be and what Nature must be *if* the claims of our science are justified; but of these claims themselves Kant has not made the criticism. I mean that he took for granted the idea of a science that is one, capable of binding with the same force all the parts of what is given, and of co-ordinating them into a system presenting

on all sides an equal solidity. He did not consider … that science became less and less objective, more and more symbolical, to the extent that it went from the physical to the vital, from the vital to the psychical (CE 359).

Bergson contends that the physical laws of scientific knowledge are, in their mathematical form, artificial constructions foreign to the real movement of nature since its standards of measurement are conventional ones created by the concerns of the human intellect and its attachment to utilitarian groupings. This does not prevent Bergson from appreciating the success of modern science; on the contrary, it is his insights into the specific character of science that enables him to appreciate the reasons for its success, namely the fact that it is contingent and relative to the variables it has selected and to the order in which it stages problems. For Bergson, philosophy needs to involve itself in special problems as we encounter in the positive sciences. The true difficulty is to create the unique solution of the problem which the philosopher has posed anew in the very effort of trying to solve it, and this involves abstracting oneself from language (from order-words) which has been made for conversation and which satisfies the requirements of common sense and social action, but not those of thinking. The genuine philosopher, as opposed to the amateur, is one who does not accept the terms of a problem as a common problem that has been definitively posed and which then requires that s/he select from the available solutions to the problem (the example Bergson gives to illustrate his point is that of Samuel Butler rejecting Darwin's solution in favour of Lamarck's) (BKW 370).

Bergson makes two major claims contra Kant: the first is that the mind cannot be restricted to the intellect since it overflows it; and second, that duration has to be granted an absolute existence, which requires thinking time on a different plane to space. According to Bergson, Kant considered only three possibilities for a theory of knowledge: (i) the mind is determined by external things; (ii) things are determined by the mind itself; (iii) between the mind and things we have to suppose a mysterious agreement or pre-established harmony. In contrast to these three options, Bergson seeks to demonstrate the need for a double genesis of matter and the intellect. It is not that matter has determined the form of the intellect or that the intellect simply imposes its own form upon matter, or even that there is some curious harmony between the two we can never explain, but rather that the two have, in the course of evolution, progressively adapted themselves one to the other and so attained a common form. He regards this adaptation as coming about naturally, '*because it is the same inversion of the same movement which creates at once the intellectuality of mind and the materiality of*

things' (CE 206). Both science and the intellect for Bergson concern themselves
with the aspect of repetition. The intellect selects in a given situation whatever
is like something already known so as to fit it into a pre-existing schema; in this
way it applies 'its principle that "like produces like"' (CE 29). It rebels against
the idea of an original and unforeseeable production of forms. Similarly, science
focuses its attention on isolable or closed systems, simply because anything 'that
is irreducible and irreversible in the successive moments of a history eludes' it
(CE 29). In cases of organic evolution, Bergson insists, foreseeing the form in
advance is not possible. This is not because there are no conditions or specific
causes of evolution but rather owing to the fact that they are built into, are part
and parcel of, the particular form of organic life and so 'are peculiar to that
phase of its history in which life finds itself at the moment of producing the
form' (CE 28). There is a need to display a readiness to be taken by surprise in
the study of nature and to appreciate that there might be a difference between
human logic and the logic of nature. The scientist has to cultivate a feeling for the
complexity of natural phenomena. In this respect we cannot approach nature
with any a priori conceptions of parts and wholes or any a priori conception of
what constitutes life, including how we delimit the boundaries of an organism
and hence define it. We must resist the temptation to place or hold nature within
our own ideas or shrink reality to the measure of them. Contra Kant, therefore,
we should not allow our need for a unity of knowledge to impose itself upon the
multiplicity of nature. Moreover, to follow the sinuosities of reality means that
we cannot slot the real into a concept of all concepts, be it Spirit, Substance, Ego,
or Will (CM 35 & 49).

Bergson argues that it 'is not enough to determine, by careful analysis, the
categories of thought; we must engender them' (CE 206). A theory of knowledge
and a theory of life are to be viewed as inseparable since if the critique of
knowledge is not accompanied by a philosophy of life – which will study the
emergence of the human intellect and the habits of the mind in its evolutionary
context of adaptation – we will uncritically accept the concepts that the intellect
has placed at our disposal and enclose our facts within a set of pre-existing
frames. We need to show how the frames of knowledge have been constructed
and how they can be enlarged and gone beyond. Instead of ending up with a split
between appearance and reality, or between phenomenon and noumenon, we
now approach epistemological issues in terms of the relation between our partial
perspective on the real, which has evolved in accordance with the vital needs of
adaptation, and a mobile whole. The sensible intuition of a homogenous time and

space that Kant establishes as transcendental forms, for example, presupposes a 'real duration' and a 'real extensity': the former are stretched out beneath the latter in order that the moving continuity can be divided and a becoming can be fixed (MM 211).

Thinking Beyond the Human Condition

Bergson conceives philosophy as the discipline that 'raises us above the human condition' (*la philosophie nous aura élevés au-dessus de la condition humaine*') and makes the effort to 'surpass' (*dépasser*) it (CM 50; IM 45). Philosophy provides us with the methods for reversing the normal directions of the mind (instrumental, utilitarian), so upsetting its habits. Because it finds itself having to work against the most inveterate habits of the mind, Bergson compares philosophy to an act of violence (IM 33, 40; CE 29). The aim of the enterprise is to expand the humanity within us and allow humanity to surpass itself by reinserting itself in the whole (it recognizes it is part of nature and the evolution of life). Intelligence is reabsorbed into its principle and comes to know its own genesis. In spite of what one might think, this makes the task of philosophy a modest one. If we suppose that philosophy is an affair of perception, then it cannot simply be a matter of correcting perception but only of extending it. Like Nietzsche before him, Bergson is seeking to draw attention to fact that humanity has constituted itself on the basis of a set of errors without being aware of this.[16] We find ourselves born or thrown into a world that is ready-made and that we have not made our own, and it when we recognize this that we are motivated to think beyond the human condition.

Bergson was motivated by what he saw as the wandering and aimless nature of much of our research into the workings of the mind, in which there is an absence of a guiding thread (CM 53). The supposition he sees at work in psychology – and by extension what we today would call the philosophy of mind – is that the mind has fallen from heaven in which its subdivision into functions and faculties (memory, imagination, conception, and perception) needs only to be recognized. In short, the fundamental question of genesis – of how things have become what they are – is absent from research. Only an inquiry into the fundamental exigencies of life will enable us to raise the most important questions, such as, for example, whether the ordinary subdivision into various faculties is natural or artificial. Should our divisions be maintained or modified? Moreover, if one of the results of the research conducted is that the exigencies of life are found to be working in an analogous fashion in humans, animals, and plants, what will be the consequences for all kinds of disciplines and modes of inquiry? Our reliance on an unconscious metaphysics has led us to cut up and distribute psychological life in an inadequate manner, one that cannot do justice to the complexity of our evolution and how the mind has been formed. There is, therefore, a need to dig down to sources and roots. Both Nietzsche and Bergson share this commitment to archaeology as a way of opening up the human condition and subjecting the mind and its habits of thinking to a genetic history.

Bergson insists that the whole cannot be approached in terms of ready-made criteria of an organic totality. Neither is the whole of nature or the evolution of the fundamental directions of life, such as the divergent tendencies of instinct and intelligence, to be thought in dialectical terms of contradiction, negation, and sublation. It is not necessary to ascribe to evolution, whether natural or historical, a logical or dialectical development. On this point Bergson has clearly been inspired by the Darwinian revolution. Bergson considered Darwin to be the greatest of all modern naturalists and held that the doctrine of evolution would impose itself on our thinking. The conception of the whole he has in mind is that of a universal mobility. True evolutionism, he says, must focus on the study of becoming but this requires that we do not follow the path of perception which would reduce an 'infinite multiplicity of becomings' to the single representation of a 'becoming *in general*' (CE 304). For Bergson the whole enjoys neither interiority nor totality; individuated forms of life have a tendency towards closure but this is never accomplished. As Bergson puts in *Creative Evolution*, 'finality is external or it is nothing at all' (CE 41). That the whole is never given but is a pure virtual should meet with our delight since it is only our habitual confusion of time with space, and the assimilation of time into space, that makes us think the whole is given, if only in the eyes of God.[17] We could say: on the level of life there is only actualization and differentiation but to make adequate sense of this we need to appeal to a conception of the whole, and what matters is the conception we evince of it. For Bergson it is the *élan vital* conceived as a 'virtual' power of self-differentiation; for Nietzsche it is the will to power conceived as a pre-form (*Vorform*) of life (a potential of energy), which is also a power of self-differentiation.[18] Without a conception of the whole we can only posit what comes into existence in mysterious and inexplicable terms of so many brute eruptions of being.

The human condition refers, then, not to an existential predicament but to accrued evolutionary habits of thought that prevent us from recognizing our own creative conditions of existence and restrict the domain of praxis to social utility. Bergson believes that there is a basis for a novel alliance between metaphysics and the new post-Newtonian sciences, insofar as both, working in concert, are able to discover the natural articulations of the universe that have been carved artificially by the intellect. The categories of stable being are not simple illusions but have their anchorage in the conditions of our evolutionary existence; space, for example, is a schema of matter which represents the limit of a movement of expansion that would come to an end as an external envelope of all possible extensions. On account of its ever-more complete demonstration of the reciprocal action of all material points upon each other science produces an insight into the universal continuity between things. We might suppose that all we need to do is to replace the notion of matter with that of force, but this is still insufficient for what is decisive are 'movements and lines of force whose reciprocal solidarity brings back to us universal continuity' (MM 200). It should, therefore, be the task of a theory of matter to find the reality hidden beneath our customary images of it and that are relative to our adaptive needs. This attempt to think beyond our customary images of matter explains why Bergson claims that every philosophy of nature ends by finding the discontinuity that our senses perceive incompatible with the general properties of matter (MM 201).

In a letter of 1903 to William James Bergson speaks of the need to transcend 'a simple logic' and 'the methods of over-systematic philosophy which postulates the unity of the whole'. If a 'truly *positive* philosophy is possible', he adds, it 'can only be found there' (BKW 358–9). This would be the opposite of a closed system of metaphysics which one could decide to take or leave. Indeed, Bergson commits himself to the possibility of a metaphysics that could progress indefinitely (M 652). The reformed metaphysics will advance by the gradual accumulation of obtained results. In other words, metaphysics does not have to be 'a take-it-or-leave-it system' that is forever in dispute and doomed to start afresh, thinking abstractly and vainly without the support of empirical science. Not only is it the case for Bergson that metaphysics can be a true empiricism, but it can also work with science in an effort to advance our knowledge of the various sources, tendencies, and directions of life. Bergson outlines what is in effect his 'superior positivism' in his Huxley lecture of 1911 on 'Life and Consciousness': 'we possess now a certain number of *lines of facts*, which do not go as far as we want, but which we can prolong hypothetically' (ME 4). This is taken up again in the

The Two Sources where he states that the different lines of fact indicate for us the direction of truth but none go far enough; the attainment of truth can only take place when the lines are prolonged to the point where they intersect (TSMR 248). He makes it clear that the conceptions of a vital impetus and of a creative evolution were only arrived by following the evidence of biology. Furthermore, he stresses that his conception is not simply a hypothesis of the kind that can be found at the basis of all metaphysical systems; rather, it aims to be 'a condensation of fact, a summing up of summings up' (TSMR 249). The knowledge we wish to develop and advance concerning evolution must 'keep to ascertained facts and the probabilities suggested by them' (TSMR 273).

Duration

To think duration is to think beyond the human condition (IM 45). My existence, including my duration, is disclosed by objects 'inferior' and 'superior', though in a certain sense interior, to me (IM 33). Take the example Bergson gives of mixing a glass of water with sugar and waiting until the sugar dissolves, which he says is a 'little fact big with meaning' (CE 9 & 339). The time I have to wait is not a mathematical time which we could apply to the entire history of the material world as if it was spread out instantaneously in space; rather, it coincides with an impatience that constitutes a portion of my duration and which I cannot protract or contract at will. This is an experience that is lived and denotes not a relative but an absolute. Furthermore, my duration has the power to disclose other durations and to encompass them ad infinitum. Bergson gives the example of a simultaneity of fluxes in which while sitting on the bank of a river, the flowing of the water, the flight of a bird, and the uninterrupted murmur in the depths of our life, can be treated as either three things or a single one (DS 36). Bergson admits that to conceive of durations of different tensions and rhythms is both difficult and strange to our mind simply because we have acquired the useful habit of substituting for duration an homogeneous and independent time (MM 207).

Bergson argues that time involves a co-existence of past and present and not simply a continuity of succession. Pure duration 'is the form which the succession of our conscious states assumes when our ego lets itself *live*, when it refrains from separating its present state from its former states' (TFW 100). Duration can be defined as 'the continuous progress of the past which gnaws into the future and which swells as it advances' (CE 4). It is irreversible since, 'consciousness cannot go through the same state twice. The circumstances may still be the same, but they will act no longer on the same person, since they find him at a new moment of his history' (CE 6). Even if states can be repeated and assume the character of being identical, this is merely an appearance, so we cannot live over and over again a single moment. We may think we can efface memory but such effacement would work on the level of our intellect, not our will. If we take time to be something positive then we have to treat it as both irreversible and unforeseeable. This conception of duration, which is that of a 'becoming' that flows out of previous forms while always adding something new to them, is very different from Spinoza's conception of the 'one complete Being' which manifests forms. For Bergson this conception denies effective action to duration (CE 352). Both Cartesian and Spinozist physics seek to establish a relation of logical necessity between cause and effect and in so doing 'do away with active duration' (TFW 208–9).

Bergson holds that duration cannot be made the subject of a logical or mathematical treatment. This is owing to its character as a continuous multiplicity, as opposed to one made up of discrete parts or elements. In *Creative Evolution* Bergson addresses the status of his construal of life in terms of an impetus. He explicitly conceives it in terms of a 'virtual multiplicity' (*virtuellement multiple*). He acknowledges that describing life in terms of an impetus is to offer little more than an image. The image, however, is intended to disclose something about the essential character of life, namely that it is not of a mathematical or logical order but a psychological one: 'In reality, life is of the psychological order, and it is of the essence of the psychical to enfold a confused plurality of interpenetrating terms' (CE 257). The contrast he is making is with space in which the multiplicity posited or found therein will be made up of discrete elements or components that are related to one another in specific terms, namely relations of juxtaposition and exteriority.

In *Time and Free Will* Bergson argues that the different degrees of a mental state correspond to qualitative changes that do not admit of simple measure or number. When we ordinarily speak of time we think of a homogeneous medium in which our conscious states are placed alongside one another as in space, and so form a discrete multiplicity. The question is whether the evolution of our psychic states resembles the multiplicity of the units of a number and whether duration has anything to do with space. If time is simply a medium in which our conscious states are strung out as a discrete series that can be counted, then time would indeed be space. The question Bergson poses is whether time can legitimately be treated as such a medium.

One way of thinking about the issue is to reflect on the nature of a psychic state and question the validity of treating it as a magnitude. Does it make sense, for example, to say that today I am twice as happy or joyous as I was yesterday? While we can distinguish between experiencing a twinge of jealousy and being obsessed by a jealous passion, would it make sense to say that the jealousy of Othello should be understood as being made up of innumerable twinges of jealousy? (TFW 73)[19] Bergson asks: 'why do we say of a higher intensity that it is greater? Why do we think of a greater quantity or a greater space?' (TFW 7) His contention is that states of consciousness cannot be isolated from one another but should be approached in terms of a multiplicity in which there is fusion and interpenetration, in short, a qualitative heterogeneity. The reason for this fusion and interpenetration is that the states of consciousness unfold themselves in duration and not, like the units of arithmetic, in space. An increasing intensity of a mental state is inseparable from a qualitative progression and from a becoming of time. The notion of an intensive magnitude 'involves an impure mixture between determinations that differ in kind' with the result that our question 'by how much does a sensation grow or intensify?' takes us back to a badly stated problem.[20] It is not that we do not count in duration; rather, we count the moments of duration by means of points in space. We perfectly comprehend the sense of there being a number that is greater than another, but can the same be said of an intensive sensation? How can a more intense sensation contain one of less intensity? Unlike the law of number the relations among intensities cannot be adequately approached in terms of those of container and contained with different intensities being superposed upon one another. Adequately understood intensity cannot be assimilated to magnitude.

Looked at from the perspective of pure duration our states can be seen to permeate and melt into another without precise outlines and without any affiliation with number, in which past and present states form a whole, 'as happens when we recall the notes of a tune, melting, so to speak, into another' (TFW 100). These are involved in qualitative changes that disclose a pure heterogeneity (continuous variation). When we interrupt the rhythm of a tune by perhaps dwelling longer than is customary on one note, it is not the exaggerated length that signals the mistake to us but rather the qualitative change caused in the whole of the piece of music.

> We can thus conceive of succession without distinction, and think of it as a mutual penetration, an interconnexion and organization of elements, each one of which represents the whole, and cannot be distinguished or isolated from it except by abstract thought. (TFW 101)

When we reduce time to a simple movement of position we confuse time with space. It is this confusion between motion and the space traversed which explains the paradoxes of Zeno. The interval between two points is infinitely divisible, and if motion is said to consist of parts like those of the interval itself, then the interval can never be crossed. But the truth of the matter is different:

> each of Achilles's steps is a simple indivisible act ... after a given number of these acts, Achilles will have passed the tortoise. The mistake of the Eleatics arises from their identification of this series of acts, each of which is *of a definite kind and indivisible*, with the homogeneous space which underlies them. (113)

Because this space can be divided and put together again according to an abstract law, the illusion arises that it is possible to reconstruct the movement of Achilles not with his step but with that of the tortoise. In truth, we have only two tortoises that agree to make the same kind of steps or simultaneous acts so never to catch one another! Within any posited motionless trajectory it is possible to count as much immobility as we like. What we fail to see is that 'the trajectory is created in one stroke, although a certain time is required for it; and that although we can divide at will the trajectory once created, we cannot divide its creation, which is an act in progress and not a thing' (CE 309). While the space traversed is a matter of extension and quantity (it is divisible), the movement is an intensive act and a quality. Bergson is insistent that it is through the quality of quantity that we form the idea of quantity without quality, not the other way round. Qualitative operations are even at work in the formation of numbers. The addition of a third unit to two others alters the nature (the rhythm) of the whole, even though our spatial habits lead us to disregard the significance of these varying aspects (TFW 123). We can appreciate why Bergson holds that metaphysics, in the negative sense of the term, begins not with Plato but with Zeno: 'Metaphysics ... was born of the arguments of Zeno of Elea on the subject of change and movement. It was Zeno who, by drawing attention to the absurdity of what he called movement and change, led the philosophers – Plato first and foremost – to seek the true and coherent reality in what does not change' (CM 141; see also 17).

Mechanism is not wholly illegitimate or simply false in Bergson's view (he does not embrace finalism since this is merely an inverted mechanism that also reduces time to a process of realization). It is a reflection of our evolved habits of representation and these are habits that conform in large measure to certain tendencies of matter. The intellect is the product of a natural evolution and has evolved as an instrument of action that exerts itself on fixed points. Intelligence, for example, does not consider transition, but prefers instead to conceive movement as a movement through space, as a series of positions in which one point is reached, followed by another, and so on. Even if something happens between the points the understanding intercalates new positions, an act that can go on ad infinitum. As a result of this reduction of movement to points in space, duration gets broken up into distinct moments that correspond to each of the positions (this is what we can call a discrete or actual multiplicity). Bergson writes:

> In short, the time that is envisaged is little more than an ideal space where it is supposed that all past, present, and future events can be set out along a line, and in addition, as something which prevents them from appearing in a single perception: the unrolling in duration (*le déroulement en durée*) would be this very incompletion (*inachèvement*), the addition of a negative quantity. Such, consciously or unconsciously, is the thought of most philosophers, in conformity with the exigencies of the understanding, the necessities of language and the symbolism of science. *Not one of them has sought positive attributes in time.* (CM 95)

If we say that time merely glides over these (material) systems then we are speaking of simple systems that have been constituted artificially through the operations of our own intellect. Such systems can be calculated ahead of time since they are being posited as existing prior to their realization in the form of possibles (when a possible is realized it simply gets existence added to it, its fundamental nature has not changed). The successive states of this kind of system can be conceived as moving at any speed, rather like the unrolling of a film: it does not matter at what speed the shots run an evolution is not being depicted. The reality here is more complex, however, but the complexity is concealed. An unrolling film, for example, remains attached to consciousness that has its own duration and which regulates its movement. The more duration marks the living being with its imprint, the more the organism must differ from a mere mechanism (CE 37).

One of the difficulties we have in accepting this conception of duration as the invention of the new is due to the way in which we think of evolution as the domain of the realization of the possible. We have difficulty in thinking that an event – whether a work of art or a work of nature – could have taken place unless it were not already capable of happening. For something to become it must have been possible all along. As Bergson points out, the word possibility can signify at least two different things and we often waver between the two senses. From the negative sense of the word, such as pointing out that there was no known insurmountable obstacle to something coming into being, we pass quickly onto the positive sense of it, in which we hold that any event could have been foreseen in advance of its happening by a mind with adequate information. In the form of an idea this is to suppose that an event was pre-existent to its eventual realization. Even if it is argued that an event, such as the composition of a symphony or a painting, was not conceived in advance, the prejudice still holds sway that such an event *could have been*, and this is to suppose that there exists a transcendent realm of pre-existing possibles. In *The Two Sources of Morality and Religion* Bergson applies this critique of the pre-existence of the possible in the real, which he now calls 'retrospective anticipation', to the domain of history. The supposition at work in our thinking of history is that things are approximating some ideal or norm – one that must stand outside history to make the judgement possible – as in the view that: 'the conceptions of justice which followed one another in ancient societies were no more than partial, incomplete versions of an integral justice as we know it today' (TSMR 72). But this is to deny that something new comes into existence in history, often by taking possession of something old and absorbing it into a new whole. It is always possible to interpret a forward movement as a progressive shortening of the distance between the starting point and the end, and then to claim that when the end has been reached the thing in question was either possible or that it had been working towards this end all along. But there is nothing that warrants this inference; it is the result of the error of 'thinking backwards'. For Bergson, this is a metaphysical doctrine (in the negative sense) that sets the theory of knowledge insoluble problems.

The reduction of the real, and of real complexity, to mathematical calculability or computation is one that Bergson locates in both nineteenth-century physics and biology. He quotes the following passage from Du Bois-Reymond's *Über die Grenzen des Naturerkennens* ('On the Limits of Our Knowledge of Nature') of 1892: 'We can imagine the knowledge of nature arrived at a point where the universal process of the world might be represented by a single mathematical formula, by one immense system of differential equations, from which could be deduced, for each moment, the position, direction, and velocity of every atom of the world' (CE 38). Time is positive for Bergson in the sense that it introduces indetermination into the very essence of life. However, our natural bent is always to construe this indetermination in terms of a completion of pre-existent possibles. The intellect, which has evolved as an organ of utility, has a need for stability and reliability. It thus seeks connections and establishes stable and regular relations between transitory facts. It also develops laws to map these connections and regularities. This operation is held to be more perfect the more the law in question becomes more mathematical. From this disposition of the intellect there have emerged the specific conceptions of matter that have characterized a great deal of Western metaphysics and science. Our mind conceives the origin and evolution of the universe as an arrangement and rearrangement of parts that simply shift from one place to another. This is what Bergson calls the Laplacean dogma that has informed a great deal of modern enquiry, leading to a determinism and a mechanism in which by positing a definite number of stable elements all possible combinations can be deduced without regard for the reality of duration (CE 38).

In *Time and Free Will* Bergson also aims to show the limitations of physical determinism by arguing that the science of energy rests on a confusion of concrete duration and abstract time. Modern mechanism holds that it is possible to calculate with absolute certainty the past, present, and future actions of a living system from knowledge of the exact position and motion of the atomic elements in the universe capable of influencing it. It is this quest for certainty that informed the science built up around the principle of the conservation of energy. To admit the universal character of this theorem is to make the assumption that the material points which are held to make up the universe are subject solely to forces of attraction and repulsion that arise from the points themselves and have intensities that depend only on their distances. Thus, whatever the nature of these material points at any given moment, their relative position would be determined by relation to the preceding moment (TFW 151).

Bergson's main concern is to demonstrate why it is illegitimate to simply extend this conception of matter to a deterministic and mechanistic understanding of psychic states (perhaps by making them reducible to cerebral states). Bergson does not deny that the principle of the conservation of energy appears to be applicable to a whole array of physico-chemical phenomena, especially the case, he notes, since the development of the mechanical theory of heat. The question he wants to pose for science, however, is whether there are new kinds of energy, different from kinetic and potential energy, which may rebel against calculation (he is thinking in particular of physiological phenomena). His principal point is to argue that conservative systems cannot be taken to be the only systems possible. For these conservative systems time does not bite into them. Without duration can these systems be said to be *living* systems? On the model of modern mechanism the isolable material point can only remain suspended in an eternal present (MM 153). While a conservative system may have no need of a past time (duration), for a living one that exists in a metastable state it is a prerequisite. For Bergson the setting up of an abstract principle of mechanics as a universal law does not, in truth, rest on a desire to meet the requirements of a positive science, but rather on a psychological mistake derived from reducing the duration of a living system to the 'duration which glides over the inert atoms without penetrating and altering them' (MM 154).

The antinomies of modern thinking, for example of determinism and freedom, stem in large measure from our imposition of symbolic diagrams upon the movement of the real, which serve to make it something uniform, regular, and calculable for us. To break free of these mental habits would make it possible to transcend space without stepping outside extensity. There is no fixed logic or established law that compels us to equate a continuous and diversified extensity with the amorphous and inert space that subtends it, and within which movement can only be constructed in terms of a multiplicity of instantaneous positions. In arguing that movement is something absolute and place is relative (Bergson argues contra Newton explicitly on this point), Bergson is claiming it to be something real and not merely an effect of measurement (the mathematical symbols of the geometrician are unable to demonstrate that it is a moving body that is in motion and not the axes and points to which it is referred). But if motion is merely relative then change must be an illusion (MM 194–5).

In his work on the philosophy of mind Bergson attempts to draw our attention to the faulty assumptions on which much of the thinking in this area is founded. For example, he seeks to show how realism ends up in the trap of idealism. To state this in brief terms of two notation systems: for the idealist the world is the product of our ideas and cannot exist independently of them. For the realist or materialist the mental is reduced to the cerebral and in this way the brain is made into the progenitor of our representations of the world. Bergson takes both to task for reducing the relation of the body to the world into one of speculative knowledge as opposed to vital activity. Realism becomes idealism when it locates perception and consciousness in a centre or some detached isolated object that has been abstractly divorced from its conditions of action in the world. Both err in making the presentation of the part – the mind or the brain – equivalent to the presentation of the whole. A great deal of neuroscience, and what passes today for the philosophy of mind (identity theory, for example), inadvertently produces an idealism of the cerebral substance by severing motor activity from the processes of perception, localizing perception in the sensory nervous elements. But this is in error in thinking: 'the truth is that perception is no more in the sensory centers than in the motor centers; it measures the complexity of their relations, and, is, in fact, where it appears to be' (MM 46). The view that Bergson wishes to combat most is that which would, in treating sensations merely as signals, in which the office of each sense is to translate homogeneous and mechanical movements into its language, posit on the one hand homogeneous movements in space and, on the other, extended sensations in consciousness. Bergson argues that the identity resides not between the cerebral and the mental or spiritual, but rather between the real action of sensory elements and the virtual action of perception (including the motor diagrams). Thus, perception is a part of things (it is not an interior, subjective vision), just as an affective sensation (such as the capacity to experience pain or pleasure) does not spring from the depths of inner consciousness by extending itself into an outer realm (affection is not a simple movement from an inner intensive state to an outer extensity), simply because it is intimately bound up with the modifications that inform the movement of one body with other bodies. Our appreciation of the movement of bodies becomes more complex when this is thought in terms of duration and the addition of memory. Although this movement has its material conditions in a nervous system – 'The greater the power of action of a body, symbolized by a higher degree of complexity in the nervous system, the wider is the field that perception embraces' (MM 56) – it cannot be reduced to its simple physical embodiment simply because the brain is part of the world. The error in treating the brain in reified terms as the material centre of consciousness is that it withdraws the objects which encase it, so also withdrawing in the process the very thing we designate as a cerebral state, simply because it is dependent on the objects for its properties (ME 198). Realism surreptitiously passes over into idealism where it posits as isolable by right what is isolated only in idea.

Intuition

What is involved in restoring the absolute? For Bergson it centres on recognizing that reality is made up of both differences of degree (the tendencies of matter) and differences of kind (the tendencies of life). We can divide a composite or mixture according to qualitative and qualified tendencies, such as the way in which it combines duration and extensity defined as directions of movements, giving us 'duration-contraction' and 'matter-expansion'. Such a method of division might be compared to a form of transcendental analysis in that it takes us beyond experience as given towards its conditions. However, we are now dealing not with the conditions of all possible experience, but rather with conditions that are neither general and abstract nor broader than the conditioned.[21] Once we make the turn in experience beyond the bias directed towards utility we reach the point at which we discover differences in kind and no longer subsume reality within utilitarian groupings. We frequently locate only differences in degree (more or less of the same thing), when in actuality the most profound differences are the differences in kind. Experience itself offers us nothing more than composites, such as time imbued with space and mixtures of extensity and duration. To think beyond our mental habits, which give us only badly analysed composites, we require a special method, and for Bergson this is the method of intuition. Without this method duration would remain a simple psychological experience. Intuition is not itself duration but rather 'the movement by which we emerge from our own duration' and 'make use of our own duration to affirm … and recognize the existence of other durations'.[22]

Given our finitude Kant claims that our mode of intuition can only be of a derivative kind and not an original one. By this he means that we have no access to an intellectual intuition. Kant allows for the fact that the way the human being intuits time and space may not be peculiar to it alone but may be something to be found among all finite beings that have a capacity of self-representation. But what he will not allow for is the possibility that we could overstep the bounds of our finitude and attain a higher intuition such as an intellectual one. This can only belong to the primordial being.[23] We can only know matter in terms of its outer relations; the inward nature of matter, that is, matter as it would be conceived by the pure understanding independently of sensuous intuition, is a phantom. The most we can do is to posit a 'transcendental object' (*Objekt*) which may be the ground of the appearance we call matter, but this is an object without quantity or substance, it is 'a mere something of which we should not understand what it is, even if someone were in a position to tell us'.[24] To be able to intuit things without the aid of our senses would mean that we could have knowledge 'altogether different from the human, and this not only in degree but as regards intuition likewise in kind'.[25] But of such non-human beings we do not know them to be possible or how they would be constituted. Kant does not deny that through observation and analysis it is possible that we can penetrate into nature's recesses, but he insists that this is nature conceived only in the aspect or dimension of its *appearance*: 'with all this knowledge, and even if the whole of nature were revealed to us, we should still never be able to answer those transcendental questions which go beyond nature', that is, beyond nature qua appearance.[26] Ultimately, Kant is led to positing a problematic noumenon, which is not the concept of any determinate object but rather bound up with the limitation of human sensibility. This provides a place for speculation with regard to there being objects outside of our specific field of intuition, objects other and different to what we are able to intuit through our particular a priori intuitions of time and space, but of their existence nothing can either be denied or be asserted.[27]

Bergson argues that in order to reach a higher mode of intuition it is not necessary, as Kant supposed, to transport ourselves outside the domain of the senses: 'After having proved by decisive arguments that no dialectical effort will ever introduce us into the beyond and that an effective metaphysics would necessarily be an intuitive metaphysics, he added that we lack this intuition and that this metaphysics is impossible. It would in fact be so if there were no other time or change than those which Kant perceived...' (CM 128) By recovering intuition Bergson hopes to save science from the charge of producing a relativity of knowledge (it is rather to be regarded as approximate) and metaphysics from the charge of indulging in empty and idle speculation. Although Kant himself did not pursue thought in the direction he had opened for it – the direction of a 'revivified Cartesianism' Bergson calls it – it is the prospect of an 'extra-intellectual matter of knowledge by a higher effort of intuition' that Bergson seeks to cultivate (CE 358). Kant has reawakened, if only half-heartedly, a view that was the essential element of Descartes's thinking but which the Cartesians abandoned: knowledge is not completely resolvable into the terms of intelligence.[28] Bergson does not, let it be noted, establish an opposition between sensuous (infra-intellectual) intuition and intellectual (what he calls an 'ultra-intellectual') intuition but instead seeks to show that there is a continuity and reciprocity between the two. Moreover, sensuous intuition can be promoted to a different set of operations, no longer simply being the phantom of an unscrutable thing-in-itself:

> The barriers between the matter of sensible knowledge and its form are lowered, as also between the 'pure forms' of sensibility and the categories of the

understanding. The matter and form of intellectual knowledge (restricted to its own object) are seen to be engendering each other by a reciprocal adaptation, intellect modelling itself on corporeity, and corporeity on intellect. But this duality of intuition Kant neither would nor could admit. (CE 360–1)

For Kant to admit this duality of intuition would entail granting to duration an absolute reality and treating the geometry immanent in space as an ideal limit (the direction in which material things develop but never actually attain).

In Bergson intuition denotes neither a vague feeling nor a disordered sympathy but a method that aims at precision in philosophy (see CM 11, 79, 88; IM 43; note, 53; ME 26). As Deleuze points out, duration would remain purely intuitive, in the ordinary sense of the word, if intuition in Bergson's sense did not exist as a method.[29] It is a complex method that cannot be contained in single act. Rather, it involves an 'indefinite series of acts', the diversity of which 'corresponds to all the degrees of being' (IM 33). The first task is to stage and create problems; the second is to locate differences in kind; and the third is to comprehend real time, that is, duration as a heterogeneous and continuous multiplicity. Bergson acknowledges that other philosophers before him, such as Schelling, tried to escape relativism by appealing to intuition (CM 30). He argues, however, that this was a non-temporal intuition that was being appealed to, and, as such, was largely a return to Spinozism, that is, a deduction of existence from 'one complete Being'.

Regarding the first task, we go wrong when we hold that notions of true and false can only be brought to bear on problems in terms of ready-made solutions. This denotes a negative freedom that reflects manufactured social prejudices where, through social institutions such as education and language, we become enslaved to 'order-words' that identify for us ready-made problems that we are forced to solve. True freedom lies in the power to decide through hesitation and indeterminacy and to constitute problems themselves. This might involve the freedom to uncover certain truths for oneself, but true freedom is more to do with invention than it is with discovery that is too much tied to uncovering what already exists, an act of discovery that was bound to happen sooner or later. In mathematics and in metaphysics the effort of invention consists in raising the problem and in creating the terms through which it might be solved but never as something ready-made. As Maurice Merleau-Ponty notes in a reading of Bergson, when it is said that well-posed problems are close to being solved, 'this does not mean that we have already *found* what we are looking for, but that we have already invented it.'[30]

False problem are of two kinds: first, those which are caught up in terms that contain a confusion of the 'more' and the 'less'; and, secondly, questions which are stated badly in the sense that their terms represent only badly analysed composites. In the first case the error consists in positing an origin of being and of order from which nonbeing and disorder are then made to appear as primordial. On this schema order can only appear as the negation of disorder and being as the negation of nonbeing (see CE 222). Such a way of thinking introduces lack into the heart of Being. Thinking in terms of the more or less errs in not seeing that there are kinds of order and forgetting the fact that Being is not homogeneous but fundamentally heterogeneous. Badly analysed composites result from an arbitrary grouping of things that are constituted as differences in kind. For example, in *Creative Evolution* Bergson contends that the cardinal error that has vitiated the philosophy of nature from Aristotle onwards is identifying in forms of life, such as the vegetative, instinctive, and rational, 'three successive degrees of the development of one and the same tendency, whereas they are divergent directions of an activity that has split up as it grew' (CE 135). He insists that the difference between them is neither one of intensity nor of degree but of kind. Life proceeds neither via lack nor the power of the negative but through internal self-differentiation along divergent lines.

It is through a focus on badly analysed composites that we are led, in fact, to positing things in terms of the more and the less, so that the idea of disorder only arises from a general idea of order as a badly analysed composite. We are the victims of illusions that have their source in aspects of our intelligence. However, although these illusions refer to Kant's analysis in the *Critique of Pure Reason*, where reason is shown to generate for itself in exceeding the boundaries of the understanding inevitable illusions and not simple mistakes, they are not of the same order. There is a natural tendency of the intellect to see only differences in degree and to neglect differences in kind. This is because the fundamental motivation of the intellect is to implement and orientate action in the world. For the purposes of social praxis and communication the intellect needs to order reality in a certain way, making it something calculable, regular and necessary.

If intuition is to be conceived as a method that proceeds via division – the division of a composite into differences of kind – is this not to deny that reality is, in fact, made up of composites and mixtures of all kinds? For Bergson, the crucial factor is to recognize that it is not things that differ in kind but rather tendencies. It is not things (their states or traits) that differ in nature, but the tendency things possess for change and development. A simple difference of degree would denote the correct status of things if they could be separated from their tendencies. The tendency is primary not simply in relation to its product but rather in relation to the causes in time that are retroactively obtained from the product itself. For example, if considered as a product, then the human brain will show only a difference of degree in relation to the animal brain. If it is viewed in terms of its tendency, however, it will reveal a difference of nature. Any composite, therefore, needs to be divided according to qualitative tendencies. Again, this brings Bergsonism close to Kant's transcendental analysis, going beyond experience as given and constituting its conditions of possibility. However, these are not conditions of all possible experience but of real experience (e.g. the inferior and superior durations we discussed above). Living systems in the universe are open systems in which liberty and contingency are real empirical features. As Deleuze notes: 'Indetermination, unpredictability, contingency, liberty always signify an independence in relation to causes.'[31]

Bergson's metaphysics of change aims to operate via differentiations and qualitative integrations, and in an effort to reverse the normal directions of the workings of thought enjoys a rapport with modern mathematics, notably the infinitesimal calculus:

> Modern mathematics is precisely an effort to substitute for the *ready-made* what is in process of *becoming*, to follow the growth of magnitudes, to seize movement no longer from outside and in its manifest result, but from within and in its tendency towards change, in short, to adopt of the mobile continuity of the pattern of things. (CM 190; see also MM 185)

Metaphysics differs from modern mathematics (the science of magnitudes), however, in that it has no need to make the move from intuition to symbol. Its understanding of the real is potentially boundless because of this: 'Liberated from the obligation of working practically for useful results, it will indefinitely enlarge the domain of its investigations' (CM 191). Metaphysics can adopt the generative idea of mathematics and seek to extend it to all qualities, 'to reality in general' (ibid.). The aim is not to bring about another Platonism of the real, as in Kant's system he contends, but rather to enable thought to re-establish contact with continuity and mobility (CM 197). A form of knowledge can be said to be relative when, through an act of forgetting, it ignores the basis of symbolic knowledge in intuition, and is forced to rely on pre-existing concepts and to proceed from the fixed to the mobile. Absolute knowledge by contrast refuses to accept what is pre-formed and instead cultivates 'fluid concepts', seeking to place itself in a mobile reality from the start and so adopting 'the life itself of things' (IM 13, 43), able to follow 'the real in all its sinuosities' (CE 363). To achieve this requires relinquishing the method of construction that leads only to higher and higher generalities and thinking in terms of a concrete duration 'in which a radical recasting of the whole is always going on' (CE 363). Bergson calls for experience to be purified of intellectualism and released from 'from the moulds that our intellect has formed' (361).

Bergson insists that his method of intuition contains no devaluation of intelligence but only a determination of its specific facility. If intuition transcends intelligence this is only account of the fact that it is intelligence that gives it the push to rise beyond. Without it intuition would remain wedded to instinct and riveted to the particular objects of its practical interests. The specific task of philosophy is to introduce us 'into life's own domain, which is reciprocal interpenetration, endlessly continued creation' (CE 178). This is different, though not opposed, to what science does when it takes up the utilitarian vantage point of external perception and prolongs individual facts into general laws. The reformed metaphysics Bergson wishes to awaken commits itself to an 'intellectual *expansion*' of thought and intuition is, in fact, '*intellectual* sympathy' (IM 32 & 40; my emphases).

Bergson's Critique of Ethical Rationalism

On a cursory reading Bergson's statement in *The Two Sources of Morality and Religion* that 'all morality is in essence biological' would seem to lend support to the criticism that his project amounts to biologism. I want to show that this is not in fact the case, and to do by looking at the critical points he make against the rationalist approach to ethics and as found largely, but not only, in Kant.

Nietzsche famously challenges any and all attempts to establish morality on a rational foundation (*Begründung*).[32] Bergson makes virtually the same point. For him it is the ease with which philosophical theories of ethics can be built up that should make us suspicious:

> if the most varied aims can thus be transmuted by philosophers into moral aims, we may surmise, seeing that they have not yet found the philosophers' stone, that they had started by putting gold in the bottom of their crucible. Similarly it is obvious that none of these doctrines will account for obligation. For we may be obliged to adopt certain means in order to attain such and such ends; but if

᾿ to renounce the end, how can the means be forced upon us? And
᾿ᵉ any one of these ends as the principle of morality, philosophers
᾿ it whole systems of maxims, which, without going so far as
᾿rative form, come near enough to it to afford satisfaction.
simple. They have considered the pursuit of these ends …
there are peremptory pressures, together with aspirations
so to extend them… . Each of these systems then already
mosphere when the philosopher arrives on the scene.

at moral philosophers treat society, and the two forces
ᵥₒ which it ᵤ ᵤ ᵤ ᵤₐbility and mobility (pressure and aspiration), as established facts. At the same time they take for granted the matter of morality and its form, all it contains and the entire obligation with which it is clothed.

Bergson wishes to expose what he regards as the essential weakness of a strictly intellectualist system of morality, which covers, he holds the majority of the philosophical theories of duty. The error of intellectualism is that it fails to appreciate the extent to which morality is a 'discipline demanded by nature' (TSMR 269). Moreover, intellectualism supposes that there is a difference of value between motives or principles and that there exists a general idea to which the real can be estimated. It is led to take refuge in Platonism in which the Idea of the Good dominates all others. For Bergson there are essentially two forces acting upon us and to which we respond as duties, namely impulsion and attraction. Without this emphasis on *forces* moral philosophy has great problems in explaining how a moral motive could take over our soul and impel it to action.

> That reason is the distinguishing mark of man no one will deny. That it is a thing
> of superior value, in the sense in which a fine work of art is indeed valuable, will
> also be granted. But we must explain how it is that its orders are absolute and why
> they are obeyed. Reason can only put forward reasons, which we are apparently
> always at liberty to counter with other reasons. Let us not then merely assert
> that reason, present in each one of us, compels our respect and commands our
> obedience by virtue of its paramount value. We must add that there are, behind
> reason, the men who have made mankind divine, and who have thus stamped a
> divine character on reason, which is the essential attribute of man. (TSMR 68)

Bergson is keen to share in philosophy's promotion of reason: 'the rational alone is self-consistent' and cannot be devalued; in civilized society morality is essentially rational (TSMR 81). The danger of reason, however, must equally be recognized: it can give us only a diagram of action and in so doing it runs the risk of rendering our decisions and deliberations automatic. As part of living a vital life we need the joy and exuberance of moral inventions and transformations. Any morality that claims reason as its basis in the guise of a pure form without matter is deluding itself; it is metaphysical in the bad sense of the word (TSMR 87). Social life cannot be taken as a fact we begin with but requires an explanation in terms of the vital necessities and imperatives of life itself. If we pursue matters of morality purely in intellectualist terms we reach a transcendental dead-end; if we place the emphasis on life, we can explain both the static and the dynamic dimensions of life, as well as both the closed and the open forms of morality and religion:

> Let us then give to the word biology the very wide meaning it should have, and will perhaps have one day, and let us say in conclusion that all morality, be it pressure or aspiration, is in essence biological. (TSMR 101)

Bergson's final text is an inquiry into the sources and origins of morality. Such an approach is possible according to him because in spite of the development of civilization and the transformations of society that have taken place in history the tendencies that are organic in social life have remained what they were in the beginning. There is an 'original nature', the bedrock of which is covered over by a 'thick humus', namely all the acquisitions of culture or civilization such as the deposits of knowledge, traditions, customs, institutions, syntax and the vocabulary of language, and even gestures (TSMR 83). If we scratch the surface and abolish everything we owe to education we find in the depth of our nature primitive humanity, or something near it. Although society and education make all the difference and overlay the natural, 'let a sudden shock paralyse these superficial activities, let the light in which they work be extinguished for a moment: at once the natural reappears, like the changeless star in the night' (TSMR 127). It is intelligence and its pride that will not admit our original subordination to biological necessities. The illusion is that intelligence is pure, unrelated to either nature or life, with no correspondence to vital needs. Intelligence wants man to be superior to his actual origins, higher than nature. And yet intelligence, in the form of science, shows man to be part of nature. However, neither Nietzsche nor Bergson is wedded to origins. Nietzsche argues that he who grows wise about origins will seek out sources of the future and new origins and he appeals to a new earth and new peoples to come.[33] For Bergson there are two moralities, one of pressure and one of aspiration. Whereas the former is one of social constraint, the morality of the city as he calls it, the latter concerns humanity's expansion that brings into existence new ways of living and new emotions.

is the image society wishes for itself (to hide the effect that in actuality all is imperfect, arbitrary, and so on). In this respect it is like the realm of Platonic ideas in the sphere of knowledge: it enables us to replace the uncertain with the certain, and the empirical with the eternal.

Kant's ethics rest on an absolute distinction between inclination and duty, or between nature and reason, which for him amounts to the difference between heteronomy and autonomy. Contra Kant, Bergson maintains that obligation is in not a unique fact incommensurate with others, 'looming above them like a mysterious apparition' (TSMR 20). Moreover, he argues that when we seek to define the essence and origin of obligation by laying down that obedience is primarily a struggle with the self, a state of tension or contraction, 'we make a psychological error which has vitiated many theories of ethics' (TSMR 20). Here there is confusion over the sense of obligation – which Bergson defines as 'a tranquil state akin to inclination' – with the violent effort we exert on ourselves now and again to break down possible obstacles to obligation:

> We have any number of particular obligations, each calling for a separate expla-
> nation. It is natural ... a matter of habit to obey them all. Suppose that excep-
> tionally we deviate from one of them, there would be resistance; if we resist this
> resistance, a state of tension or contraction is likely to result. It is this rigidity
> which we objectify when we attribute so stern as aspect to duty. (TSMR 21)

Bergson appreciates that when we resist resistance – the temptations, passions, and desires – we need to give ourselves reasons. There is the call of an idea, and autonomy (the exertion of self-control) takes place through the medium of intelligence. However, 'from the fact that we get back to obligation by rational ways it does not follow that obligation was of a rational order' (TSMR 22).

Bergson stresses the social origins of obligation. When we neglect this we posit an abstract conception of our conformity to duty (we obey duty for the sake of duty, Kant says). The 'totality of obligation', by which Bergson means our moral habits taken as a whole, represents a force that if it could speak would utter: 'You must because you must' (TSMR 23). What intelligence does is to introduce greater logical consistency into our lines of conduct. However, is it not the case that we never sacrifice our vanity, passions, and interests to the need for such consistency? We go wrong not when we ascribe a spurious independent existence to reason but when we conceive it as the controlling power or agency of our action: 'We might as well believe that the fly-wheel drives the machinery' (TSMR 23). Bergson is not denying that reason intervenes as a regulator to assure consistency between rules and maxims. His point is that it oversimplifies what is actually taking place in moral agency. Reason is at work everywhere in moral behaviour. Thus, an individual whose respectable behaviour is the least based on reasoning, as someone acts in accordance with sheepish conformity, introduces a rational order into his conduct from the mere fact of obeying rules that are logically connected to one another.

Bergson makes the striking claim that 'an absolutely categorical imperative is instinctive or somnambulistic, enacted as such in a normal state...' (TSMR 26) The 'totality of obligation' is, in fact, the *habit of contracting habits*, and this is a specifically human instinct of intelligence. Let us imagine that evolution has proceeded along two divergent lines with societies at the extremities of each. On the one hand, the more natural will be the instinctive type (such as ants or bees). On the other hand, there is the society where a degree of latitude has been left to individual waywardness. For nature to be effective in this case, that is, to achieve a comparable regularity, there is recourse to habit in place of instinct. Bergson then argues:

> Each of these habits, which may be called 'moral', would be incidental. But the aggregate of them, I mean the habit of contracting these habits, being at the very basis of societies and a necessary condition of their existence, would have a force comparable to that of instinct in respect of both intensity and regularity. (TSMR 26–7)

No matter how much society progresses through refinement and spiritualization this original design will remain. For Bergson then, social life is immanent, if only as a vague ideal, in instinct and intelligence. The difference in human societies is that here it is only the necessity of a rule that is the cardinal natural thing the two moralities: the former consists in impersonal rules and formulas, the latter incarnates itself in a privileged personality who becomes an example, such as exceptional human beings, be they Christian saints, sages of Greece, prophets of Israel, or the Arahants of Buddhism. Whereas the first morality works as a pressure or propulsive force, the second morality has the effect of an appeal. In it new life is proclaimed that goes against what nature prescribes, be it the survival of the fittest or the will to power of the strongest or the weakest. Here Bergson departs from Nietzsche's often brutally naturalist approach to ethics that must struggle harder to meet the charge of biologism.[34]

Bergson insists that in the second morality it is not simply a question of replacing egoism with altruism. It is not simply a question of the self now saying to itself, 'I am working for the benefit of mankind', simply because such an idea is too vast and the effect too diffuse. So what is taking place and being asked of the self? In the closed morality of pressure the individual and social are barely distinguishable: it is both at once and at this level spirit moves around a circle. Can we say that operative in the open soul subject to the open morality of aspiration there is the love of all humanity? For Bergson this would not go far enough since the openness can be extended to animals, plants, and all nature. It could even do without these since its form is not dependent on any specific content: '"Charity" would persist in him who possesses "charity," though there be no other living creature on earth' (TSMR 38). It is a psychic attitude that, strictly speaking, does not have an object. It is not acquired by nature but requires an effort and transmits itself through feeling. Think, for example, of the attraction or appeal of love and its passion in its early stages. It resembles an obligation (we must because we must) and perhaps a tragedy lies ahead, with a whole life facing the prospect of being wrecked, wasted, and ruined. This does not stop our responding to its call or appeal. We are entranced, as in cases of musical emotion that introduces us into new feelings, and as passers-by are forced into a street dance. The pioneers in morality proceed in a similar fashion: 'Life holds for them unsuspected tones of feeling like those of some new symphony, and they draw us after them into this music that we may express it in action' (TSMR 40).

The error of intellectualism is to suppose that feeling must hinge on an object and that all emotion is little more than the reaction of our sensory faculties to an intellectual representation. In music, Bergson notes, the emotions are not linked to any specific objects of joy, of sorrow, of pity, or of love. The difference he wants us to think about is between an emotion that can be represented (in images and through objects) and the creative emotion that is beyond representation and amounts to a real invention. States of emotion caused by certain things are ordained by nature and are finite or limited in number; we recognize them quite easily because their destiny is to spur us on to acts that answer to our needs. Bergson is not blind to the illusions of love and our propensity to psychological deception. However, he maintains that the effect of creative emotion is not reducible to this because here we are faced with emotional states that are distinct from sensation, that is, they cannot be reduced to being a psychical transposition of a physical stimulus. For Bergson such an emotion informs the creations not only of art but of science and civilization itself. It is a unique kind of emotion, one that precedes the image, virtually containing it, and is its cause (TSMR 47). His position is not equivalent, he insists, to a moral philosophy of sentiment, simply because we are dealing with an emotion that is capable of crystallizing into representations, even into an ethical doctrine. Moreover, he insists that if a new emotion, such as charity, wins over human beings this is neither because some metaphysics has enforced its moral practice nor because the moral practice has induced a disposition towards its alleged metaphysical claims. It is an attraction we are freely responding to in such cases and on the level of both intelligence and will (TSMR 49).

Bergson acknowledges that many will find this account of the second morality difficult to accept: is it not the domain of the irrational par excellence? Bergson is keen to challenge the assumption that the superhuman can be born only out of reactive forces or energies and he credits the inspirers of humanity with 'overflowing vitality' (TSMR 95). Neither of the two moralities exists in a pure state today: the first has handed on to the second something of its compulsive force, while the latter has diffused over the former something of its aroma.

this is incapable of producing real movement. Rather, real movement involves an action in which we find the impression of a coincidence, real or imaginary, with the generative effort of life (TSMR 55).

Bergson's thinking has its normative dimension in this positing of an open morality. While the first morality has its source in nature, the second has no place in nature's design. Nature may have foreseen a certain expansion of social life through intelligence but only of a very limited kind:

> Nature surely intended that men should beget men endlessly, according to the rule followed by all other living creatures; she took the most minute precautions to ensure the preservation of the species by the multiplication of individuals; hence she had not foreseen, when bestowing on us intelligence, that intelligence would at once find a way of divorcing the sexual act from its consequences, and that man might refrain from reaping without forgoing the pleasure of sowing. It is quite another sense that man outwits nature when he extends social solidarity into the brotherhood of man. (TSMR 56–7)

For Bergson the two forces of pressure and aspiration are to be treated as fundamental data and are not exclusively moral; rather, they have their sources in the twin tendencies of life: preservation and enhancement or overcoming (ibid., 96). There cannot be an absolute break with nature since this is never possible. Rather: 'It might be said, by slightly distorting Spinoza, that it is to get back to *natura naturans* that we break away from *natura naturata*' (TSMR 58).

century European thought. For Marx, writing in the 1840s, and in defiance of Hegel's negative assessment, Epicurus is the 'greatest representative of the Greek enlightenment',[1] while for Jean-Marie Guyau, writing in the 1870s, Epicurus is the original free spirit, 'still today it is the spirit of old Epicurus who, combined with new doctrines, works away at and undermines Christianity'.[2] For Nietzsche, Epicurus is one of the greatest human beings to have graced the earth and the inventor of 'heroic-idyllic philosophizing'.[3] Here my focus is on the reading of Epicureanism to be found in Bergson's commentary on Lucretius's remarkable poem, *De Rerum Natura*. For Bergson the task Lucretius sets himself is a pioneering one, one that will serve humanity, in particular making the Romans aware of previously unknown or misunderstood truths. In order to demonstrate these truths with precision it was necessary for Lucretius to be acquainted with Greek philosophy, especially the teaching of Epicurus.

In what follows I propose to highlight some of the central features of Bergson's commentary of Lucretius's text, *De Rerum Natura*. Bergson's commentary should be of interest to us for a number of reasons: (1) it is interesting that Bergson, typically represented as part of a French spiritualist tradition, should embark on this encounter with Epicurean materialism and atomism at the beginning of his philosophical career; (2) he encounters Lucretius in a way that I think resonates with any reader coming to Lucretius's text for the first time: there is the clear recognition of the brilliance of the text as well as of the tremendous challenges it presents to us as mortal subjects; (3) in recent years, and largely through the work of Pierre Hadot, there has been a great deal of interest in the idea of 'philosophy as a way of life', and we find such a conception of philosophy at work in Bergson's appreciation of Lucretius.[4] Bergson makes us aware of the offensive character of the text, noting that both Christians and pagans agreed on leaving Lucretius's teaching aside: in excluding the supernatural from the universe and denying any divine intervention in human affairs he had caused offence to Christians, while in speaking out violently as a poet against their gods, he had forfeited the right to be cited as an authority by the pagans. It is largely with advances in modern science, and on account of a growth in our enlightenment sensibilities, that we moderns can come to a renewed appreciation of the text and its main ideas. Nevertheless Lucretius continues to pose a challenge to us: we have to accept that the universe not only is not the work of the gods but it is also not in any way made for us; that it has been shaped haphazardly by the coming together of atoms, and that all things, including the earth, are destined to disappear. What is the function of philosophy and the ultimate aim of wisdom in the face of our insights into the nature of the universe? For Bergson, the science of Lucretius is fundamentally a melancholic one, and in what follows I want to show why he holds to this view in his reading of, and encounter with, the text. Indeed, it is only the French text that makes it clear that Bergson conceives the poem as 'profoundly melancholic' (*mélancolie profonde*) since the English translation from 1959 alters the order of the original text, and it is the point about melancholy that the text begins with and indicates that this is Bergson's main concern in his commentary. This opening of Bergson's commentary does not appear in the expurgated English edition until well into the translation.[5] For Bergson the teaching is 'sad and disheartening' since it raises the fundamental question, 'why persist in living?' if life is nothing more than a treadmill that leads nowhere and desire never finds a fulfilment. Moreover, pleasures are deceptive and no joy is untainted, and all striving is in vain.

I

Let me begin with citing some lines from *De Rerum Natura*. I cite from the opening of book two:

> What joy it is, when out at sea the stormwinds are lashing the waters, to gaze from the shore at the heavy stress some other man is enduring! Not that anyone's afflictions are in themselves a source of delight; but to realize from what troubles you yourselves are free is joy indeed. What joy, again, to watch opposing hosts marshalled on the field of battle when you yourself have no part in their peril! But this is the greatest joy of all: to possess a quiet sanctuary, stoutly fortified in the teaching of the wise, and to gaze down from that elevation on others wandering

makes it clear that the superior mode of existence attained is a modest existence, one enjoyed with a tranquil mind.[8]

For Lucretius, the object of philosophy is the cultivation of health and he speaks of philosophy as a form of treatment that can be administered;[9] it is a therapeutics, one that has specific illnesses and afflictions to cure, notably the fear of the active gods and the fear of death as well as the whole realm of superstition. Lucretius thinks that his Roman brethren suffer from what he calls the dead weight of superstition and are haunted by the fear of eternal punishments after death. A thoroughgoing and clear-sighted programme of naturalism is needed in order to emancipate the mind from subjection to fear and superstition. On several occasions in the book Lucretius provides the following lines as a refrain of learning:

> The dread and darkness of the mind cannot be dispelled by the sunbeams, the shining shafts of day, but only by an understanding of the outward forms and inner workings of nature.[10]

We are not to ask of the universe 'what does it mean?' since it means nothing, there is only the dance of the eternal return of atoms and the void; rather, we are to ask, 'how does it work?' Lucretius writes in book five of his text:

> So many atoms, clashing together in so many ways as they are swept along through infinite time by their own weight, have come together in every possible way and realized everything that could be formed by their combinations.[11]

True piety for Lucretius, as an Epicurean, consists in the serene contemplation of such a universe.[12]

His is a philosophy of immanence: nature is a self-producing positive power, eternally self-creating and self-destroying; the elements postulated at the base of nature work bottom up, in which the diverse products of nature are generated rather than assumed as already given.[13] The immanence at work is a radical one for it means that no 'divine power' has created the universe;[14] that there is no 'divine plan';[15] and that, I quote:

> our world has been made by nature through the spontaneous and casual collision and the multifarious, accidental, random, and purposeless congregation and coalescence of atoms whose suddenly formed combinations could serve on each occasion as the starting point of substantial fabrics – earth and sea and sky and the race of living creatures. On every ground, therefore, you must admit that there exist elsewhere other clusters of matter similar to this one which the ether clasps in ardent embrace.[16]

We can note the influence of Epicurus on Lucretius: virtue is related to pleasure and this pleasure consists in peace of mind, being the privilege of the sage. Epicurus has understood that human beings have materially everything they need to live and more, and yet humankind brings suffering upon itself, enslaving itself to superstition, fear, and desire or the 'deplorable lust for life', as Lucretius calls it. We could reflect here on the various paeans to Epicurus that structure the text, in which Epicurus is presented as a noble saviour-like figure freeing human beings from the inauthentic life – excessive pride, lust, aggression, self-indulgence, and indolence – and inspiring them to a new way of life, including an ethics of refined egoism and the cultivation of the self (see especially the opening of book six, the final book of the text).

Let me stress once again the naturalism informing the ethical doctrine: it rids philosophy of supernatural explanations with its scientific principles of nothing springing from nothing and nothing ever being destroyed. The emphasis throughout the book is on explaining phenomena through natural causes, so lightning is to be explained in such terms and not as a divine warning. Nothing springs from nothing since for anything to be created specific germs are required: a set of conditions and time. As noted, the teaching has radical aspects: for example, the soul is nothing more than matter and is subject to death since it is made of subtle atoms scattered throughout the body, and is therefore as material as the body and without which it cannot exist. Death is radical in its finality and Lucretius is uncompromising in his account of this: it denotes the end of our existence and yet is not to be feared for the reasons that Epicurus has provided and that Lucretius rehearses in dramatic fashion in the denouement to book three of the text.

b. That old age is forced to succeed youth by an eternal law.
c. That beings necessarily reproduce at the expense of other beings.
d. That the movement of atoms is eternal and the formation of new worlds continues eternally.
e. We do not need to marvel at the creation of life since the laws of matter are all we need to explain everything.
f. Finally, that humankind is not separate from nature and is not in any way a special case or exception to the laws of material existence. It is destined to perish since, as a result of the movement of atoms, everything will one day disintegrate. The atoms, converted into dust, will be drawn together again, and new combinations of atoms will produce new worlds, and on it will go throughout eternity.

Nietzsche, as I have noted, refers to the poet as the 'sombre Lucretius', and Bergson holds that he produces a melancholic philosophy of nature and of life; indeed, for Bergson this is where Lucretius departs from his great master, Epicurus. Let me now turn to Bergson's commentary.

II

Bergson's encounter with the text is of a specific kind. For example, at the start of his commentary he makes it clear that he does not propose to refute a philosophical system, such as we find in Epicurean teaching, but to understand the system: what are its main claims? How does it argue for them? What are its achievements? And what philosophical challenge does it present to us? He proposes to read the poem as a whole and not focus on the descriptive passages alone since, he argues, the most gripping passages of the poem, such as the depiction of the life of primitive humans, the effects of lightning, and plague of Athens, are there to try and make us comprehend a significant philosophical principle. Right at the beginning of the commentary he notes the fundamental dimension of Epicurean teaching (and that also had such an effect on other nineteenth-century readers such as Nietzsche), namely to liberate the human mind that is plagued by fear and superstition: 'religion, guilty of many crimes, has kept mankind in constant dread of death'.[20] In short, Epicurean teaching has an essentially practical function, its chief aim being that of restoring calm to the human mind. Bergson stresses here the inspiration of Epicurus on Lucretius, in which virtue is related to pleasure and in which pleasure consists of peace of mind and is the privilege of the sage. Epicurus has understood that the human has materially everything it needs to live and more and yet it brings suffering upon itself, being enslaved by desire, superstition, and fear. Epicurus teaches that our happiness depends not on external things but on our state of mind. Bergson also notes the naturalistic character of this teaching: it rids philosophy of supernatural explanations with its key scientific principles of nothing springing from nothing and nothing ever being destroyed (principles first bright to light, Bergson notes, by Democritus). The Epicurean achievement, so amply displayed in *De Rerum Natura*, is to attempt a genuinely scientific explanation of the workings of universe: 'What proves that nothing springs from nothing is that anything, to be created, requires a specific germ, set of conditions, and time'.[21] Bergson describes Lucretius's theory of atoms as 'one of the most beautiful creations of antiquity'.[22] Later in the commentary he describes atomism as a 'profound philosophical system' in which the best explanation of the universe is the simplest one.[23] Moreover, the system of Democritus, who invents atomism, is 'perhaps the most perfect expression of materialism'.[24] Epicurus adopts and modifies the atomic theory, and here Bergson notes both Epicurus's 'abysmal ignorance of scientific things' and 'the originality of his approach'. In the hands of Epicurus the aim of philosophy is not, strictly speaking to instruct human beings but to soothe them. Bergson also notes that for Lucretius, Epicurus was not just a sage but the 'matchless sage and great benefactor of mankind'.[25] More than this Epicurus is a god for Lucretius with his 'sublime discoveries'.[26]

Bergson notes that each of the six books that make up the poem feature a remark or observation about philosophy in general or about Lucretius's particular aim. Book two, in particular, he notes, commences with a magnificent eulogy of

Memory and *Creative Evolution*. Bergson ends his initial treatment of the poem by noting the tremendous challenge of the ideas presented in it: first, the gods, though they exist, do not interfere in any way with the things in this world and therefore it is childish to live in fear of them; and, second, all living things are subject to growth and eventually disappearance, and here Bergson notes the poignancy of Lucretius's insights – the same is true of our planet earth (which is a living being for Lucretius, notes Bergson), as this too will one day fall to dust.

The main idea of the text Bergson treats next, and treats extensively throughout the commentary, is that of Lucretius on death. He notes the salient features of the teaching: that the soul is nothing more than matter and therefore this soul is subject to death since it is made up of subtle atoms scattered throughout the body and is, therefore, as material as the body. However, Bergson goes on to note that Lucretius was not able to completely destroy belief in the immortality of the soul since this belief is stronger than his philosophical arguments. What Lucretius does develop though, Bergson says, is an insight into one of the sources of the belief in the immortality of the soul, namely 'the instinctive tendency which every living being has to perpetuate itself indefinitely in time.'[29] Ultimately, Bergson locates in Lucretius's text a melancholy science and teaching, and he rightly draws our attention to the remarkable and emphatic ending of book three of the text: 'Life is nothing more than constant movement that leads nowhere, than desire that is never fulfilled', and so on.[30] Indeed, in the text, at the very close of book three, Lucretius speaks of the 'lust for life' as 'deplorable' since it 'holds us trembling in bondages to uncertainties and dangers' and says that the 'unquenchable thirst for life keeps us always on the gasp'.[31] As a way of indicating the noble way to face one's demise and inevitable death, Lucretius holds up the lives of Democritus and Epicurus as examples: the former approached ripe age by making a willing sacrifice to death with his unbowed head, while the latter, the master himself, endured intense pain in his final days and yet only looked back with pleasure on his life and friendships.

I now wish to comment on how Bergson construes what we might call Lucretius's 'modernity'. For him this consists in two things: the first is the attempt to account for the origin of the first living beings; the second is to develop insight into the adaptation of their organs to their needs. Regards the first point, Bergson notes that an adequate explanation defeated Lucretius – he falls back, he says, on a myth, namely that all living things spring from the earth as the mother of all things – and goes on to explain the appearance of the first living organisms. Regards the second point, Bergson thinks that Lucretius's answer anticipates that provided by Darwin. I quote:

> Of a multitude of living organisms that spring up haphazardly, the only ones to survive are those capable of providing for their needs and adapting themselves to their environment. In these beautiful descriptive passages Lucretius's imagination is given full reign. Latin literature offers nothing superior to the last half of Book V.[32]

What can be said of the birth of living beings, including the human, is that it was due to chance. The human is not different from the rest of the animal kingdom in this regard; being weaker than other animals, the human has evolved slowly and painfully through a struggle that has involved intelligence and will, resulting in a social order and civilization. Bergson departs from Lucretius here, attributing to the human an ethical superiority: 'The more humble our origin, the more praise we deserve for becoming what we are.'[33]

A specific feature of Bergson's interpretation of Lucretius is the emphasis I have already alluded to on the melancholy character of *De Rerum Natura*. Bergson thinks melancholy pervades the book and is, along with the sublime, its most striking feature: the teaching is 'sad and disheartening' since it raises the fundamental question, 'why persist in living?' if life is nothing more than a treadmill that leads nowhere and desire never finds a fulfilment. Moreover, pleasures are deceptive and no joy is untainted, and all striving is in vain. Now this sounds a lot like Schopenhauer, but his doctrine is nowhere mentioned in the text: 'We spend the best part of our lives in pursuing vain honours or in cultivating land that is barren and indifferent to our toil. Then comes senescence and with it the childish fear of death.'[34] We are tortured by our visions of death, in which all hope and joy disappear. Although death is the end the spectacle of civil strife had an enormous impact on his thinking; from a young age Lucretius witnessed bloody struggles, for example, those arising from the rivalry between Marius and Sylla and that can be seen as a prelude to the violent upheavals that cast a dark shadow over the Roman republic. Bergson notes that the first lines of the poem are a prayer to Venus. It is no surprise, Bergson thinks, that Lucretius should extol the virtues of philosophy (which affords peace and sanity of mind) compared to the vanities of the pursuit of power and wealth. Lucretius attacks those who are full of ambition and intrigue, and Bergson cites him: 'Let them sweat and bleed in the narrow road where their ambition writhes.'[36] Bergson notes that, like his great mentor, Lucretius stood apart from public affairs and public life. However, he maintains that Lucretius's melancholy is not simply a result of his alienation from the world or the time he inhabited. In addition, he does not think that Lucretius reduces philosophy to being little more than a means of consolation. Knowledge is not simply a refuge or a consolation in terms of strife; rather, it is the object of life itself; wars and disasters are ills because they divert the attention of humans from the only noble preoccupations worthy of the mind. Philosophy is noble because, says Bergson, it frees us from social ambition and competition. As a philosopher Lucretius liberates himself from indignation and anger; he feels only pity for those who fail to see where genuine happiness lies and thus unknowingly afflict great harm on themselves.

I have mentioned that Bergson is interested in Lucretius's thinking on the clinamen or the swerve, since it seems to grant a degree of freedom to human existence. However, Bergson also notes the deterministic character of Lucretius's materialism. He notes that Lucretius is a thinker with an abiding love of nature and who observes it closely. We need to be enlightened by a great truth according to Lucretian teaching: behind the smiling and picturesque face of nature and beyond the infinitely diverse phenomena that constantly change, we discover pre-established, unchangeable laws, ones that work uniformly and constantly, yielding predetermined effects. This means, of course, that nothing in the workings of the universe is fortuitous and that there is no place for nonconformity: 'Everywhere there are collective or compensatory forces, mechanically linked causes and effects. A number of invariable elements have existed throughout eternity; the inexorable laws of nature determine how they combine and separate; these laws are rigidly prescribed and adhered to.'[37] Bergson thus sees as the dominant feature of Lucretius's poem this stress on events being mathematically predictable since they are the inevitable consequence of what has preceded. For Lucretius, then, at least on Bergson's reading, nature is bound by a contract, with each phenomenon being mathematically predetermined and predictable. Ultimately for Bergson recognition of this is the main source of the melancholy of Lucretius. He argues that the concept of the rigidity of natural laws obsesses and saddens the poet. Let me quote Bergson at some length:

> Unable to see anything in the universe except cumulative or compensatory forces and convinced that whatever is results naturally and inevitably from whatever has been, Lucretius takes pity on the human race. Man stands helpless in the face of blind, unchanging forces that are and will continue throughout eternity to be at work. Man is the accidental product of a wretched combination of atoms brought temporarily together by inexorable natural laws and destined eventually to be torn apart by the same forces. Does he have a purpose in the universe? We think that matter was made for us, as if we were not subjected to its selfsame laws. We think that friendly or jealous gods protect or persecute us, as if unpredictable alien forces could intervene in nature, or as if we were not borne along in the all – embracing stream by inexorable laws of matter. This is the source of Lucretius' melancholy and of his compassion for mankind.[38]

What of Lucretius's achievements as an observer of nature, and what are the weaknesses in his approach? Bergson notes that in the poem the role of science is just as important as the role of philosophy. He notes several shortcomings though in Lucretius's approach to nature and in his physics. The poet, he claims, fails to liberate his mind completely from mythological notions and occasionally falls back on the pagan notion that nature is animate and personal: 'He would of course condemn a theory which suggests the earth is an animate being; yet we created or destroyed.'[41]

Bergson's commentary ends with an appreciation of the main challenges presented by Lucretius's materialism and naturalism. The movement of atoms is eternal and the formation of new worlds will continue eternally. The earth has been formed relatively recently, engendering plants and then animals. We do not need to marvel at the creation of life or living beings since the laws of matter can explain everything. Humankind is not separate from nature and certainly not a special case or exception to the laws of material existence; it is destined to perish since as a result of the movement of atoms everything will one day disintegrate: 'The atoms, converted into dust, will be drawn together again; new combinations of atoms will produce new worlds; and so it goes, throughout eternity.'[42] Bergson notes the eternally recurrent aspect of the doctrine (not that we, as humans, have any consciousness of this since, as Lucretius points out, we lack the memory of our previous existences): 'Atoms, which are constantly moving about, uniting and disuniting, will naturally yield every possible combination during the infinite course of the centuries.'[43]

Concluding Thoughts

In spite of his reliance on Epicurus's teaching, including the science and the ethics, Bergson sees Lucretius as singularly original. He is original in his conception of the nature of things and in his conception of human nature. For Bergson,

Lucretius differs from Epicurus in being an enthusiastic observer of nature, showing a gift for its picturesque aspect (its 'fleeting, transitional variations'). Moreover, he appreciates simultaneously both the pattern of nature that appeals to the geometrician and that which appeals to the artist: he admires the beauty of nature and understands it, but this does not stop him from analysing it and breaking it apart anatomically into fibres and cells. This ability on the part of Lucretius to grasp the two-sided character of things is for Bergson the source of the originality of his poetry and his philosophy. For Bergson, Lucretius is not like Democritus: he does not depict collections of atoms in their stark nakedness but decks them out in natural or in fancied colours. Moreover, his descriptions of the universe are not cold but 'imbued with an oratorical fervour that stimulates and sways'.[44] Indeed, Bergson speculates that Lucretius would not have written his text if he had seen in Epicureanism little more than a dry and self-centred doctrine, 'contrived for the purpose of bringing to man the calm placidity of the beast and ridding him of his most noble anxieties'.[45]

Lucretius differs from Epicurus in as much as Epicurus did not study nature or physical phenomena simply for the purpose of increasing knowledge and instructing his followers in the nature of things. Bergson notes that Epicurus disdainfully rejects the idea that we acquire and enjoy knowledge for its own sake; rather, the whole purpose of knowledge is to banish gods from nature and defeat superstition. Bergson even goes so far as arguing that the Epicurean doctrine leads, in fact, to futility in the study of any question that is not directly linked to everyday life and the attainment of happiness or peace of mind.

For Bergson we cannot ignore the fact that the theory of atoms offers a poetic conception of the universe. What he means by this is that it cannot but have a deep impact on our imaginations, in which nature takes on a new majesty, and with every description pointing to an eternal truth. Bergson well appreciates the sublime quality of Epicureanism, especially as we find it articulated in Lucretius's text.[46]

Finally, what of Bergson's major claim that Lucretius's materialism is fundamentally melancholic? For Bergson this is where Lucretius departs from Epicurus. The doctrine of Epicurus, he argues, excludes melancholy and sadness as these would only continue to trouble the mind when the whole point of practising philosophy as a way of life is to attain a state of undisturbed serenity or what Bergson describes as a placid state of joyfulness that may not be intense but is nevertheless permanent. Lucretius draws different conclusions from the theory of the atom according to Bergson. We are subject to rigid natural laws

This, he thinks, is what the closing description of the book is meant to do: if we have not learnt the ultimate lesson and attained philosophical serenity over the most intense physical pain and suffering, then we cannot face the nature of the universe with truly Epicurean equanimity.[48]

in turn is modelled on the fiction of a unitary, timeless self. Both Spinoza and Nietzsche regard it as a notion with a pernicious influence. For Spinoza it is bound up with our ignorance of nature and of the real causes of our action.[1] For Nietzsche it is part of the 'metaphysics of the hangman', being an invention of the weak and vengeful who need to believe in the idea of a doer separate from its deeds so as to blame the strong for being what they are and so hold them accountable for their strength.[2] The idea of free will is bound up, then, with simple-minded and illusory conceptions of the will. As we shall see, though, Bergson offers a highly subtle and sophisticated defence of 'free will' in his first published book – in French the title of the book runs as *Essai sur les données immédiates de la conscience* ('Essay on the immediate data of consciousness') – where freedom involves breaking with the habits and conventions that govern the life of the social ego or what Bergson calls our superficial self. With regard to the significance of the book's title one commentator helpfully noted that with the word *données* (data) Bergson intends something that is the opposite of 'construction':

and the reference it always arouses in the mind … is to a fact, assumed or ascertained, which is to serve as a starting-point for research. Such facts are primitive terms, ultimate principles, beyond which, as Pascal would say, our analysis cannot proceed. It is no longer a case of constructing the world, to make it conform, willy-nilly, to a system, as the Germans do; it is a case of ascertaining precisely what is given, which is a much more exacting and praiseworthy task.[3]

We need to bear this in mind as we proceed since it is clear that for Bergson duration is a fact of experience, and he does not seek to build an elaborate system or philosophy of construction to account for it.

Bergson approaches questions concerning freedom in the context of the rise of the physical sciences as the dominant paradigm of knowledge in modern culture. In particular he challenges the uncritical transference of a physicalist model of reality to the domain of psychology and to psychical life. In short, he advances a conception of freedom in response to the claims of scientific determinism. In *Time and Free Will* Bergson restricts his argument to this level, defending the becoming of psychical life with its qualities of voluntary and free action against the claim that everything that exists is determined in accordance with mechanical laws of cause and effect. For Bergson freedom is bound up with the reality of duration, and for him this has the status of a fact of experience. If we adequately understand what duration is, then we can advance the claim that a durational life is as factual a reality as what the physicist claims for physical reality. Bergson does not appeal to anything mysterious to support his insights into duration, neither does he suppose there is a fixed, unitary self that remains the same over and above all change. Freedom consists in our becoming in time and we are nothing other than this becoming. Bergson's account does not contain everything that one might wish for in a theory of freedom – it has nothing to say on collective action and the actualization of freedom in this manner, for example – but it does succeed in posing in original terms questions concerning the relation between time, freedom, and the self. There are also problems with his account as we will see.

For Bergson the problem of freedom is in large part bound up with the legacy Kant bequeaths to modern thought. In some of its fundamental aspects Kant's project is a response to the rise of Newtonian physics and mechanism in the modern age. Kant accepted the Newtonian picture as an accurate picture of the world and thought that metaphysics had to be reconfigured in the wake of the Newtonian revolution. But, as he himself puts it in the preface to the second edition of the *Critique of Pure Reason* (1787), he is led to deny knowledge in order to make room for faith. In short, the traditional ideas of metaphysics, such as God, the immortality of the soul, and free will, cannot lay claim to knowledge but they can be posited as postulates of pure practical Reason and are valid only when conceived in these terms. However, this saving of metaphysics comes at a great price: freedom has to be placed in a noumenal realm, a realm beyond phenomenal appearance, and this is a realm outside time. In *Time and Free Will* Bergson picks up this difficulty presented to philosophy by Kant and endeavours to demonstrate that freedom is time and that without this identification it cannot be said to be anything real at all. Moreover, for Bergson time is the domain of freedom since the reality of time means that all is not given and not everything that happens can be calculated in advance and

We are in the habit of misconstruing ourselves. This is true, for Bergson, of both common sense and science. Two problems or obstacles stand in the way of our comprehension of freedom qua our becoming in time or duration: language and space.

Language imitates our spatial habits of representation: it compels us to establish sharp and precise distinctions or discontinuity between material things, which proves useful for social life. It is not until the chapter on the two multiplicities that this is properly explained and clarified: we have a natural inability to conceive of a multiplicity other than the discrete or discontinuous kind, and what we need to think, but struggle to do so, is the continuous multiplicity where the elements exist in a confused state and relations of fusion and interpenetration. To adequately understand what 'free will' is we need to overcome the confusion that informs the debates between determinists and their opponents: we confuse duration with extensity, succession with simultaneity, and quality with quantity.

In chapter 1 of the text Bergson poses a simple question: How can a more intense sensation contain one of less intensity? Is this a good problem to focus on? He seeks to expose the error of psychophysics that consists in the view that intensities are magnitudes and so lend themselves to precise measurement and calculation. This is to treat them on the order of extensive magnitudes. It makes sense to compare the difference in quantity between two tables; but does it make sense to say I feel twice as jealous today as I did yesterday? And yet this is what the science of Bergson's day would have us do. The error, though, is not peculiar to science since we commonly set differences of quantity between internal states, saying I am more or less warm, more or less sad, etc.

In numbers we form a series in which the greater contains the lesser; how do we form a series of this kind with intensities without supposing they can be superposed on each other? Do we not have to suppose that an intensity can be assimilated to magnitude? Bergson's question, then, is whether a psychic state can be treated as a magnitude.[6] Bergson himself asks: 'Why do we say of a higher intensity that it is greater? Why do we think of a greater quantity or a greater space?' (TFW 7) His contention is that states of consciousness cannot be isolated from one another but should be approached in terms of a concrete multiplicity, in which there is fusion and interpenetration, in short, a qualitative heterogeneity. The reason for this fusion and interpenetration is that the states of consciousness unfold themselves in duration and not, like the units of arithmetic, in space. An increasing intensity of a mental state is inseparable from a qualitative progression and from a becoming of time. As Deleuze points out, the notion of an intensive magnitude 'involves an impure mixture between determinations that differ in kind' with the result that our question 'by how much does a sensation grow or intensify?' takes us back to a badly stated problem.[7]

Bergson seeks to promote a dynamic way of looking at things in opposition to the confusions that guide common sense and science. For example, he maintains that when we penetrate 'the depths of consciousness', we see that it is illegitimate 'to treat psychic phenomena as things which are set side by side' (TFW 8–9). However, he appreciates that a dynamic appreciation of things is repugnant to what he calls 'reflective consciousness' simply because such a consciousness prides itself on thinking in terms of clean-cut distinctions, such as the ones we can easily express in words and in things with well-defined outlines, just like the ones that are perceived in space. His fundamental argument is that we are, in fact, dealing with changes in quality rather than of magnitudes. Bergson gives examples of the emotions of hope, joy, and sorrow in an effort to demonstrate that what we are dealing with in our emotional life are qualitative changes, changes that alter the nature of the experience in question, and not with increases in magnitude. He also deals with aesthetic and moral feelings in the same manner, such as grace, the feeling of the beautiful, and the moral sentiment of pity. He notes in the latter example that the transition from a feeling of repugnance to one of fear, then from this fear to a feeling of sympathy, and finally from sympathy to humility, denotes a qualitative progress in what we take to be an increasing intensity of a sentiment (TFW 19).

This is what we are doing, then, in setting up a pure intensity as if it were a magnitude: in the idea of intensity we find the image of a present contraction and therefore a future expansion, of a kind of compressed space, and this leads chapter that has treated the relation between intensity and multiplicity, in which Bergson seeks to show that our idea of intensity is situated at the junction of two streams: one of which is the idea of extensive magnitude (something we can compare and measure precisely, such as the difference in size between two blocks of wood) and the other is the image of an inner multiplicity that does not lend itself to calculation.

Let us see how Bergson seeks to expose the illusion of number. This is the illusion that generates a confusion of quality with quantity, of intensity with extensity. Chapter 2 of *Time and Free Will* begins with the claim that number may be defined as a synthesis of the one and the many conceived as a collection of discrete units, in which every number is the 'one' of a simple intuition. The unity of a number is that of a sum in that it covers a multiplicity of parts each of which can be taken separately. However, this characterization is insufficient since it fails to recognize that the units of a collection of numbers are identical. In other words, the question has to be posed: just what is the difference between the units of a number if the units are identical? Bergson's answer is that numbering or counting relies upon the intuition of a multiplicity of identical parts or units, so that the only difference between them can reside in their position in space.[8] The components or elements of an actual or discrete multiplicity have to be differentiated; otherwise they would form a single unit. Bergson gives the example of a flock of sheep and invites us to carry out the following operation: we can count them and say there are fifty and in counting them as a collection of units we neglect their individual differences (which are known to the farmer whose flock they are); then we can say that although we have a grouping of sheep they differ in that they occupy different positions in space. Now this requires an intuition of space. This is what Kant sought to demonstrate in his transcendental aesthetic by showing that space has an existence independent of its content and arguing that it cannot be treated as an abstraction like other abstractions of sensation. This is a demonstration that Bergson regards as correct as far as it goes (TFW 92–5). How do I form the image of a singular collection of things? Do I place the sheep side by side in an ideal space or do I repeat in succession the image of a single one? It is certain that I am building up a composite picture in which I retain the successive images and this retention is required if the number is to go on increasing in proportion to my building up of the collection of units. Bergson's contention is that this act, in which I am juxtaposing the images being built up, takes place not in duration but in space. It is not that we do not count in duration; rather, the point is that we count the moments of duration by means of points in space.[9]

Numbers evoke curiosity in that every number is both a collection of units (the number one being a sum of, or divisible into, fractional quantities) and is itself a unit. Taken as a unit in itself the whole of any number can be grasped by a simple and indivisible intuition. Such intuition leads us to the belief that all numbers are made up of indivisible components; all we are doing here, however, is building up levels of discreteness (adding, subtracting, multiplying, and dividing discreteness). Any unit of a number is potentially implicated in an actual or discrete multiplicity, and within such a multiplicity when the elements change they do not change in kind (they might grow smaller or bigger, but this is pure quantity and not quality). When I equate the number three to the sum of 1 + 1 +1 there is nothing to stop me from regarding each of the units as indivisible, but the reason for this is simply that I choose not to make use of the multiplicity that is enclosed within each of the units (I could choose to compose the number from halves or quarters). If it is conceivable that a unit can be divided into as many parts as we want then it is shown to be extended as a magnitude. Only when a number assumes a completed state do we think that the whole displays the features of continuity, and this then settles into a general illusion with respect to numbering (we overlook the discontinuity of number). This explains why Bergson is keen to draw our attention to the difference between number in the process of formation and a formed number: 'The unit is irreducible while we are thinking it and the number is discontinuous while we are building it up; but, as soon as we consider number in its finished state, we objectify it, and it then appears to be divisible to an unlimited extent' (TFW 83). Number applies to the sphere of 'objectivity' in the sense that new elements or components can be added or substituted at any time but without this addition or subtraction our experience (TFW 97). Abstract space has to be seen as a limit-conception, that is, as a result of the needs of action and not reified as an indomitable feature of the human standpoint.[10]

We can now return to the central argument of *Time and Free Will*: we perfectly comprehend the sense of there being a number that is greater than another, but can the same be said of an intensive sensation? How can a more intense sensation contain one of less intensity? Unlike the law of number the relations among intensities cannot be adequately approached in terms of those of container and contained with different intensities being superposed upon one another. Adequately understood an intensity cannot be assimilated to magnitude.

Is Time Space?

The question to be posed now is the following: can duration be treated as a discrete multiplicity, that is, are states of consciousness external to one another and spread out in time as a spatial medium? Looked at from the perspective of pure duration our states can be seen to permeate and melt into another without precise outlines and without any affiliation with number, in which past and present states form a whole, 'as happens when we recall the notes of a tune, melting, so to speak, into another' (TFW 100). These are involved in qualitative changes that disclose a pure heterogeneity (continuous variation). When we interrupt the rhythm of a tune by perhaps dwelling longer than is customary on one note, it is not the exaggerated length that signals the mistake to us but rather the qualitative change caused in the whole of the piece of music.

> We can thus conceive of succession without distinction, and think of it as a mutual penetration, an interconnexion and organization of elements, each one of which represents the whole, and cannot be distinguished or isolated from it except by abstract thought. (TFW 101)

Because we have the idea of space we set our states side by side so as to perceive them simultaneously: we project time into space, express duration in terms of extensity, and succession assumes the form of a continuous chain. A decisive movement or shift takes place in our thinking, although one we are ordinarily not aware of:

> Note that the mental image thus shaped implies the perception, no longer successive, but simultaneous, of a *before* and *after*, and that it would be a contradiction to suppose a succession which was only a succession, and which nevertheless was contained in one and the same instant. (TFW 101)

The important point is this: we could not introduce order into terms without first distinguishing them and then comparing the places they occupy. As Bergson writes, 'if we introduce an order in what is successive, the reason is that succession is converted into simultaneity and is projected into space' (TFW 102). Moreover, since the idea of a reversible series in duration, even of a certain order of succession in time, itself implies the representation of space it cannot be used to define it.

Reducing time to simple movement of position means confusing time with space. It is this confusion between motion and the space traversed which explains the paradoxes of Zeno. The interval between two points is infinitely divisible, and if motion is said to consist of parts like those of the interval itself, then the interval can never be crossed. But the truth of the matter is different:

> each of Achilles's steps is a simple indivisible act ... after a given number of these acts, Achilles will have passed the tortoise. The mistake of the Eleatics arises from their identification of this series of acts, each of which is *of a definite kind and indivisible*, with the homogeneous space which underlies them. (TFW 113)

Because this space can be divided and put together again according to any kind of abstract law, the illusion arises that it is possible to reconstruct the movement of Achilles not with his step but with that of the tortoise. In truth, we have only two tortoises that agree to make the same kind of steps or simultaneous acts so never to catch one another. Let us now take the paradox of the flying arrow that at any point is not in flight. If the arrow is always at a point when is it ever in flight or mobile? Instead, we might ask, what is it in this example that leads us to saying of these varying aspects) (TFW 123).

In Bergson's first published text duration, conceived as a pure heterogeneity, is presented as an aspect of a synthesizing consciousness; that is, its reality is something solely psychological. Bergson contrasts psychic time with clock time. It is the latter that treats time as a magnitude (TFW 107–8). Motion, however, in so far as it is a passage from one point to another, 'is a mental synthesis, a psychic and therefore unextended process ... If consciousness is aware of anything more than positions, the reason is that it keeps the successive positions in mind and synthesizes them' (TFW 111). The conclusion is reached in *Time and Free Will* that the interval of duration exists only for us and on account of the interpenetration of our conscious states (TFW 116). Outside ourselves we find only space, and consequently nothing but simultaneities, 'of which we could not even say that they are objectively successive, since succession can only be thought through *comparing* the present with the past'. The qualitative impression of change cannot, therefore, be felt outside consciousness. Duration and motion are not objects but 'mental syntheses' (TFW 120). In our consciousness states permeate one another, imperceptibly organize themselves into a whole, and bind the past to the present. Conceived as a virtual, qualitative multiplicity this duration 'contains number only potentially, as Aristotle would have said' (TFW 121).

The danger in the account Bergson gives, one which he appears to implicitly acknowledge, is that it fails to appreciate the extent to which even a homogeneous space presupposes dimensions of space that have qualitative differences. As Lindsay points out, if we take away the possibility of determinations in space then space itself becomes nothing and cannot provide the basis of counting.[11]

Certainly space has to be regarded as that which has infinite divisibility, but such a characterization only serves to indicate that each division is made in definite ways and that a definite division of provisional units implies some kind of heterogeneity. If objects were, as a matter of fact, completely identical and devoid of qualitative differences then no discrimination would be possible at all: 'Without counting and discrimination we could not have the conception of that which is merely divisible.'[12] So, while we can think of qualitative differences becoming more and more like mathematical points, if they disappeared completely so too would the ground upon which spatial relations are constructed. Lindsay then notes that if the same is true of time then, *mutatis mutandis*, 'time and space may be homogeneous media and yet sufficiently distinguished as the limits of duration and extensity; as the limits of two mathematical functions may be nothing and yet distinguishable in terms of the functions which they limit.'[13] Space and time cannot then be taken to be, in their homogeneous aspect, a priori realities (intuitions of sensibility) but have to be seen as emergent and exigent features of social action. As the mental diagram of infinite divisibility abstract space and abstract time are the result of the solidification and division we effect on a moving continuity in order to secure a fulcrum for our action and to introduce into it real changes. This necessity of making this move is clearly argued for, and contra Kant, by Bergson in *Matter and Memory* (MM 211). The real is made up of both extensity and duration, but this extent is not that of some infinite and infinitely divisible space, the space of a receptacle, that the intellect posits as the place in which and from which everything is built. It is necessary, then, to separate a concrete extension, diversified and organized at the same time, from 'the amorphous and inert space which subtends it' (MM 187). This is the space that we divide indefinitely and within which we conceive movement as a multiplicity of instantaneous positions. Homogeneous space is not, then, logically anterior to material things but posterior to them.

The Errors of the Associationist Model of the Mind

Bergson's book makes a bold claim: all determinism, even physical determinism, involves a psychological hypothesis: both psychological determinism and refutations of it rest on an inaccurate conception of duration. Moreover, our conceptions of matter and how it behaves may tell us more about the operations of our human mind than about matter itself. We have an 'associationist' rose would have a qualitatively different experience. Thus, the kind of plurality involved in a mental life is that of a qualitative heterogeneity. Our mental life is not composed of atomic elements. This atomism is a widespread view of matter and it also informs how we commonly conceive of time as made up of discrete instants that are analogous to mathematical points (think again of Zeno's paradoxes). Bergson maintains, however, that the mind does not work by a linear series of discrete events that bring each other about by laws of association.

Why do these habits of associationism and atomism exist? Bergon's answer is that they exist for the convenience of language and the promotion of social relations. Our language gives weight to discrete entities and is structured in terms of subject and predicate. As social beings we need to control and manipulate objects and things, to work on them for utilitarian ends, so it becomes a custom or habit to view the entire material universe in these terms. But this is to overlook the interconnected links that bind things together and also to neglect duration as a continuous heterogeneity.

Let me seek to demonstrate with the aid of a simple diagram how Bergson works out the relation between time and free will. Bergson claims that while we are deliberating over an action the self is changing and modifying the feelings that agitate it. A dynamic series of states is thus formed that permeate one another and which lead, through a process of natural evolution, to a free act. Where determinism goes wrong is in conceiving of non-durational self that simply glides across feelings that have a fixed form. This, however, is to deprive a self of living activity. It is only by making an artificial extraction from the actual flow of time that we can pose issues of action in abstract terms, such as the action

I took could not have taken place in any other way. We are simply unaware and our habits conceal the durational conditions of our existence.

Let us take the example of the equal possibility of two contrary actions in which I hesitate between X and Y and go in turn from one to the other. The example and diagram I am using is taken from Bergson's text (TFW 176).

The deterministic or mechanistic view that Bergson is seeking to expose as flawed is the one that rests on the assumption of an impartially active ego or self that hesitates between two inert and solidified courses of action. Let us say we decide in favour of OX over OY: well, the mechanist assumes that OY will remain, and vice versa; if I choose OY, then the line OX remains open, waiting in case the self decides to retrace its steps so as to make use of it. It is in this sense that we say that the contrary action in each case was equally possible.

Christophe Bouton has argued that in Bergson's philosophy 'the tree of possibilities, with all its ramifications, can have no other meaning than that of a spatialization of duration. It arises not out of time but out of space.'[14] He is correct to note that in Bergson's account duration is an organic evolution and involves a process of maturation, in which, as in Bergson's own words, the free life in order to prove that man is capable of choosing without a motive. (TFW 170)

For Bergson freedom is elusive for good reasons: 'Freedom is the relation of the concrete self to the act which it performs. This relation is indefinable, just because we *are* free. We can analyse a thing but not a process; we can break up extensity but not duration' (TFW 219). To say that the free act is one that once done might have been left undone is to imply an equivalence between concrete duration and its spatial symbol. And to say that a free act is one that could not be foreseen even though all the conditions were known in advance is again to deny the positive or creative reality of duration. In short, every demand for an explanation of the conditions of freedom comes back to the question: Can time adequately be represented by space? The answer is yes if we are dealing with time flown and no if we are speaking of 'time flowing'.

The Force of Time

Bergson's key claim is that time is force, it is an energy.[17] However, durational time is completely different from the force and energy of concern to the physicist, notably, the law of the conservation of energy. Science cannot deal properly with the reality of flowing time but only with the time that has already flown. This flowing time can only be approached in terms of a specific conception of multiplicity in which the relations between elements are ones of fusion and interpenetration. Bergson makes a distinction between the reality where the law of the conservation of energy holds sway and the domain of life:

The instinctive belief in the conservation of one identical quality of matter, and of force, depends on the fact that inert matter does not seem to exist in time, or at least does not conserve any trace of past time. But this is not the case in the realm of life. Here duration in time seems to act as a cause, in which the idea of putting things back in their place after a certain period of time is absurd: regression in time has never occurred in a living being. (TFW 124)

In a system ruled by conservation past time constitutes neither a gain nor a loss, but it is always a gain for a living being. Time makes a difference, and it may be the only reason why difference and not sameness exists. Life does not live like a material point that remains in an eternal present. Time, then, is the field of difference in which the future is not given in the present. As such, it is the site of the new and the novel. Here the new cannot be conceived without the thickness of durational time.

Duration, then, is for Bergson the great unthought of Western philosophy, and it names this novel force of becoming. To explain the reality, the fact, of the experience of duration Bergson retains a focus and a stress on the immediate data of consciousness, as the book's title in French has it, that is, on consciousness before it has been led astray by social convention and linguistic habits. For such a consciousness or awareness the given is not, as it is in Kant, simply an empty uniform location for the representation of objects. Rather, it is a heterogeneous real in which the perception of qualitative differences takes place and where the experience of qualities is unique each time. The inner states of experience do not have boundaries like the external things we posit in space; rather they overflow into one another even as they succeed one another. Here there can be no clear separation between our present state and anterior states. To illustrate the point Bergson likes to give the example of melody in music: when I listen to music I don't just hear a set of discrete, isolable sounds; rather, I make connections and linkages, and I retain past notes as I am listening to a present note. I thus hear a 'whole' of music no matter how complicated this whole may be. Our experience of listening to music, then, involves qualitative changes and serves as an effective example of what Bergson means by the continuous and confused kind of multiplicity.

Bergson on the Self

Suzanne Guerlac has argued that by extending scientific models of reality to ourselves we transform ourselves into reified things: 'If we try to measure and decision'.[19]

Bergson, then, speaks of a free self as a rare self: this is a self that is outside of automatism and that challenges in its actions everyday social reality. An action can be said to free to the extent that it is the expression of the 'fundamental self' and our 'whole personality'. Two selves then, characterize us: we are, in a reworking of Kant, both a conscious automaton (we have much to gain by being so) and a free self. Unlike Kant, however, Bergson does not place the free self outside of the domain of time. Bergson follows through to its logical conclusion his main insight into the relation between time and free will: for an action to be free I must maintain that I myself am the *author* of it. But, we need to ask: just what is this 'self' that authorizes action? And, under what conditions does it come to articulate itself?

In my view Bergson does not provide the reader with a wholly clear conception of this active, authorizing self and this shows the extent, I think, to which the matter of the self remains somewhat elusive in his writings.[20] For him it essentially consists in what he calls 'personality' and it is the 'whole personality' that is at play in any given free action. The contrast once again is with the associationist model of the mind that reduces the self to nothing more than an aggregate of conscious states (sensations, feelings, and ideas). Bergson is highly critical of this model since it gives us only a 'phantom self': 'if he sees in these various states no more than is expressed in their name, if he retains only their impersonal aspect, he may set them side by side for ever without getting anything but a phantom self, the shadow of the ego projecting itself into space' (TFW 165). In contrast to this impersonal model Bergson maintains that each one of us is a 'definite person' (TFW 165) in which the whole personality is present in our conscious states. This whole personality is one that is constantly growing and forming itself, and it can be said to be the 'author' of a free act when it expresses 'the whole of the self' (TFW 166). This insight leads Bergson to claim that freedom is not an absolute, but admits of degrees. This is an important qualification to his account of freedom and the conception of the self he supposes since it clearly recognizes that not all elements of our being are so incorporated as to form a unitary and fully integrated self: not everything that forms us blends perfectly 'with the whole mass of the self' (TFW 166). Furthermore, even if we wish to appeal to 'character' to explain the expression of our whole personality in free acts, we have to recognize that this 'character is still ourselves' (TFW 172). Moreover, this character changes imperceptibly every day and 'our freedom would suffer if these new acquisitions were grafted on to our self and not blended with it' (TFW 172). When this blending takes place we can say that the change that has supervened in our character belongs to us, and in Bergson's words, 'we have appropriated it' (TFW 172).

Bergson's analysis of the self, in terms of a focus on what constitutes our coherence and in terms of processes of incorporation and assimilation, strikes me as highly suggestive. It argues that there is a core 'fundamental self' that we can attune ourselves to and be true to, as the following set of insights clearly indicate:

> Here will be found within the fundamental self, a parasitic self which continually encroaches upon the other. Many live this kind of life, and die without having known true freedom. But suggestion would become persuasion if the entire self assimilated it; passion, even sudden passion, would no longer bear the stamp of fatality if the whole history of the person were reflected in it … It is the whole soul, in fact, which gives rise to the free decision: and the act will be so much the freer the more the dynamic series with which it is connected tends to be the fundamental self. (TFW 166–7)

Bergson, then, takes to task our reliance upon the habitual self that has been formed by education, language, and socialization. This is the self-conceived in terms of the discrete mode of multiplicity: 'We generally perceive our own self by refraction through space, that our conscious states crystallize into words, and that our living and concrete self thus gets covered with an outer crust of clean-cut psychic states, which are separated from one another and consequently fixed' (TFW 167). The key challenge Bergson presents to a thinking about the self, it seems to me, is the question he focuses on concerning incorporation ideas' (TFW 169) This is our 'fundamental self' seeking to express itself through the mass of solidified feelings and thoughts that constitute our habitual self, and is perhaps a classic statement in favour of a notion of 'authenticity'. As Bergson notes, 'It is at the great and solemn crisis, decisive of our reputation with others, and yet more with ourselves, that we choose in defiance of what is conventionally called a motive, and this absence of any tangible reason is the more striking the deeper our freedom goes' (TFW 170). Freedom, we might say, is radically open and has to be so by definition.

Conclusion

Bergson's *Time and Free Will* is a brilliant, wide-ranging critique of the illusions of consciousness that prevent us from appreciating the character of our durational selves and the reality of our freedom. It remains today a fertile, if unduly neglected, source for thinking about freedom and the self and there are aspects of Bergson's argument that have yet to be fully explored (such as his conception of the incorporating self). Genuine freedom is a rare phenomenon for Bergson and for the greater part of our existence we live 'outside ourselves, hardly perceiving anything of ourselves but our own ghost, a colourless shadow' (TFW 231) In this quest for autonomy or genuine selfhood Bergson makes the decisive point: unless we act for ourselves we will lose our autonomy and be *acted upon*. Here our life unfolds in space rather than in time: we live for the external world and not for ourselves, and 'we are "acted" rather than act ourselves' (TFW

231). We have a chance of taking repossession of ourselves by getting back into pure duration. As Suzanne Guerlac wisely notes, the problem of freedom is not, so we learn from a Bergsonian inquiry into it, solely a philosophical problem, but equally a question of desire, making it a problem that concerns social life and even a political education:[21] do we in fact *desire* our freedom?

Still, as Bouton has noted, Bergson's account suffers from some serious difficulties. Bouton points out that in order to be true to itself it looks as though the genuinely free self, according to Bergson, has to remain inactive and largely contemplative. This is because 'spatialization is both the condition of action, destined to find its way into the world, and what hides, betrays the author of the action, the profound ego'.[22] So, while Bergson may have overcome Kant's predicament – where freedom is placed outside the realm of time altogether – he faces in turn a genuine puzzle of his own: How is the true and free self to become itself when all its actions are destined to become events in space? As Bouton puts it, a free action is one that modifies and even disturbs 'the totality of images and events that constitute the world even while being entangled in them. But by the same token, every act realized in the world brings with it a sacrifice of the singularity of the ego in favour of an impersonal and common reality'.[23]

In order to think in a radical manner certain ingrained habits of the mind need to be overcome and conquered, habits which also inform how science approaches the real, such as: (1) the view that change is reducible to an arrangement or rearrangement of parts or that change merely involves a change of position regarding unchangeable things; (2) the view that the irreversibility of time is only an appearance relative to our ignorance and that the impossibility of turning back is only a human inability to put things in place again; (3) and, that time has only as much reality for a living system as an hour-glass. We are fixated on reducing time to instants (mathematical points), but this is to deny time any positive reality. Bergson's lesson is clear: time is not space and yet as part of our human condition we are fixated on living and thinking as if it were.

1. What is the relation between past and present? Is it merely a difference in degree, or it possible to locate the difference between them as one of kind? If we can do the latter, what will this reveal about memory?
2. What is the status of the past? Is it something merely psychological or might it be possible to ascribe an ontological status to it? In other words, what is the reality of the past?

Matter and Memory (first published in 1896) is widely recognized as Bergson's major work. William James, a great admirer of Bergson's work, described it as effecting a Copernican revolution that was comparable to Kant's *Critique of Pure Reason*. Although the text fell into neglect in the second half of the twentieth century, it exercised a tremendous influence on several generations of French philosophers, including Emmanuel Levinas, Maurice Merleau-Ponty, Jean-Paul Sartre, Paul Ricouer, and Gilles Deleuze. In addition, there have been important engagements with the text, and with the phenomenon of Bergsonism, in the writings of critical theorists such as Walter Benjamin, Theodor Adorno and Max Horkheimer. If Bergson's texts are being rediscovered today this is largely as a result of the influence of Deleuze's writings on current intellectual work. The current interest being shown in Bergson is not, however, confined to fashionable developments in continental philosophy. Bergson is gaining a renewed presence in psychology and the philosophy of mind. I devote most of this chapter to an explication of the main ideas we encounter in Bergson's text and conclude this chapter with my comments on the reception of Bergson's ideas in some key strands of twentieth-century thought.

Bergson's approach to memory was highly innovative. He was one of the first thinkers to show the importance of paying attention to different types of memory (episodic, semantic, procedural), and he sought to provide a sustained demonstration of why memory cannot be regarded as merely a diluted or weakened form of perception. Bergson is close to Freud insofar as both are committed to the view that a radical division must be made between memory and perception if we are to respect the radical alterity of the unconscious. Bergson regards memory a privileged problem precisely because an adequate conception of it will enable us to speak seriously of unconscious psychical states. In this respect Bergson anticipates the arguments Freud put forward four years later in the *Interpretation of Dreams*.[1] Gilles Deleuze contends that Bergson introduces an ontological unconscious over and above the psychological one, and it is this which enables us to speak of the being of the past and to grant the past a genuine existence. The past is not simply reducible to the status of a former present, and neither can it be solely identified with the phenomenon of psychological recollection.[2] However, as one commentator has rightly noted, Bergson's conception of the unconscious does not concern itself with the problems of psychological explanation that so occupied the attention of Freud.[3]

Bergson always sought to think time in terms of duration (*durée*), the preservation or prolongation of the past and entailing the co-existence of past and present. He insists that a special meaning is to be given to the word memory (MM 222). Jean Hyppolite notes that the new sense that memory comes to have in Bergson's thought consists in conceiving its operation in terms of a synthesis of past and present and with a view to the future.[4] This goes against the prevailing conception which conceives memory as a faculty of repetition or reproduction, in which the past is repeated or reproduced in the present and is opposed to invention and creation. For Bergson memory is linked to creative duration and to sense. As Bergson notes, if matter does not remember the past since it repeats it constantly and is subject to a law of necessity, a being that evolves creates something new at every moment (MM 223).

But just how are we to draw this distinction between past and present? Following Bergson we can note:

1. Nothing is *less* than the present moment, if we understand by this the indivisible limit which separates or divides the past from the future.
2. This, however, is only an 'ideal' present; the real, concrete, 'live' present is different and necessarily occupies a tension of duration. If the essence of time is that it goes by, that time gone by is the past, then the present is the

of Martin Heidegger and Gaston Bachelard, criticized Bergson for conceiving duration as cohesion, and so failing to develop an account of the separations and ruptures of time, including the ecstasies of past, present, and future. However, as Jean Hyppolite points out, Bergson's second major work, *Matter and Memory*, was precisely an attempt to raise this problem and to resolve it.[6] In his Huxley lecture of 1911 on life and consciousness Bergson makes it clear that consciousness is both memory (the conservation and accumulation of the past in the present) *and* anticipation of the future (ME 8).

Bergson's treatment of memory is not without difficulties or problems. But it is a valuable resource for mapping memory, and in this chapter I wish to explicate its novel and distinctive features. As we shall see, Bergson's presentation contains some highly unusual and unorthodox aspects, at least when one first encounters them and struggles to give them a sense.

Matter and Memory

In *Matter and Memory* Bergson seeks to establish the ground for a new rapport between the observations of psychology and the rigours of metaphysics (by metaphysics Bergson means that thinking which endeavours to go beyond the acquired and sedimented habits of the human mind, which for him are essentially mechanistic and geometrical in character). His argument on memory is not advanced in abstraction from consideration of work done on mental diseases, brain lesions, studies of the failures of recognition, insanity and the whole pathology of memory. He poses a fundamental challenge to psychology in seeking to show that memories are not conserved in the brain. We have to hear him carefully on this point. In not wishing to privilege the brain as the progenitor of our representations of the world Bergson shows that he has an affinity with phenomenological approaches. He conceives perception and memory, for example, in the context of the lived body, conceives of cognition as fundamentally vital not speculative, and grants primacy to action or praxis in our relation to the world.

Bergson's argument rests on two hypotheses being put to work: pure perception and pure memory. Imagine a perception without the interlacing of memory (impossible but helpful). Imagine a memory that is not actualized in concrete and specific memory-images and thus not reducible to our present recollection: less impossible perhaps but equally helpful. The central claim of the book is that while the difference between matter and perception is one of degree the difference between perception and memory is one of kind. Regarding the first: unless we see it in this way the emergence of perception out of matter becomes inexplicable and mysterious. Regarding the second: unless we see it this way then memory is deprived of any unique and autonomous character and becomes simply a weakened form of perception (indeed Locke calls memory a secondary perception). Bergson's argument for the autonomy of memory is twofold:

1. It is a thesis on the active character of perception, the interest of which is vital and not speculative. In cases of failed recognition it is not that memories have been destroyed but rather that they can no longer be actualized because of a breakdown in the chain that links perception, action, and memory.

2. It is also an argument regarding time conceived as duration: independent recollections cannot be preserved in the brain, which only stores motor contrivances, since memories are 'in' time, not in the brain which is seated in the present. Since memories concern the past (which always persists and exists in multiple modes), an adequate thinking of memory must take the being of memory seriously.

It is as if Bergson is saying: memory is not in the brain but rather 'in' time, but time is not a thing, it is duration, hence nothing can be 'in' anything. Hence his argument, curious at first, that when there takes place a lesion in the brain it is not that memories are lost, simply that they can no longer be actualized and translated into movement or action in time. Memory and psychological recollection are not which involves an impairing of attention to outward life. Bergson thus resists interpretations of disorders like aphasia in terms of a localization of the memory-images of words. Bergson is not, of course, denying that there exists a close connection between a state of consciousness and the brain. His argument is directed against any reified treatment of the brain in separation from the world it is a part of and from life treated as a sphere of praxis or activity. He thus argues against the idea that if we could penetrate into the inside of the brain and see at work the dance of the atoms which make up the cortex we would then know every detail of what is taking place in consciousness. The brain is in the world and it is only a small part of the life of the organism, the part that is limited to the present.

Bergson's starting point is to criticize the notion of some detached, isolated object, such as the brain, as the progenitor of our representation of the world. The brain is part of the material world. Thus, if we eliminate the image that is the material world we at the same time destroy the brain and its cerebral disturbances. The body is in the aggregate of the material world, an image that acts like all other images, receiving and giving back movement. The body is a centre of action and not a house of representation. It exists as a privileged image in the universe of images in that it can select, within limits, the manner in which it will restore what it receives.[8] The nervous system, Bergson argues, is not an apparatus that serves to fabricate or even prepare representations of the world. Its function, rather, is to receive stimulation, to provide motor apparatus, and to present the largest possible number of such apparatuses to a given stimulus. The brain is thus to be regarded as an instrument of analysis with regard to a received movement and an instrument of analysis with regard to executed movement. Its office is to transmit and divide movement. Let us posit the material world as a system of closely linked images and then imagine within it centres of action represented by living matter – that is, matter which is contractile and irritable – and around these centres there will be images that are subordinated to its position and variable with it. This is how we can understand the relation between matter and its perception and the emergence of conscious perception. Matter, therefore, can be approached in terms of the aggregate of images; the perception of matter is these same images but referred to the eventual (possible or virtual) action of one particular image, my body. It is not, therefore, a question of saying simply that our perceptions depend upon the molecular movements of the cerebral mass; rather, we have to say that they vary with them, and that these movements remain inseparably bound up with the rest of the material world. We cannot conceive of a nervous system living apart from the organism which nourishes, from the atmosphere in which the organism breathes, from the earth which that atmosphere envelopes, and so on.

Bergson insists: 'There is no perception which is not full of memories' (MM 33). With the immediate and present data of our senses we mingle a thousand details out of our past experience. Why does he use the hypothesis of an ideal perception? He comes up with the idea of an impersonal perception to show that it is this perception onto which are grafted individual accidents and which give an individual sense to life; owing to our ignorance of it, and because we have not distinguished from it memory, we are led to conceive of perception mistakenly as a kind of interior, subjective vision which then differs from memory simply in terms of its greater intensity. At the end of chapter 1 Bergson turns his attention to memory and insists that the difference between perception and memory needs to be made as a difference in kind. He fully acknowledges that the two acts, perception and recollection, always interpenetrate each other and are always exchanging something of their substance as if by a process of endosmosis. So, why does he insist on drawing the difference as one of kind? He has a number of reasons: first and foremost, he wants to make the difference between past and present intelligible and to ascribe a genuine ontological character to the past (the past is real in its past-ness); second, he wants to develop an adequate understanding of the phenomenon of recognition (in what situations does my body recognize past images?); and finally, he wants to explain the mechanism of the unconscious.

So, what are Bergson's claims about memory? First, that in actuality memory is inseparable from perception; it imports the past into the present

present (solving a problem, overcoming an obstacle in the environment). It is only in the form of motor contrivances that the action of past can be stored up. Past images are preserved in a different manner. The past survives, then, under two distinct forms: in motor mechanisms and in independent recollections. Both serve the requirements of the present. The usual or normal function of memory is to utilize a past experience for present action (recognition), either through the automatic setting into motion of mechanisms adapted to circumstances, or through an effort of the mind which seeks in the past those conceptions that are best able to enter into the present situation. Here the role of the brain is crucial: it will allow only those past images to come into being or become actualized that are deemed relevant to the needs of the present. A lived body is one embedded in a flux of time, but one in which it is the requirements of the present that inform its constant movement within the dimension of the past and horizon of the future. If the link with reality is severed, in this case the field of action in which a lived body is immersed, then it is not so much the past images that are destroyed but the possibility of their actualization, since they can no longer act on the real: 'It is in this sense, and in this sense only, that an injury to the brain can abolish any part of memory' (MM 79).

Let us consider in a little more detail how Bergson conceives the contraction of the past taking place as a way of addressing the present. Here I draw on the helpful account provided by Patrick McNamara. When a level of the past gets contracted the contraction is experienced by present consciousness as an expansion simply because its repertoire of images and moments of duration are increased and intensified.[9] Memory enables us to contract in a single intuition

multiple moments of time. In this way it frees us from the movement of the
flow of things and from the rhythm of mechanical necessity. The activation of
memory involves a series of phases. First, there is a relaxation of the inhibitory
powers of the brain; this is followed by a proliferation of memory-images that can
flood the cognitive system; and then, finally, there takes place a selection phase
in which the inhibitory processes are once again called upon. The proliferation
of images opens up a plurality of possible states of affairs and possible worlds;
the process of actualization, however, requires contraction to take place in order
to contextualize a cue and provide an adequate response to the problem in the
environment that has been encountered. What is selected may not, however, be
the 'best match or the most optimal solution to a current perception'.[10] Bergson
does not subscribe to a straightforwardly Darwinian model of the selection
process at work in memory.

Bergson's theory of memory rests on understanding these contractions and
expansions in relation to the syntheses of past and present. However, our grasp
of this theory remains inadequate so long as we do not appreciate its addition of
a third term, that of pure memory. Bergson provides in fact a tripartite theory
with a pure memory advanced alongside those of habit- and representational-
memory. How do we arrive at this third term of memory?

When we learn something a kind of natural division takes place between the
contractions of habit and the independent recollection of events that involve
dating. If I wish to learn a poem by heart I have to repeat it again and again
through an effort of learning, in which I decompose and recompose a whole. In
the case of specific bodily actions and movements, habitual learning is stored
in a mechanism that is set in motion by some initial impulse and that involves
releasing automatic movements within a closed system of succession and
duration. The operations of independent recollection are altogether different.
In the formation of memory-images the events of our daily life are recorded
as they take place in a unique time and provide each gesture with a place and a
date. This past is retained regardless of its utility and practical application. The
past is preserved in itself and, at the same time, contracted in various states by
the needs of action that are always seated in an actual present. This repetition
of memory-images through action merits the ascription of the word memory
not because it is involved in the conservation of past images but rather because
it prolongs their utility into a present moment. The task of this kind of memory
is to ensure that the accumulation of memory-images is rendered subservient
to praxis, making sure that only those past images come into operation that can

Not only is there more than one kind of memory, but memory-images enjoy more than the one kind of existence, being actualized in multiple ways: 'Memory thus creates anew the present perception, or rather it doubles this perception by reflecting upon it either its own image or some other memory-image of the same kind' (101). Our life moves – contracts, expands, and relaxes – in terms of circuits and it is the whole of memory that passes over into each of these circuits but always in a specific form or state of contraction and in terms of certain variable dominant recollections: 'The whole of our past psychical life conditions our present state, without being its necessary determinant' (148). We shift between virtual and actual states all of the time, never completely virtual or completely actual.

Bergson holds that perception and memory interlace and all memories must become actualized in order to become effectively real (127). Personal recollections make up the largest enclosure of our memory. He writes: 'Essentially fugitive, they become only materialized by chance, either when an accidentally precise determination of our bodily attitude attracts them or when the very indetermination of that attitude leaves a clear field to the caprices of their manifestation' (106). The pathology of memory has its basis in an appreciation of the vitality of memory. Memory, Bergson argues, has distinct degrees of tension or of vitality. Pathology confirms this insight: 'In the "systematized amnesias" of hysterical patients', he writes, 'the recollections which appear to be abolished are really present, but they are probably all bound up with a certain determined tone of intellectual vitality in which the subject can no longer place himself' (170). He further notes that there are always dominant memories for us, which exist as 'shining points round which the others form a vague nebulosity' (171). These shining points get multiplied to the extent to which our memory is capable of expansion. The process of localizing a recollection in the past does not consist in simply plunging into the mass of our memories as into a bag in order to draw out memories closer and closer to each other and between which the memory to be localized may find its place. Again, he finds helpful the pathology of memory:

> In retrogressive amnesia, the recollections which disappear from consciousness are probably preserved in remote planes of memory, and the patient can find them by an exceptional effort like that which is effected in the hypnotic state. But, on the lower planes, these memories await, so to speak, the dominant image to which they may be fastened. A sharp shock, a violent emotion, forms the decisive event to which they cling; if this event, by reason of its sudden character, is cut off from the rest of our history, they follow it into oblivion (171).

In short, Bergson has posited an assemblage made up of three components: pure memory, memory-images, and perception. The latter is never simply a contact of the mind with a present object but is impregnated with memory-images; in turn these images partake of a pure memory that they materialize or actualize and are bound up with the perceptions that provide it with an actual embodiment.

Perception and Memory

For Bergson it is necessary to dispel a number of illusions that shape and govern our thinking about memory, a key one being that memory only comes into existence once an actual perception has taken place. This illusion is generated by the requirements of perception itself, which is always focused on the needs of a present. While the mind or consciousness is attending to things it has no need of pure memory that it holds to be useless. Moreover, although each new perception requires the powers afforded by memory, a reanimated memory appears to us as the effect of perception. This leads us to suppose that the difference between perception and memory is simply one of intensity or degree, in which the remembrance of a perception is held to be nothing other than the same perception in a weakened state, resulting in the illegitimate inference that the remembrance of a perception cannot be created while the perception itself is being created or be developed at the same time (Bergson ME 160–1).

It is by recognizing the virtual character of pure memory that we can perhaps better appreciate that the difference between perception and memory is one of kind and not merely degree. Memory is made up of memory-images but the this very splitting, for the present moment, always going forward, fleeting limit between the immediate past which is now no more and the immediate future which is not yet, would be a mere abstraction were it not the moving mirror which continually reflects perception as a memory. (ME 165)

It is because the past does not simply follow the present but coexists with it that we can develop an explanation of paramnesia or the illusion of *déjà-vu*, in which there is a recollection of the present contemporaneous with the present itself. The illusion is generated from thinking that we are actually undergoing an experience we have already lived through when in fact what is taking place is the perception of the duplication we do not normally perceive, namely of time into the two aspects of actual and virtual. There is a memory of the present in the actual moment itself. I cannot actually predict what is going to happen but I feel as if I can: what I foresee is that I am going to have known it – I experience a 'recognition to come', I gain insight into the formation of a memory of the present (if we could stall the movement of time into the future, this experience would be much more common for us; we can note that current empirical research on the phenomenon of *déjà-vu* focuses on the regions of the brain involved in producing it and explains it in terms of gaps in our attentive system).

This difference between past and present can be explained in the following terms: our present is the 'very materiality of our existence' in the specific sense that it is 'a system of sensations and movements and nothing else' (MM 139). This system is unique for each moment of duration, 'just because sensations and movements occupy space, and because there cannot be in the same place several things at the same time' (ibid.). One's present at any moment of time is sensory–

motor, again in the specific sense that the present comes from the consciousness of my body: actual sensations occupy definite portions of the surface of my body. The concern of my body, manifest in the consciousness I have of it, is with an immediate future and impending actions. By contrast one's past is essentially powerless in the specific sense that it interests no part of my body conceived as a centre of action or praxis. No doubt, Bergson notes, it begets sensations as it materializes, but when it does so it ceases to be a memory and becomes something actually lived by passing into the condition of a present thing. In order for such a memory to become materialized as an actual present I have to carry myself back into the process by which I called it up, 'as it was virtual, from the depths of my past'. Bergson insists that this pure memory is neither merely a weakened perception nor simply an assembly of nascent sensations. When conceived in terms of the latter, memory becomes little more than the form of an image contained in already embodied nascent sensations. Let us once again clarify the difference between the present and the past: it is because they are two opposed degrees that it is possible to distinguish them in nature or kind.

Bergson's innovation, then, is to suggest that a recollection is created alongside an actual perception and is contemporaneous with it: 'Either the present leaves no trace in memory, or it is twofold at every moment, its very up-rush being in two jets exactly symmetrical, one of which falls back towards the past whilst the other springs forward towards the future' (ME 160). The illusion that memory comes after perception arises from the nature of practical consciousness, namely the fact that it is only the forward-springing jet that interests it. Memory becomes superfluous and without actual interest: 'In a general way, or *by right*, the past only reappears to consciousness in the measure in which it can aid us to understand the present and to foresee the future. It is the forerunner of action' (175). Because consciousness is bound up with an attentiveness to life, to action, it 'only admits, legally' those recollections which provide assistance to the present action (177). This explains Bergson's interest in the anomalies (illegalities) of the life of a *esprit*, such as deliriums, dreams, and hallucinations, which, Bergson insists, are positive facts that consist in the presence, and not in the mere absence, of something: 'They seem to introduce into the mind certain new ways of feeling and thinking' (151).

The past can never be recomposed with a series of presents since this would be to negate its specific mode of being. To elaborate an adequate thinking of time, including the time of the present, requires that we make the move to an ontological appreciation of the past. Psychological consciousness is born and realized, we might as well look for darkness beneath the light (MM 135). Bergson contends that this is, in fact, one of the chief errors of the school of associationism, which dominated the study of memory in the second half of the nineteenth century: 'placed in the actual, it exhausts itself in vain attempts to discover in a realized and present state the mark of its past origin, to distinguish memory from perception, and to erect into a difference in kind that which it condemned in advance to be but a difference of magnitude' (MM 135) What is in need of explanation is not so much the cohesion of internal mental states but rather 'the double movement of contraction and expansion by which consciousness narrows or enlarges the development of its content' (MM 166). Associationism conceives the mechanism of linkage in terms a perception remaining identical with itself, it is a 'psychical atom which gathers to itself others just as these happen to be passing by' (165). In Bergson's model of recollection, however, the linkages and connections forged by the mind are not simply the result of a discrete series of mechanical operations. This is because within any actual perception it is the totality of recollections that are present in an undivided, intensive state. If in turn this perception evokes different memories,

> it is not by a mechanical adjunction of more and more numerous elements which, while remaining unmoved, it attracts round it, but rather by an expansion of the entire consciousness which, spreading out over a larger area, discovers the fuller details of its wealth. So a nebulous mass, seen through more and more powerful telescopes, resolves itself into an ever greater number of stars (165–6).

The first hypothesis, which rests on a physical atomism, has the virtue of simplicity. However, the simplicity is only apparent and it soon locks us into an untenable account of perception and memory in terms of fixed and independent states. It cannot allow for movement within perception and memory except in artificially mechanical terms, with memory traces jostling each other at random and exerting mysterious forces to produce the desired contiguity and resemblance.[11] Bergson's theory of memory in terms of pure memory, memory-images, and actual perception, is designed to provide a more coherent account of how associations actually take place and form in the mind.

We find ourselves, largely out of force of habit, compelled to determine or ascertain the place or space of memory: Where is it? How can the past, which has ceased to be, preserve itself if not in the brain? Bergson does not deny that parts of the brain play a crucial role in our capacity for memory and in the actualization of memory. Memories cannot be in the brain (except habit-memory), because the brain occupies only a small slice or section of becoming, namely the present: 'The brain, insofar as it is an image extended in space, never occupies more than the present moment: it constitutes, with all the rest of the material universe, an ever-renewed section of universal becoming.' Moreover, the difficulty we have in conceiving the survival of the past – which has ceased to be useful but not ceased to be – comes from the fact that

> we extend to the series of memories, in time, that obligation of *containing* and *being contained* which applies only to the collection of bodies instantaneously perceived in space. The fundamental illusion consists in transferring to duration itself, in its continuous flow, the form of the instantaneous sections which we make in it. (MM 149)

Our reluctance to admit the integral survival of the past has its origin in the very bent of our psychical life – 'an unfolding of states wherein our interest prompts us to look at that which is unrolling, and not at that which is entirely unrolled' (150). As Deleuze points out in *Bergsonism*, the question 'where are recollections preserved?' involves a false problem by supposing a badly analysed composite.[12] Why suppose that memories have to be preserved somewhere? Furthermore, a fundamental feature of Bergson's novel empiricism is to insist on there being different lines of fact; as Deleuze insists, whereas the brain is situated on the line of 'objectivity', recollection is part of the line of 'subjectivity'. It is thus 'absurd to mix the two lines by conceiving of the brain as the reservoir or the substratum of recollections'.[13] For Bergson memory is primarily affective, and as soon as we attempt to isolate the effects of memory, setting out time in space and confusing the different lines of fact, they become lifeless.

a young Jean-Francois Lyotard argued that phenomenology separates itself from Bergsonism on the question of time by replacing a flowing time in consciousness with a consciousness that positively constitutes time for itself.[19] This critique of Bergson has been challenged in recent theoretical work where he is seen as having closer affinities with post-phenomenological notions of agency and subjectivity to be found, for example, in the work of so-called post-structuralist figures such as Jacques Derrida and Gilles Deleuze.[20] Bergson's work, especially *Matter and Memory*, is seen as containing valuable resources for calling into question the primacy of the 'For-Itself' and its idealistic stress on the unitary and transparent character of self-consciousness.[21] On this point Levinas goes as far as underlining the importance of Bergsonism 'for the entire problematic of contemporary philosophy' on account of the fact that it is no longer a thought of a 'rationality revealing a reality which keeps to the very measure of a thought'. In effecting a reversal of traditional philosophy by contending the priority of duration over permanence, Bergson provides thought with 'access to novelty, an access independent of the ontology of the same'.[22]

Walter Benjamin is one thinker to have appreciated the rich character of Bergson's treatment of memory and its significance for our understanding of certain critical aspects of modernity. In his essay 'On Some Motifs in Baudelaire', first published in 1939 in the *Zeitschrift für Sozialforschung*, in which he develops a wide-ranging treatment of Proust, Freud, and Baudelaire, the disintegration of the aura and the shock experience, he situates Bergson's text in the context of attempts within philosophy to lay hold of the '"true" experience' in opposition to the manufactured kind that manifests itself in the 'standardized, denatured life of the civilized masses'. For Benjamin, Bergson's 'early monumental work', as he describes it, towers above the body of work associated with the philosophy of life of the late nineteenth century – he mentions the work of Wilhelm Dilthey – on account of its links with empirical research and the richness of its account of the structure of memorial experience.[23] Bergson's text needs to be taken to task, however, on account of its failure to both understand its own historical conditions of possibility and reflect on its historical determinations.[24] On this issue Benjamin goes on to note some important differences in the figuration of the experience of memory we find in Bergson's text and in Proust's great modern novel, *In Search of Lost Time*. Benjamin contends that Bergson's conception of *duration* is estranged from history,[25] and this point informs Max Horkheimer's critical engagement with Bergson. Horkheimer acknowledges that he owes 'decisive elements' to Bergson's philosophy for his own thinking, but argues that Bergson offers a metaphysics of time that privileges an interior spiritual world, rests on a disavowal of human history, and suffers from a biological realism.[26]

It is interesting to note that the critical reception of Bergson we find in the works of critical theorists such as Horkheimer is similar to that we find in phenomenology, namely that his thinking on memory is seen to grant too much importance to its contemplative aspects over its critical and intentional ones. For phenomenologists this manifests itself in an alleged failure to account for the synthesizing powers of an intentional subject (Bergson grants intention to memory itself over and above the subject; the subject is implicated in memory; 'subjectivity is never ours, it is time ... the virtual', as Deleuze puts it).[27] For critical theorists, by contrast, it reveals itself in the failure to provide a constructivist, and activist, account of history and historical agency (Bergson is oblivious, Horkheimer says, to the meaning of theory for historical struggle). To what extent these criticisms are fair, and to what extent they have been called into question by more recent intellectual developments, are questions that cannot be treated here. I would simply point out that Bergson set himself a specific task in *Matter and Memory* – taking the psychology of his day to task on account of what he regarded as its inadequate and impoverished approach to the life of memory – which, to a large extent, he fulfilled and admirably so, and it is necessary to respect the integrity of his project (which is not to say that all kinds of critical questions cannot, and should not, be asked of it). It is quite clear that Bergson's heart lies not with contemplation but with creative action. His complaint is there is *too much* contemplation in philosophy. In his prescient final text *The Two Sources of Morality and Religion*, published in 1932, Bergson on mind and memory to instructive and productive use in his important study, *Mind and Variability: Mental Darwinism, Memory, and Self* (1999), while the attempt by Israel Rosenfield in his *The Invention of Memory* (1988) to expose the view that we can remember because we have fixed memory-images permanently stored in our brains for what it is – a myth (that of localization) – continues the work Bergson began over a century ago.[29] This is echoed in McNamara's study, when he writes for example: 'The representational-instructionist view of memory is still what I would call the modern standard view of the nature of memory. It and its related "trace theory" of how the brain "stores" memory constitute the background assumptions of much of modern research into memory.'[30] In his book, *Memory, History, Forgetting*, one of the most important studies of memory in recent years, Paul Ricoeur acknowledges the original and innovative character of Bergson's thinking on memory. For Ricoeur, Bergson is 'the philosopher' to have best understood the close connection between the survival of images and the phenomenon of recognition.[31] Furthermore, with this insight into the survival of images, which require that we acknowledge that memory has the character of endurance, Ricoeur believes that Bergson's thinking holds the resources required for understanding the working of forgetting, even if Bergson himself was only able to think this in terms of effacement. It is the self-survival of images that can be considered as a figure of fundamental forgetting. Ricoeur poses the question, 'On what basis, then, would the survival of memories be equivalent to forgetting?'[32] His answer is to propose that forgetting be conceived not simply in terms of the effacement of traces, but rather in terms of a reserve or a resource: 'Forgetting then designates the *unperceived* character of the perseverance of memories, their removal from the vigilance of consciousness.'[33] Going by this conception, forgetting can be understood not simply as an inexorable destruction, but as an immemorial resource.

Bergson's great text is significant for a number of reasons, including its attempts to demonstrate the ontological status of the past, to provide a genuinely dynamical model of memory's operations, to show the virtual character of (pure) memory, and, finally, its advancement of the argument that memory is not simply the mechanical reproduction of the past but it is also sense. Without memory life is, quite literally, devoid of meaning. *Matter and Memory* is a text we are still catching up with.

to the philosophy of life.' The primary aim of the text though is to show the need for a fundamental reformation of philosophy. Bergson wants to show the limits of mechanism, and how, through an appreciation of the evolution of life, philosophy can expand our perception of the universe. Aspects of Bergson's attempt to expand human perception in the text may not be to the taste of many contemporary readers, keen, as they no doubt are, to shy away from any romance of evolution. On this point it might be claimed that Bergson remains faithful to philosophy's vocation as the product of wonder: 'The effort after the general characterization of the world around us is the romance of human thought.'[2] However, even if today we feel no affinity with this aspect of Bergson's thinking about evolution, I want to show that we can still gain a great deal of instruction from his attempt to get us closer to the realities of life and to creative evolution.

On the Ambition of *Creative Evolution*

In the English-speaking world *Creative Evolution* appears to have the status of an optional text in Bergson's oeuvre.[3] This is in marked contrast to its French reception where thinkers from Georges Canguilhem to Maurice Merleau-Ponty and Gilles Deleuze undertook close readings of the text.[4] Deleuze's philosophy of difference is developed in significant part from out of a reading of *Creative Evolution*. So long as we lack an encounter with this text we remain ignorant of crucial aspects of Bergson's attempt to reform and transform philosophical thinking and practice. Bergson's ambition with this text is clearly stated towards the end of chapter 2. It is worth citing what he says almost in full so as to have a grasp of why he is so interested in evolution:

> We shall see that the problem of knowledge ... is one with the metaphysical problem, and that both one and the other depend on experience. On the one hand, indeed, if intelligence is charged with matter and instinct with life, we must squeeze them both in order to get the double essence from them; metaphysics is therefore dependent upon the theory of knowledge. But, on the other hand, if consciousness has thus split up into intuition and intelligence, it is because of the need it had to apply itself to matter at the same time as it had to follow the stream of life. The double form of consciousness is then due to the double form of the real, and the theory of knowledge must be dependent upon metaphysics. In fact, each of these two lines of thought leads to the other; they form a circle, and there can be no other centre to the circle but the empirical study of evolution. It is only in seeing consciousness run through matter, lose itself there and find itself there again, divide and reconstitute itself, that we shall form an idea of the mutual opposition of the two terms, as also, perhaps of their common origin. But, on the other hand, by dwelling on this opposition of the two elements and on this identity of origin, perhaps we shall bring out more clearly the meaning of evolution itself. (CE 178–9)

Here we clearly see in evidence the complexity of Bergson's philosophical position: it concerns itself with epistemology and metaphysics, in which metaphysics is said to be dependent on epistemology and then epistemology is said to be ultimately dependent on metaphysics. For Bergson there are two principal ways by which we can know something: first, by going around it, and, second, by 'entering into it', and the latter is the province of metaphysics as he conceives it (CM 133). Bergson wants to attend to both matter and life, and to both intuition and intelligence, and thinks he can illuminate all of this through 'the empirical study of evolution'.[5]

Although the ambition of the inquiry is clearly stated in the passage I have just cited, in his actual introduction to the text Bergson also acknowledges that a philosophy of the kind he seeks will not be made in a day. Rather, and unlike philosophical systems that are the work of an individual genius, such a philosophy can be developed only through the collective and progressive effort of a number of thinkers and observers that complete and correct each other. In his appraisal of the work of the physiologist Claude Bernard, Bergson cites approvingly Bernard's mistrust of philosophical and scientific systems: 'Systems tend to enslave the human mind' (CM 176).[6] The attempt to embrace the totality of things in simple formulae needs to be abandoned. This is not without of materialism and to imagine it can persist in such a direction: 'It seeks quite naturally a mechanical or geometrical explanation of what it sees' (CM 237). Such an attitude Bergson regards as a survival of preceding centuries, one that harks back to an epoch when science was conceived largely as geometry. The significance of the science of the nineteenth century is that it places at the centre of its inquiry the study of living beings. He concedes that even here science may still be governed by mechanics but, as he makes clear a few years later in *Creative Evolution*, what we are dealing with here is a mechanics of transformation, which is a mechanics that cannot be developed by relying upon geometrical schemas of thought. Change, transformation, and evolution are bound up with living and open systems. With this critical reference to 'materialism' it seems clear that Bergson invariably treats it as an essentially mechanistic modelling of reality that deals with systems into which time does not bite. The focus is on aspects of repetition in which the intellect selects in a given situation whatever is like something it already knows so as to fit it into a pre-existing mould or schema; in this way it applies the principle that 'like produces like'. It naturally rebels against the idea of an originality and unforeseeability of forms. Similarly, classical science focuses its attention on isolable or closed systems simply because anything that is irreducible and irreversible in the successive moments of a history eludes it. In cases of organic evolution Bergson insists that foreseeing the form in advance is not possible. This is not because there are no conditions or specific causes of evolution, but rather owing to the fact that they are built into the particular form of organic life and peculiar to that phase of its history in which life finds itself at the moment of producing the form.

Creative Evolution is a text that engages with the history of philosophy and the history of science and does so in terms of their ancient and modern aspects. The two key philosophical figures engaged with in the text are Aristotle and Kant, though there are also important engagements with the likes of Spinoza and Fichte. Indeed, on one level it is possible to read *Creative Evolution* as an attempt to refute Spinoza and dispel the entrancing effect his logical conception of reality has over modern minds. For a system like Spinoza's, Bergson notes, true or genuine being is endowed with a logical existence more than a psychological or even physical one: 'For the nature of a purely logical existence is such that it seems to be self-sufficient and to posit itself by the effect alone of the force immanent in truth' (CE 276). Spinozism is an attempt to make the mystery of existence, such as why minds and bodies exist, vanish and instead of making actual observations of nature the philosopher advances a logical system in which at the base of everything that exists is a self-positing being dwelling in eternity.[7] In contrast to this logical system Bergson intends to develop a conception of efficient causality that includes within it duration and free choice.

The Challenge of the New Biology

What challenge did Bergson think the new biology presented? First, and most obviously, there is the rejection of Aristotle's thinking. In his discussion of the development of animal life in chapter 2 of *Creative Evolution* he says that the cardinal error that has vitiated almost all philosophies of nature from Aristotle onwards lies in seeing in vegetative, instinctive, and rational life, successive degrees in the development of one and the same tendency. In fact, they are 'divergent directions of an activity that has split up as it grew' (CE 135). This is in accord with one crucial aspect of his conception of life, namely that it does not proceed by the association and addition of elements but by dissociation and division. Bergson argues that one of the clearest results of modern biology is to have shown that evolution has taken place along divergent lines. This means that it is no longer possible to uphold the biology of Aristotle in which the series of living beings is regarded as unilinear. Aristotle belongs to the science of the ancients that rests, he says, on a 'clumsy interpretation of the physical in terms of the vital' (CE 228). All of this is of no small concern to Bergson given that in his essay on Ravaisson he clearly sympathizes with the latter's preference for Aristotle over Plato. Indeed, he even describes Aristotle as the among species and distributed amongst individuals without losing anything of its force, rather intensifying in proportion to its advance' (CE 26).

One of the most important aspects of Bergson's approach to evolution in the book, and elsewhere, is his insistence that we should resist the temptation to shrink nature to the measure of our ideas. He makes this clear, for example, at the end of his essay on Claude Bernard. In *Creative Evolution* he insists that we need to display a readiness to be taken by surprise in the study of nature and learn to appreciate that there might be a difference between human logic and the logic of nature: 'What is absurd in our eyes is not necessarily so in the eyes of nature' (CM 206). We cannot approach nature with any a priori conceptions of parts and wholes or any a priori conception of what constitutes life, including how we delimit the boundaries of an organism and hence define it. We must resist the temptation to place or hold nature within our own ideas or shrink reality to the measure of them. We should not allow our need for a unity of knowledge to impose itself upon the multiplicity of nature. To follow the sinuosities of reality means that we cannot slot the real into a concept of all concepts, be it Spirit, Substance, Ego, or Will. Bergson notes that all thought becomes lodged into concepts that congeal and harden and we have to be aware of the dangers presented by this. He regarded Schopenhauer's 'will to life', which we might think of as a precursor of the *élan vital*, as an empty concept supported by a barren theory of metaphysics. It is in *Creative Evolution* that Bergson proposes the need for thought to undergo a fundamental reform and education: 'It is not enough to determine, by careful analysis, the categories of thought; we must engender them.' (CE 207). This statement comes in the wake of an engagement with Kant, one of several that feature in the book. Bergson asks, 'Created by life, in definite circumstances, to act on definite things, how can it [the logical form of thought] embrace life, of which it is only an aspect?' (CE x). Life challenges the essential categories of thought: unity, multiplicity, mechanical causality, and intelligent finality all fall short. A consideration of life in its evolutionary aspects makes it virtually impossible to say where individuality begins and ends, whether the living being is one or many, whether it is the cells that associate themselves into an organism or the organism that dissociates itself into cells. 'It would be difficult to cite a biological discovery due to pure reasoning.' All the moulds in which we seek to force the living crack: 'They are too narrow ... too rigid, for what we try to put into them' (CE x). Unity and multiplicity, or the one and the many, are categories of inert matter; the vital impetus can be conceived neither as pure unity nor pure multiplicity. If we take as an example the most rudimentary organisms that consist of only a single cell we find already 'that the apparent individuality of the whole is the composition of an *undefined* number of potential (*virtuelles*) individualities potentially (*virtuellement*) associated' (CE 261).

Bergson conceives metaphysics as a mode of knowledge that can advance by the gradual accumulation of obtained results. In other words, metaphysics does not have to be a take-it-or-leave-it system that is forever in dispute, thinking abstractly and vainly without the support of empirical science. Not only is it the case for Bergson that metaphysics can be a true empiricism, but it can also work with science in an intellectual effort to advance our knowledge of the various sources, tendencies, and directions of life. In his Huxley lecture of 1911 on 'Life and Consciousness' he writes: 'We possess now a certain number of *lines of facts*, which do not go as far as we want, but which we can prolong hypothetically' (ME 4). This is taken up again in *The Two Sources of Morality and Religion*, where he states that the different lines of fact indicate for us the direction of truth but none go far enough; the attainment of truth can only take place when the lines are prolonged to the point where they intersect (TSMR 248). He insists that the knowledge we wish to develop and advance concerning evolution must 'keep to ascertained facts and the probabilities suggested by them' (TSMR 273). Bergson's originality consists in placing life at the centre of the study of nature. It is perhaps Whitehead who best articulates the task here when he writes that *the modern problem of philosophy and of science is, 'the status of life'.*[8] For Bergson, however, life can no longer be thought about independently of the empirical study of evolution.

that have been placed at our disposal. It means we think within pre-existing frames. We need, then, to ask two questions: first, how has the human intellect evolved (since it does not simply think for the sake of it but has evolved as an organ of action and utility)? and second, how can we enlarge and go beyond the frames of knowledge available to us?

Bergson has a specific conception of the human intellect and of matter. The intellect has moulded itself on the geometrical tendency of matter and so as to better further its instrumental manipulations of matter. His chief claim is that the intellect has to be viewed within the context of the evolution of human life and that when we do this we can better grasp its limits and also how to think beyond it. The task, in short, is to attempt to think beyond the representational and spatial habits of the intellect. For Bergson perhaps the chief function of philosophy is to expand our perception of the world and the universe. Although Whitehead contests Bergson's view that the intellect has an inherent tendency to spatialize, he does think that 'the history of philosophy supports Bergson's charge that the human intellect "spatializes the universe"', ignoring the fluency of life and analysing the world in terms of static categories and a static materialism.[9]

Bergson's criticism in *Creative Evolution* is chiefly directed at what he calls 'evolutionist philosophy', by which he specifically means the work of Herbert Spencer. The problem with this philosophy is that it uncritically extends to the phenomena of life the same methods of explanation that have yielded successful results in the case of the study of unorganized matter. Bergson accuses this evolutionism, which in Kantian fashion claims only to come up with a symbolical image of the real in which the essence of things will always escape us, of an excess of humility. He says this because he thinks that it is possible for us to go beyond the human state and enlarge our perception so as to provide us with an insight into the depths of life. He also insists that this is not easy to do.

Here we see the character of Bergson's interest in evolution. It forms an essential part of his very conception of what philosophy is: an attempt at an enlarged perception where we think beyond the human condition. The problem with the mechanistic and geometrical understanding is that 'it makes the total activity of life shrink to the form of a certain human activity which is only a partial and local manifestation of life' (CE xii). In the text itself Bergson argues that matter itself is to be characterized by certain tendencies, such as spatiality, so when the human intellect thinks in these terms, it represents an aspect of the real. Bergson's point is that this is only one aspect.

How, though, is it possible to think beyond the human condition and outside of its particular framing of reality? This is where Bergson appeals to evolution itself and stresses that the line of evolution that has culminated in the human is not the only line. His idea seems to be a radical one, namely that there are other forms of life-consciousness that express something that is immanent and essential in the evolutionary movement, and the critical task is to then bring these other forms into contact or communication with the human intellect. Bergson poses the question: would not the result be a consciousness as wide as life? What does he have in mind? The reader has to wait until the later chapters in the book before being fully able to comprehend him. Bergson suggests that it is possible to cultivate, through intellectual effort, a perception of life where we experience something of the very impetus of creative life itself or what he describes as the push of life and that has led to the creation of divergent forms of life from a common impulsion, such as plant and animal. In short, philosophy is that discipline of thinking that tries to make the effort to establish contact with the vitality and creativity of life and involves novelty, invention, process, and duration. As I have noted, he does not pretend that it is easy to do this; on the contrary, he stresses that it is necessary to perform a certain violence on ourselves so as to break with our evolved habits of representation and established patterns of thought. In the introduction to *Creative Evolution* he tackles the objection that may be raised against the project he invites us to pursue: will it not be through our intellect and our intellect alone that we perceive the other forms of consciousness? In answer to this objection he points out that this would be the case *if* we were pure intellects, but the fact is, he thinks, we are not. Around our conceptual and logical modes of thought, and that have moulded themselves different tendencies. This also helps us to understand why he is keen to maintain a separation between physics and chemistry on the one hand and biology on the other, and explains the attraction biology has for him. Basically, for Bergson physics and chemistry proceed as if historical time did not count and in which aspects of the present are calculable as functions of the past. This is not the case, he thinks, with biology. He writes:

> Nothing of this sort in the domain of life. Here calculation touches, at most, certain phenomena of organic *destruction*. Organic *creation*, on the contrary, the evolutionary phenomena which properly constitute life, we cannot in any way subject to a mathematical treatment. It will be said that this impotence is due only to our ignorance. But it may well equally express the fact that the present moment of a living body does not find its explanation in the moment immediately before, that *all* the past of the organism must be added to that moment, its heredity – in fact, the whole of a very long history. (CE 20)

Bergson associates life with the phenomena of organic creation such as growth, maturation, ageing, and so on. A living body is characterized by continuity of change, the preservation of the past in the present, and by real duration. But he does not have a single conception of life. However, he does appear to think that to explain evolution we need a special principle of life and that it is something distinct from the properties of matter. What exactly is this?

From the beginnings of his teaching career – for example, the lectures on the 'Metaphysics of Life' from 1887 to 1888 and delivered at Clermont-Ferrand – Bergson was keen to reflect on the origin and nature of life and to contest what he took to be the dogmas of materialism. He notes that a living body differs from brute matter by the fact that it displays a kind of initiative and that when we examine life, even in its rudimentary state, we observe new characteristics that cannot be mathematically foreseen: 'Two seeds placed in the same ground and that present the same aspect to scientific observation will not behave in the same way.'[10] For Bergson, then, what should impress itself upon us in the study of life is the capacity living bodies display for responding to problems in their environment in a manner that is not pregiven or predictable. The initiative they display is, 'opposed to the fatal and disorganizing action of physical and chemical laws', and he cites Xavier Bichat's well-known definition of life as 'the assemblage of the forces that resist death'[11] (he will return to this fatalistic aspect of the world if left to itself in his 1911 lecture on 'Life and Consciousness', ME 12). Bergson also wishes to draw attention to the complexity of a living organism, in which, when we observe its growth and development, we can observe a 'marvellous coordination' of elements that together seem to tend toward a single goal', including the diverse functions of digestion, circulation, and respiration.[12]

Bergson provides a potted history of materialism, referring to Lucretius and Epicurus, and Cartesians and Spinozists (who are not, he notes, straightforward materialists since their systems display idealist tendencies), and notes that it is in the nineteenth century that the mechanistic theory of life claims to be based on scientific facts and evidence, and he refers in particular to Büchner, Moleschott, and especially Haeckel (in a lecture of 1912 Bergson also notes the contribution made by the likes of La Mettrie, Helvétius Bonnet, Cabanis, and so on, ME 39). Bergson's main quarrel with materialism is that it deprives life of its specific characteristics and construes life in terms of a universal mechanism. He holds materialism to be an arbitrary hypothesis with questionable scientific evidence to support its claims. He never challenges the idea that a living body, such as the human body, is made up of the same physical and chemical forces as the rest of nature or the claim that it is made up of elements of brute matter. He does not wish to agree with Bichat that life is in a struggle with the forces of inorganic nature since his main point is that these forces do not behave in the same way in the presence of brute matter and living matter: 'Up to a certain point, the effect is indeterminate.'[13]

In his early lectures, then, we see Bergson taking materialists to task for the attempt, as he sees it, of suppressing from matter all initiative and spontaneity and imagining at work in nature a universal mechanism. These are his principal claims against materialism and they do not appear to change in the evolution of his writings. Life in *Creative Evolution* appears to work in an essentially twofold to generation. Life appears to have at least a twofold sense in Bergson, denoting (i) a current of creative energy that is precipitated into matter and wrests from it what it can; (ii) the durational phenomena of organic creation as outlined above. A few other points are worth noting about Bergson on life. First, although he refers to life as an energy that has entered into the habits of inert matter, he acknowledges that with respect to the phenomena of the simplest forms of life it is difficult to declare them to be solely physical and chemical since they may contain vital features. Second, although he maintains that at the root of life we find an effort to 'engraft on to the necessity of physical forces the largest possible amount of *indetermination*', this does mean that this effort of life results in some free creation of energy (CE 114). Bergson unreservedly accepts that this kind of creation is not possible. For him the force or energy of life is a limited one.

Is Bergson, then, a straightforward vitalist, that is, a thinker who appeals to a special principle of life and a mysterious one at that? The matter is complicated by several things: (i) he does not completely deny mechanism and speaks of a 'mechanism of the whole'; and (ii) he does not wish to contest the identity between inert matter and organized matter (CE 31). Bergson explicitly broaches the issue of vitalism about halfway into his first chapter, addressing the stumbling block of vitalistic theories (CE 42). He does not uncritically embrace a vital principle but says only that although such a principle may not explain much it serves as a label fixed to our ignorance, one that mechanism invites us to ignore. Bergson has an important reason for being hesitant with vitalistic claims; chiefly, in nature 'there is neither purely internal finality nor absolutely distinct individuality' (CE 42). In short, where would we locate the vital principle? It cannot be in the individual since this is not sufficiently independent or cut off from other things, and finality cannot be restricted to the individuality of the living being: 'If there is finality in the world of life, it includes the whole of life in a single, indivisible embrace' (CE 43). The problem in thinking through the nature of life and its special character becomes acute once we recognize that both mechanism and finalism are only external views of our conduct and reflect human modes of thinking. Bergson states his own position as follows, and it reveals his commitment to genuine freedom in evolution, both of the individual and of life itself:

> This does not mean that free action is capricious... . To behave according to caprice is to oscillate mechanically between two or more ready-made alternatives and at length to settle on one of them; it is no real maturity of an internal state, no real evolution. (CE 47)

Bergson thinks 'we are all born Platonists' (CE 49). By this he means the human need to fit reality into the ready-made garments of our ready-made concepts: 'The idea that for a new object we might have to create a new concept, perhaps a new method of thinking, is deeply repugnant to us' (CE 48). As in his introduction he now appeals to an expansion of our intellectual habits and forms of thought and so as to develop an idea of the whole of life: 'such is the philosophy of life to which we are leading up. It claims to transcend both mechanism and finalism' (CE 50). Bergson, in fact, conceives of philosophy as an effort to dissolve into the whole. Of course, what is not clear at this stage in his argument is why we should endeavour to think in terms of the whole and for what ends. This dissolving has to be seen as the ultimate end of the task of thinking beyond the human condition.

Bergson now attempts to give an indication of the key principle of his demonstration. He conceives of life as 'the continuation of one and the same impetus, divided into divergent lines of evolution' (CE 53). The development of life has taken place in terms of a dissociation of tendencies, ones that were unable to grow beyond a certain point without becoming mutually incompatible. Not until chapter 3 does Bergson deal in a concerted fashion with questions of contingency. He notes at this point in the book that there is no reason why we cannot imagine evolution as having taken place in the one single individual being and having only the one dimension. However, it is a fact that on earth evolution has taken place through millions of individuals and along divergent lines. He further maintains that something of the whole abides in each one of evolution's parts, and that this common element may explain the presence of identical organs in significantly different organisms and forms of life. In short, attention to the fact that this does not explain the whole of the matter, especially in terms of the development of complexity (e.g. the evolution of the eye from the pigment-spot of lower organisms to the complicated eye of the vertebrates). So, when we speak of the gradual formation of the eye, taking into account all that is connected with it, such as the formation of the various systems (nervous, muscular, osseous) that are continuous with the apparatus of vision in the case of vertebrate animals, we have to be speaking of something different from the direct action of light: 'One implicitly attributes to organized matter a certain capacity *sui generis*, the mysterious power of building up very complicated machines to utilize the simple excitation that it undergoes' (CE 72).

This is a key statement in the book and raises the question of just what conception of life Bergson himself appeals to in order to account for the development of complexity. The answer seems to reside in his appeal to a 'psychological cause' or what he calls 'an inner directing principle' (CE 76). This, I think, is the key argument he evinces:

> The evolution of the organic world cannot be predetermined as a whole. We claim, on the contrary, that the spontaneity of life is manifested by a continual creation of new forms succeeding others. But this indetermination cannot be complete; it must leave a certain part to determination. An organ like the eye, for example, must have been formed by a continual changing in a definite direction. Indeed, we do not see how otherwise to explain the likeness of structure of the eye in species that have not the same history. Where we differ from Eimer is in his claim that combinations of physical and chemical causes are enough to secure the result. We have tried to prove, on the contrary, by the example of the eye, that if there is 'orthogenesis' here, a psychological cause intervenes. (CE 86)

By 'psychological cause' Bergson is referring to an impetus of life: this impetus, he says, is sustained along the divergent lines evolution has taken, and is the fundamental cause of variations that are responsible for the creation of new species. He once again engages with mechanism and finalism, claiming that it is necessary to think beyond both perspectives since they are only 'standpoints to which the human mind has been led by considering the work of man' (CE 89). His key criticism is that finalism is too anthropomorphic since it compares the labour of nature to that of a workman who proceeds by thinking of an assemblage of parts 'with a view to the realization of an idea or the imitation of a model' (CE 88). Although mechanism legitimately reproaches finalism on this point, it too proceeds with an equally questionable method: it gets rid of an end pursued or an ideal model, but it holds to the view that nature works like a human being that brings parts together. Contra mechanism Bergson maintains that: '*Life does not proceed by the association and addition of elements, but by dissociation and division*' (CE 89).

Life is being spoken of in terms of an impetus, says Bergson, simply because 'no image borrowed from the physical world can give more nearly the idea of it' (CE 257). An image borrowed from psychology provides us with insight into life as the enfolding of a plurality of interpenetrating terms and tendencies. Bergson perhaps best explains why he thinks we need to have this notion of tendencies and conceive them psychologically in chapter 2 of the book. From it I cite the following so as to clarify what he means:

> The elements of a tendency are not like objects set beside each other in space and mutually exclusive, but rather like psychic states, each of which, although it be itself to begin with, yet partakes of others, and so virtually includes in itself the whole personality to which it belongs. (CE 118)

A tendency can be conceived as the push or thrust (*poussée*) of an indistinct multiplicity, which is indistinct only when considered in retrospect, for example when the multitudinous views we take of its past undivided character enable us to see it composed of elements created by an actual development. Forms of life (groups and species) should be defined not by the possession of certain characters but by their tendency to emphasize them: 'Taking tendencies rather than states into account, we find that vegetables and animals may be precisely defined and distinguished, and that they correspond to two divergent developments of life' (e.g. the divergence shown in the method of alimentation) (CE 106). He specifically states that in accounting for the dissociation of tendencies there is everything is coherent, where there are arrests and setbacks of evolution, and so on. The vital impetus informing evolution is, as Bergson sees it, a limited immanent force and is at the mercy of materiality. Bergson seeks to illustrate his point by inviting us to reflect on our own existence, from which we know that our attempts at freedom are dogged by automatism. This is not an accidental feature of our quest for freedom but an essential part of it since in the very movement by which our freedom is actually affirmed there is created the habits that stifle it. This means that freedom can only be practised through the renewal of a constant effort. Bergson thinks this discordance between the dead and the living, or between the mechanical and the vital, or the habitual and the free, is to be explained in terms of what he calls 'an irremediable difference of rhythm' (CE 128). Bergson expresses himself poetically to clarify this difference, writing of the living turning upon themselves like eddies of dust raised by the passing wind. Although we need to grant a stability to living organisms we also need to conceive of them as counterfeiting immobility, so leading us to treat them as things rather than systems implicated in a process. It is when we envisage the evolution of life as a whole that we are able to see the difference at work: this is the difference between life in general and the relatively stable but transient forms in which it is manifested. Indeed, Bergson thinks that 'the living being is above all a thoroughfare, and that the essence of life is in the movement by which life is transmitted' (CE 128). However, although life can legitimately be regarded as a continually growing action, we have to acknowledge that actual evolution shows species existing in self-absorption, in which they fall into a partial sleep and ignore the rest of life.

Bergson and the Hard Problem of Science: What is Life?

For Bergson matter and life are different tendencies of reality, although it is clear that we are not to think of life without its relation to materiality. Philosophy for Bergson must attend to both matter and life. Bergson's achievement is to have given us a conception of the evolution of life in terms of its extraordinary intricacy and complexity. He has developed new modes of thinking needed for the effort to conceive of nature in the wake of modern theories on the evolution of life. Although he conducts an ambitious enterprise in *Creative Evolution* he is always careful to qualify his remarks, to provide elaborate demonstrations, and to arrive at precision wherever it is possible. Bergson's challenge to the doctrine of static materialism is clear and there are contemporary theoretical biologists who share his principal view, namely that life is something sui generis.[15]

Although Bergson engages with the entire history of materialism in his writings, his thinking on evolution is largely directed at what he sees as the intellectual currents prevailing in his own time, namely the dogmatic materialism that deprives living beings of initiative and that imposes on reality a universal mechanism. Bergson never doubts that there is mechanism in the universe and readily acknowledges that it serves to capture certain features of reality. Not everything in reality is unforeseeable, incalculable, spontaneous and free! His critical point is that mechanism fails to account for all aspects of reality, and one way he thinks we can demonstrate this is by marking a distinction between matter and life, with the former being defined as 'inertia, geometry, necessity', and the latter as freedom, choice, and unpredictable movement (ME 12). All living beings are the subject of both matter and life; we are not to think of the two independently or as separate from one another. Both (matter and life) have to be understood as tendencies and they are implicated in one another. The evolution of life on earth cannot be understood without paying close attention to this implication. Bergson rejects the idea of a Life Force at work in evolution precisely because it fails to pay attention to the empirical details of evolution (this differs from the *élan vital* in that it works as a transcendent principle, not one that is immanent to an evolutionary movement). The challenge for him, then, is to attempt to think of evolution in terms of an initial common impulsion that has led to the divergent forms of life we observe and to attempt to think of evolution in a way that avoids the pitfalls of both mechanism and finalism in their anthropomorphic forms. Although one may have serious especially if one wishes to advance a philosophy of life that makes the effort to think life beyond the human condition. Is Bergson sufficiently attentive, though, to the ways in which Darwinism challenges our dominant modes of thought? On the one hand, I think he is and he is inspired by it. He takes seriously its critique of radical finalism and incorporates the key lessons into his own thinking about evolution, including the insight that there is no idea or plan of evolution. On the other hand, he is insistent that Darwinism does not attend to some fundamental aspects of our appreciation of nature, such as the need to account for the evolution of life. I have sought to show that Bergson cannot straightforwardly be labelled a vitalist. Moreover, although the notion of a vital impetus may be a problematic one, and one that science is right to eschew, this should not be at the expense of disregarding the importance of Bergson's insights into duration and his attempt to get us to reflect on the sense of life in terms of a fundamental sympathy with it. This is not at all to fall prey to anthropomorphism but precisely the opposite: it is an effort to think beyond the human condition. Bergson thinks this is the function of philosophy, in which the task is not to complete science and add to it more generalities and of some alleged higher order; rather, the task is to extend our perception of the universe so as to attempt to get closer to life. However, although Bergson thinks this task is peculiar to philosophy and of no interest to the scientist, it is possible that contemporary science, especially in the form of complexity thinking, is also committed to this endeavour.

Bergson's decision to focus on biology as the science of living beings, and his attempt to raise the question of life, is, when seen the light of the fundamental intellectual prejudices of modern science, a bold enterprise. As Robert Rosen points out in his seminal study, *Life Itself*, physics, as we largely know it today, is the science of mechanism. Theoretical physics, he contends, has beguiled itself with a quest for what is universal and general. Moreover, because the physicist perceives that most things that make up the universe are not organisms, and not alive in any conventional sense, it is held that organisms are negligible and to be ignored in the quest for universality.[16] On the one hand, it is held that biology can add nothing new to physics and, on the other hand, that living beings can be entirely understood as specializations of physical universals; all that remains is to specify 'the innumerable constraints and boundary conditions that make organisms special'.[17] The implication of the belief in the unlimited uniformity of mechanical behaviour, as well as universality of mechanical laws, is that all forces or energies can be studied in the same manner, with the added implication that all of inanimate nature could be studied through simple laboratory situations and with such humble laboratories serving as 'proxies for the entire universe'.[18] If biology uncritically adopts this mechanism as its model – for example, by approaching the organism as a machine – it radically simplifies and, more than this 'we literally kill life'.[19] For Rosen, adopting the mechanistic approach means losing the entailment we need to understand the organism; in the case of organisms 'almost everything about is entailed by something else about them'.[20] The presupposition of mechanism proves devastating here since it confines us to fragments, 'pieces that individually can be regarded as mechanisms all right but that cannot be articulated or combined within those confines'.[21]

Although Rosen is not a vitalist – he rejects both vitalism and evolutionism – he echoes something of Bergson's concerns about dogmatic materialism when he argues, 'Life is material, but the laws framed to describe the properties of matter give no purchase on life'.[22] Physics denies that there is a difference between organic systems and material systems, and any perceived conjunction today between physics and biology, 'so fervently embraced by biology in the name of unification', is blind to the manner in which it is caught up 'in a philosophy of naïve reductionism'.[23] It is on account of his attention to the complexity of life and natural phenomena that Bergson now has an appeal to several contemporary theoretical biologists working at the cutting-edge of research in biology today, including the likes of Brian Goodwin and Mae-Wan Ho.[24]

quite go into the category of the many nor yet into that of the one; that neither mechanical causality nor finality can give a sufficient interpretation of the vital process' (CE 177). It is clear that in Bergson's thinking a distinction is to be made between what philosophical notions can claim when they function in concert with science and what validity they have when they are being developed on their own plane. A philosophy of life provides a vision and an intuition of life that may well be considered otiose by science. The possibilities of thinking cannot be dictated to by the requirements of science, however, simply because for Bergson its own praxis is an approximation of the real and not the whole explanation of it. In *Creative Evolution*, for example, Bergson outlines an appreciation of life in which the duty of philosophy is said to be one of examining the living 'without any reservation as to practical utility', and it is to do this by liberating itself from forms and habits that are strictly intellectual: 'Its own special object is to speculate, that is to say, to see' (CE 196). For Bergson this means that philosophy invades the domain of experience and it is in the absolute that we live and move and have our being. Philosophy, then:

> Busies herself with many things which hitherto have not concerned her. Science, theory of knowledge, and metaphysics find themselves on the same ground. At first there may be a certain confusion. All three may think they have lost something. But all three will profit from the meeting. (CE 198)

Bergson evidently takes science extremely seriously and seeks, ultimately a synthesis of philosophy and science. Although our knowledge could be incomplete, it is, once we move in the absolute, neither simply external nor simply relative: 'It is reality itself, in the profoundest meaning of the word, that we reach by the combined and progressive development of science and of philosophy' (CE 199). Instead of the factitious unity imposed on nature by the understanding from outside we are in search of an inward, living unity. The specific task of philosophy is to go beyond the level of knowledge attained by the pure understanding, which fails to comprehend the extent to which it itself has been cut out from reality in terms of the double genesis of matter and intellect. Some identical process has cut out matter and the intellect from a stuff or real that contains both, and it is into this reality that we seek dissolve into and get back to more and more completely, and 'in proportion as we compel ourselves to transcend pure intelligence' (CE 199). In terms of some actual experience what we plunge back into is duration: the ethical or existential task – since Bergson's philosophy of life has this aspect to it – is to come into our self-possession and highest possible freedom, reaching and accessing 'a duration in which the past, always moving on, is swelling unceasingly with a present that is absolutely new' (CE 199–200). To reform philosophy is, ultimately, to get us to a point where we are able to intuit duration and so move closer to the realities of (our) creative evolution.

this text Bergson pursues, at least in part, an innovative naturalistic approach to morality, one that some commentators have seen as an early attempt at a socio-biological approach to the topic. This claim, however, needs to be treated with a high degree of caution: although Bergson certainly thinks we need to reintegrate the human being into nature so as to develop an adequate understanding of core aspects of morality, he clearly does not think that the possibilities of the human animal, qua ethical animal, are completely reducible to this level. As John Mullarkey has astutely noted, Bergson's sociobiology is not conformist in that it does not seek to legitimize natural essences but rather aims at the continual creation of new social forms.[1] Nevertheless, I think Bergson's neglected text can connect in pertinent ways with work in this field. Consider Bergson's key claim that morality has developed in terms of both closed and open forms and then consider the following from a recent essay entitled 'Darwinian Evolutionary Ethics: Between Patriotism and Sympathy' by Peter Richerson and Robert Boyd:

> The great moral problem of our time is how to grow larger-scale loyalties to fit the fact that the world is now so famously a global village, while at the same time creating tribal-scale units that reassure us that we belong to a social system with a human face. The existence of weapons of mass destruction and the need to manage important aspects of the environment as a global commons threaten catastrophe if we fail in this project.[2]

Although Bergson uses a different and more rigorous philosophical language to investigate the sources and future of morality, the claim made by Boyd and Richerson is in tune, at least in part, with insights Bergson advanced in the early 1930s.

Still, as Paola Marrati has argued, Bergson's appeal to biology should not be confused with any form of social Darwinism or evolutionary sociology. The appeal in Bergson to go 'beyond the human condition' does not mean stripping humanity of its bodily, animal life in favour of a purely spiritual, ghostly existence. In Bergson our biological form of embodiment, including our animality, is not to be despised. Moreover, in Bergson life is identified 'with a tendency to change, with an essential mobility, an aspiration to novelty that runs through all living forms'.[3] If there is a privilege to be accorded to the human animal it resides in a greater capacity for change and freedom. However, as Marrati ably argues, this capacity does not open up an ontological gap, say in the manner of Kant or Heidegger, and humanity is not separated from the rest of the living world. Indeed, Bergson sees rationality as rooted in life 'to the extent that life as such is endowed with a highly cognitive competence: the capability of solving problems'.[4] In Bergson a fundamental biological category is that of the problem, not simply need: 'Nutrition, before being a need to be satisfied, is a problem to be solved.'[5]

Like Jean-Marie Guyau (1854–88) before him, Bergson can be interpreted as a philosopher who is keen to naturalize Kant on ethics and so as to render less mysterious the nature of obligation. For Guyau questions of duty and obligation cannot be placed in a region above that in which science and nature move, while for Bergson obligation is no unique fact incommensurate with the rest of nature in the case of the human animal. However, neither Guyau nor Bergson is reductive in pursuing a naturalistic approach. Guyau locates progress in morality taking place through the evolution of human sociability.[6] The task is to probe into the origin of morality, as well the history and future of human society, outside the perspectives of historicism and an abstract rationalism: 'Human history – the becoming of societies, of morality, of forms of political organization – is a part of the movement of the evolution of life and shares with it a radical lack of teleology.'[7] Rather than locating morality in abstract and ahistorical reason, Bergson will endeavour to show that reason is a product of the evolution of life: 'Reason belongs to evolution's becoming, a becoming that produces new ideas and new concepts at the same time as it produces new forms of life'.[8] Bergson, as we shall see, is prepared to acknowledge the fact of moral progress in human evolution but also holds that humanity carries with it a dark secret in the form of the war-instinct and for him this necessitates that today humanity needs to make a decision about its future existence. Bergson is an important figure in modern ethics since he recognizes that both the biological and phenomenological realms doubts whether he would publish a book on ethics simply because he doubted whether if he could attain conclusions as demonstrable as those of his other texts. Philosophy proceeds by a definite method and can legitimately claim as much objectivity as the positive sciences, though of a different kind.[10] Bergson was, therefore, in search of an approach to ethics that would satisfy the ambition he had set for philosophy: that of achieving precision (CM 11).

On its initial reception Bergson's text was read as an attempt to show the importance of the release of dynamic moral energies, smashing, as it were, the narrow framework of the rationalist and idealist ethics, and outlining 'an ethics which does not shut man in on himself, but reveals and respects in it the well-springs of moral experience and of moral life.'[11] Furthermore, Maritain claimed that against the idealist attitude Bergson's text belonged to the cosmic attitude that shows the human being to be situated in a universe that spreads beyond itself in every direction, seeing in the moral life a particular case of universal life. Bergson, Maritain claimed, has recognized the dependence of moral philosophy on the philosophy of nature, linking the destinies of the philosophy of human action to a philosophy of the universe.[12] However, in more recent readings Bergson's emphasis on the philosophy of life and nature as a foundation for ethics has been called into question and a different picture has emerged as to what might be going on in the text. Frédéric Worms, for example, has strongly argued against a straightforward vitalistic reading of Bergson on ethics and the double source of morality. The danger, as he sees it is one of giving an overly simplistic meaning to Bergson's statement that all morality is in essence biological. More specifically, the danger is one of attributing to

Bergson a substantialist metaphysics of life – of the *élan vital* – from which the sources of morality can be derived and reduced to. What this neglects is the fact that morality is a specifically human experience and has a specific place in human life.[13] In no way does Bergson maintain that social and political forms of organization are biologically determined.[14]

In what follows I want to illuminate the meaning of Bergson's statement that in essence all morality – by which he means the two main sources of morality in pressure and aspiration – is biological and examine the issue of biologism in the case of Bergson on ethics.[15] Bergson's contribution to ethics, I show, is essentially twofold: first, he shows that obligation is not a unique fact incommensurate with others, and second, he shows the importance of moral creativity in human life and which enables agents to escape the threat of nihilism or a meaningless universe.

Bergson on the Origins of Morality and the Character of Obligation

The aim of Bergson's opening first chapter, which focuses on morality, is twofold: first, to search for pure obligation and, in the process, significantly narrow down our conception of what morality is; and, second, to follow the same method but make a reverse movement, this time upwards, to the extreme limit, in order to show what complete morality looks like.

In its origins morality is the pressure of prohibition that we are habituated to, in the same way that necessity works in nature. Although analogous these are not the same; as Bergson notes, an organism subject to laws it must obey is one thing, a society composed of 'free wills' is another (we have inflexibility in one case, flexibility in the other). In the case of human life there is a *habit* of obligation. From an initial standpoint, then, social life can be defined as a system of more or less deeply rooted habits that correspond to the needs of a community, habits of command and obedience in the form of an impersonal social imperative.

As with all habits we feel a sense of obligation. Social obligation is a special kind of pressure and habit: 'Society, present within each of its members, has claims which, whether great or small, each express the sum-total of its vitality' (TSMR 11). Bergson is not claiming that society is nature, or that the regularity established in the two orders is of the same kind: for a start, society is a collection

There is not simply the duty to obey social commands, but also the awareness that it is possible to evade the social imperative and yet one feels the debt. The important point is this: obligation comes as much from 'within' as from 'without'. Bergson thinks there is a point reached where it becomes virtually impossible to distinguish between the individual and society. Obligation first binds us to ourselves, or rather to the superficial or surface self, the social self: 'To cultivate this social ego is the essence of our obligation to society.' The social ego is a form of self-recognition:

> Were there not some part of society in us, it would have no hold on us ... [the individual] is perfectly aware that the greater part of his strength comes from this source, and that he owes to the ever-recurring demands of social life that unbroken tension of energy, that steadiness of aim in effort, which ensures the greatest return for his activity. But he could not do so, even if wished to, because his memory and his imagination live on what society has implanted in them, because the soul of society is inherent in the language he speaks. (TSMR 15)

The verdict of conscience is that given by the social self (it is not the only kind of conscience: as we shall see, there are deeper sources for our moral feelings). Our debt or obligation to society is to cultivate our social ego: unless some part of society was within us it could have no hold on us. It can take a violent break to reveal clearly the extent of the nexus of the individual to society, for example the remorse of the criminal. The criminal loses his identity, does not know who he is anymore, such is the nature of his transgression, and this is generated by his own conscience. His desire is not so much to evade punishment but to wipe out the past, to deny the knowledge of what he has done, as though the crime had not really taken place. The criminal thus feels more isolated than does someone waking up to find himself stranded on a desert island. He could re-join society if he confessed to his crime and became the author of his own condemnation.

All kinds of intermediaries exist that ensure that the relation of individuals to society is smooth, easy, natural, and effortless: family, a trade or profession, the parish or district we belong to, etc. These are sources of fulfilling our obligations and paying our debts to society. Here duty, therefore, can be defined as a form of non-exertion, passive acquiescence. There are two cases when the ease of it all is broken: from the perspective of the individual's moral distress and from the perspective of society (e.g. war and the excessive demand it places on individuals, such as self-sacrifice).

Can we say that duty implies an overcoming of self: 'obedience to duty means resistance to self'? (TSMR 20) Can we not readily see this in cases of the natural disobedience of the child and the necessity of its education; by acts of rebellion in one's normal ties that bind (extramarital flings, school truancy, and days off work)? Bergson has a problem with this way of thinking about morals: 'When, in order to define obligation, its essence and its origin, we lay down that obedience is primarily a struggle with self, a state of tension or contraction, we make a psychological error which has vitiated many theories of ethics' (TSMR 20). This is because we are encouraging confusion over the sense of obligation – 'a tranquil state akin to inclination' – with the violent effort we exert on ourselves now and again to break down possible obstacles to obligation. In a highly innovative move contra Kant, Bergson maintains that, 'Obligation is in no sense a unique fact, incommensurate with others, looming above them like a mysterious apparition' (TSMR 20). Moreover: 'We have any number of particular obligations, each calling for a separate explanation. It is natural ... a matter of habit to obey them all. Suppose that exceptionally we deviate from one of them, there would be resistance; if we resist this resistance, a state of tension or contraction is likely to result. It is this rigidity which we objectify when we attribute so stern as aspect to duty' (TSMR 21). Bergson appreciates that when we resist resistance – temptations, passions, and desires – we need to give ourselves reasons. There is the call of an idea, and autonomy or the exertion of self-control takes place through the medium of intelligence. However, 'from the fact that we get back to obligation by rational ways it does not follow that obligation was of a rational order' (TSMR 22). He says that he will come back to this point in a fuller discussion of ethical theories. For now, a distinction is made between a that demands we make a superhuman effort of legislating and conforming to a categorical imperative: 'There is no need to be a hero of pure reason to fulfil our many duties.'[17] Intelligence introduces greater logical consistency into our lines of conduct. However, is it not the case that we never sacrifice our vanity, passions, and interests to the need for such consistency? We go wrong not when we ascribe a spurious independent existence to reason but when we ascribe to it the controlling power or agency of action: 'We might as well believe that the fly-wheel drives the machinery' (TSMR 23). Bergson is not denying that reason intervenes as a regulator to assure consistency between rules and maxims but claiming that it oversimplifies what is actually taking place in the becoming of a moral agent. Reason is at work everywhere in moral behaviour. Thus, an individual whose respectable behaviour is the least based on reasoning (sheepish conformity, for example) introduces a rational order into his conduct from the mere fact of obeying rules that are logically connected to one another. This may require social evolution and the refinement of mores. This is because a principle of economy governs logical coordination (extraction and selection). By contrast, nature is lavish, and the closer a community stands to nature we will find greater the proportion of unaccountable and inconsistent rules. The point, then, is that the essence of obligation is something different from the requirement of reason. Bergson stresses this point in order to show the natural sources of obligation and duty. The conclusion is reached: 'an absolutely categorical imperative is instinctive or somnambulistic, enacted as such in a normal state...' (TSMR 26). The totality of obligation is, in fact, the habit of contracting habits; this is a specifically human instinct of intelligence. How do we arrive at this insight?

Let's imagine evolution has proceeded along two divergent lines with societies at the extremities of each. On the one hand, the more natural will be the instinctive type (such as ants or the bee hive). On the other hand, there is the society where a degree of latitude has been left to individual choice or waywardness. For nature to be effective in this case, that is, to achieve a comparable regularity, there is recourse to habit in place of instinct. Now comes the key part of Bergson's argument:

> Each of these habits, which may be called 'moral', would be incidental. But the aggregate of them, I mean the habit of contracting these habits, being at the very basis of societies and a necessary condition of their existence, would have a force comparable to that of instinct in respect of both intensity and regularity. (TSMR 26–7)

However much society progresses (in terms of its refinement, social complexity, and spiritualization) this original design will remain. For Bergson social life is immanent, if only as a vague ideal, in instinct and intelligence. The difference in human societies is that it is only the necessity of a rule that is the only natural thing (and rules are not laid down by nature). The conclusion reached is that obligation is a kind of virtual instinct, similar to that which lies behind the habit of speech. Obligation needs to lose its specific character so we recognize it as among the most general phenomena of life. Obligation is the form assumed by necessity in the realm of human social life.

How can we say that this source of morality is still active in civilized societies? Bergson has a number of reasons. His principal one is to claim that both primitive and civilized societies are, in essence, closed societies. To appreciate the necessary insight we need to turn away from any kind of moral idealism. It is this idealism that would give us civilized society from the start. We cannot, however, begin by assuming that society is an accomplished fact, as when we lay down as a duty the respect of life and property of others as a fundamental demand of social life; for what society do we have in mind? What if we look at the matter through more realistic lens? We know that in times of war, murder, pillage, perfidy, and cheating are deemed to be not only lawful but also praiseworthy: 'Fair is foul, and foul is fair' (Macbeth's witches). Instead of listening to what society says of itself, to know what it thinks and wants we need to look at what it does.[18] Surely war and vice are exceptions and abnormalities? But then, as Bergson points out, disease is as normal as health, and peace is often a preparation for war. However much society endows man, whom it has trained to discipline, with all it has acquired during centuries of civilization, it still has need of the primitive dignity – both religion through God and philosophy through Reason do this – is take a (spiritual) leap: we don't come to such ideas by degrees, say in the manner of 'the expanding circle'.[19] Let me now explore the nature of this second morality, or what Bergson calls 'complete morality'.

The Open Soul and Creative Emotion

Bergson maintains that morality comprises two different parts. The first part follows from the original structure of human society and the second part finds its explanation in a principle that explains this structure. In the case of the first morality it is obligation that represents the pressure exerted by the elements of society upon one another and as a way of maintaining the shape of the whole, and this pressure has an effect that is prefigured in each one of us by a system of habits that go to meet it. Here the whole is comparable to an instinct and has been prepared by nature, so we have human social life. In the case of the second morality obligation remains but takes the form of an aspiration or an impetus, 'of the very impetus which culminated in the human species, in social life, in a system of habits which bears a resemblance more or less to instinct' (TSMR 55). Here the primitive impetus comes into play directly, Bergson says, and no longer simply through the medium of the mechanisms it had set up and at which it had provisionally halted. On the one hand, then, nature has set down the human along a particular path of evolution (sociability); on the other hand, the human animal has gone beyond what is prescribed for it in nature and here it follows the activity of an impetus, which is a model for creation and invention. Bergson will speak of this new aspect of morality as a coincidence with the generative effort of life, or in terms of a contact with the generative principle of the human species.

We need to mark the difference between the two moralities as a difference in kind since the tendency in each case is quite different (closed and open): the first consists in impersonal rules and formulas; the second incarnates itself in a privileged personality who becomes an example. These are exceptional human beings and include Christian saints, the sages of Greece, the prophets of Israel, and the Arahants of Buddhism. The first morality works as a pressure or propulsive force, the second has the effect of an appeal. New life and a new morality are proclaimed: loyalty, sacrifice of self, spirit of renunciation, charity. Are these not all at work in closed morality? Of course; what changes is the 'spirit' animating these notions. For Bergson it is not simply a question of replacing egoism with altruism; it is not simply a question of the self now saying to itself, I am working for the benefit of mankind since the idea is too vast and the effect too diffuse. In the closed morality the individual and social are barely distinguishable: it is both at once and at this level the 'spirit' moves around a circle that is closed on itself. Can we say that operative in the open soul is the love of all humanity? This does not go far enough since it can be extended to animals, plants, and all nature. It could even do without them since its form is not dependent on any specific content: '"Charity" would persist in him who possesses "charity," though there be no other living creature on earth' (TSMR 38). It is a psychic attitude that, strictly speaking, does not have an object. It is not acquired by nature but requires an effort. It transmits itself through feeling: think of the attraction or appeal of love, of its passion, in its early stages and which resembles an obligation (we must because we must); perhaps a tragedy lays ahead, a whole life wrecked, wasted, and ruined. This does not stop our responding to its call or appeal. We are entranced, as in cases of musical emotion that introduces us into new feelings, 'as passers-by are forced into a street dance'. The pioneers in morality proceed in a similar fashion: 'Life holds for them unsuspected tones of feeling like those of some new symphony, and they draw us after them into this music that we may express it in action' (TSMR 40). We obey the call or appeal of love, and this shows us the passion of love or a great emotion, for good or ill.

Does Bergson show himself to be an irrationalist here? His argument is against intellectualism: 'It is through an excess of intellectualism that feeling is made to hinge on an object and that all emotion is held to be the reaction of our sensory faculties to an intellectual representation' (TSMR 40). Take the example of music: are the emotions expressed linked to any specific objects are distinct from sensation, that is, they cannot be reduced to being a psychical transposition of a physical stimulus. There are two kinds: (1) where the emotion is a consequence of an idea or mental picture; and (2) where the emotion is not produced by a representation but is productive of ideas (Bergson calls them infra and supra-intellectual, respectively). A creative emotion informs the creations not only of art but of science and civilization itself. It is a unique kind of emotion, one that precedes the image; it virtually contains it, and is its cause. This position is not equivalent, Bergson insists, to a moral philosophy of sentiment, simply because we are dealing with an emotion that is capable of crystallizing into representations, even into an ethical doctrine. It concerns the new.

Bergson acknowledges that many will find this account of the second morality difficult to accept but maintains that there is no need to resort to metaphysics to explain the relation between the two moralities. Neither exists in a pure state today: the first has handed on to the second something of its compulsive force, while the latter has diffused over the former something of its perfume. Nevertheless, there are some important differences to be maintained: the former is fixed to self-preservation, and the circular movement in which it carries round with it individuals, as if revolving on the same spot, is a vague imitation, through habit, of the immobility of instinct. The latter is a self-overcoming or the conquest of life. In the first morality we attain pleasure (centred on the well-being of individual and society), but not joy. By contrast, in the open morality we experience progress that is experienced in the enthusiasm of a forward movement. There is no need, Bergson insists, to resort to a metaphysical theory to account for this: it is not an issue of picturing a goal we are trying to achieve or envisaging some perfection we wish to approximate. It is an opening out of the soul, a breaking with nature, a moving of the boundaries of itself and the city.

Whereas the first morality has its source in nature, the other kind has no place in nature's design. Nature may have foreseen a certain expansion of social life through intelligence, but only of a limited kind. But it has gone so far as to endanger the original structure. More concretely:

> Nature surely intended that men should beget men endlessly, according to the rule followed by all other living creatures; she took the most minute precautions to ensure the preservation of the species by the multiplication of individuals; hence she had not foreseen, when bestowing on us intelligence, that intelligence would at once find a way of divorcing the sexual act from its consequences, and that man might refrain from reaping without forgoing the pleasure of sowing. It is in quite another sense that man outwits nature when he extends social solidarity into the brotherhood of man; but he is deceiving her nevertheless, for those societies whose design was prefigured in the original structure of the human soul, and of which we can still perceive the plan in the innate and fundamental tendencies of modern man, required that the group be closely united, but that between group and group there should be virtual hostility.... (TSMR 56-7)

However, an absolute break with nature is never possible or even conceivable: 'It might be said, by slightly distorting Spinoza, that it is to get back to *natura naturans* that we break away from *natura naturata*' (TSMR 58). The circle of a closed existence is broken not through preaching love of one's neighbour since we do not embrace humanity by a mere expansion of our narrower feelings. The understanding of the open soul discloses Bergson's commitment to real movement. This cannot take place by a series of discrete stages, as in Zeno's paradoxes, which cannot produce real movement, but via an action in which we find the impression of a coincidence, real or imaginary, with the generative effort of life. When this takes place the obligation felt has the force of an aspiration in the sense of the vital impetus.

Why do we have such a problem in recognizing and speaking about this other morality? Bergson thinks it is because we are Zenoists and do not know how to think real or genuine movement. We can stop short of action in making the transition from the closed and the open, or immobility and movement or e-motion. There can be a waning of the vitality of impetus. We can halt at the point of intelligence. In leaving the closed the sentiment most likely to be adopted is the ataraxia of the Epicureans and the apatheia of the Stoics. Here we are moving from a detachment from the old life to a new attachment to life, but we reach religion called for?'[21] The first morality is a morality of social cohesion and belongs to closed societies as their definition: 'A society is closed because its essence is to include a certain number of individuals and to exclude all others.'[22] We might suppose, as is widespread in thinking about morality, that the whole of obligation and institutionalized religions can be broadened in such a way as to include the whole of humanity in a system of moral and civic habits. Bergson, however, argues against this idea of the expanding circle. As Marrati powerfully puts it:

> Bergson knows well that in each nation there is much talk about duties toward humanity … and that these duties are made out to be the natural prolongation, so to speak, of duties toward the family, the institution, or the state, as if there were only a quantitative difference but no gap, no tension. Yet, according to Bergson, this discourse is nothing but a façade, whether it be pronounced in good or in bad faith. It is enough to look at what happens when a war breaks out: borderless human fraternity gives way to an outburst of violence, everything is allowed against the enemy – murder, pillage, rape, torture, cruelty. To respond that these are exceptional and rare events is but a delusion.[23]

As she points out, the manifestation of violence illustrates the nature of closed societies and shows the dark face of morality and religion in which the exclusion that founds our societies is neither neutral nor vaguely benevolent but essentially hostile. Again, Marrati expresses it astutely when she notes that human societies rest neither on utilitarianism nor a contract 'but on a biologico-evolutionary "social instinct," of which the closure of the social group is an essential aspect'.[24] The belief or idea that we can move from love of the family and of the nation to a love of humanity 'by a continuous broadening of our sympathy, by the progress of a sentiment that would grow while remaining the same, is a mistake with grave consequences.'[25] The leap Bergson appeals to does not simply give us the love of humanity in general since such an object is vague and diffuse. In fact, there is no determined or determinable object once this leap beyond the closed mentality has been made. Instead, we need to think of their being two quite different *sources* of morality, so strictly speaking there is neither continuity nor rupture: 'The opening is nothing but a tendency or an attitude, and it is precisely in this sense that the opening is essentially mystical ... the opening *as* opening does not have an object. Every object assigned to it from the outset, even if it were the entire universe, would close it.'[26] This should not be taken to imply that an open morality is not relevant to all kinds of different objects according to situation and context. Bergson's key claim is that moral creators and mystics are first and foremost figures of action: 'The force of mysticism is a force of agency.'[27]

Marrati claims that the universal has no figure but is empty. Such an emptiness does not denote anything structural, however, since it is primarily and essentially a movement, one 'without pre-established direction and without continuity'.[28] Although this is to write in non-Bergsonian terms such an insight captures in a fertile manner just how we can conceive the universal in productive terms. Although there are no guarantees we are not devoid of hope or the promise of a different future (as Bergson points out, any optimism on our part has to be empirical):

> Without being willing to subscribe to a philosophy of history or to a universalism of pure reason, Bergson puts the emphasis on the new, the unforeseeable, which is never contained in the past, not even as possible. He trusts the powers of time and of life, which are nothing but a production of the new – all along knowing that these forces are fragile and that nobody can guarantee us a better future.[29]

Bergson between Biology and Phenomenology

For Bergson the two forces he has been tracing are fundamental data and not strictly or exclusively moral. Rather, they are the sources of the twin tendencies of life (preservation and enhancement or overcoming). There are two ways of teaching and the attempt to get hold of the will: by training and by the mystic way. The former inculcates impersonal habits, the second takes place through the imitation of a personality, even a spiritual union. Social life cannot be taken that is, of reducing the ethical to the biological. Let me now deal explicitly with this issue.

Frédéric Worms has raised doubts about the wisdom of a straightforward vitalistic reading of Bergson's statement that in essence all morality is biological. For him it is important to appreciate that ethics is a decidedly human affair and this means, in part, that ethics is inseparable from phenomenology. For example, obligation is 'the experience of something that necessitates in us as if coming from life, but still implies an elementary consciousness at least to be felt, which is the beginning of reflection and discussion, if not of complete liberty'.[30] In short, then, we can say that Bergson's account of ethics refers to a quasi-biological experience of the human being that also presupposes a phenomenology of ethical life:

> *our life is, via obligation, present to our consciousness and takes the moral aspect*
> *of duty*, specific to humanity. Even if 'closed', even if incapable of leading to the
> open society of humanity as such ... this first kind of ethics is nevertheless not
> grounded on metaphysical presupposition, but on the contrary on a conscious
> and quasi-phenomenological experience.[31]

We are not, Worms claims, to be seen as prisoners of a life that is exterior to our lives (for example, life as a metaphysical substance and of which we are the mere vehicles). While there is most definitely a contact with life's energy, we also 'remain ... on the strict level of human experience and immanence'.[32] Our actual lives are lived in terms of a double meaning corresponding to the double experience of obligation, and this duality 'means that we cannot reach a primitive and absolute unity by taking "life" as a general and infinite substance, and annihilating our own life as such within it'.[33] Bergson makes it clear that he regards dynamic morality to be essentially the work of human genius. While the first kind of morality, the static kind, is characteristic of a group of habits that can be seen as the counterpart of certain instincts in animals, the second kind of morality involves individual initiative, intuition, and emotion, 'susceptible of analysis into ideas which furnish intellectual notations of it and branch out into infinite detail' (TSMR 64). True, Bergson does say that the inventive efforts that characterize the domain of human life, and that have resulted in the creation of new species, have found in humanity, and humanity alone, 'the means of continuing its activity through individuals, on whom there has devolved, along with intelligence, the faculty of initiative, independence and liberty' (TSMR 119). This suggests that humanity is a representative of life conceived as an inventive vital impetus, but, at the same time, there is no suggestion that in the field of ethical life we are not dealing with specifically historical problems faced by humanity and that have required the constitution of new legal codes and invention of new political ideals and orders.

Is Bergson thinking in terms of analogy when he attempts to conceive morality in terms of biology and a notion of life? Although Bergson's text can be read as an anticipation of sociobiology, in which it is held that nature has set down the human species along a particular path of evolution, he specifically states the obligations laid down by a human community introduce a regularity that has 'merely *some analogy* to the inflexible order of the phenomena of life' (TSMR 11). The situation is more complex with respect to the second morality since here Bergson seems to conceive it in terms of a realization of the vital impetus of life. However, at one point in the text Bergson says that the leaders of humanity, the ones who have broken down the gates of the city, '*seem* indeed thereby to have placed themselves again in the current of the vital impetus' (TSMR 57). Moreover, the break with nature, which is what these figures represent, takes place through a genius of the will: 'Through these geniuses of the will, the impetus of life, traversing matter, wrests from it, for the future of the species, promises such as were out of the question when the species was being constituted' (TSMR 58). He argues that although there is a break with one nature, that of the closed and the *natura naturata*, there is not a break with all nature, with the *natura naturans*. The path of evolution, whether natural or human, cannot be anticipated and Bergson is not, I think, positing teleology; it has happened that humanity has broken with animal closure and gone beyond what nature prescribed for it.[34] While this process can be likened to an impetus of life, the change has been larger, calls for a bigger soul' and 'mechanism should mean mysticism' (TSMR 310). Bergson has been criticized for neglecting the possessive and destructive death wish,[35] and indeed he claims that the vital impetus, which knows nothing of death, is fundamentally optimistic (TSMR 140; see also 260-1 on 'empirical optimism'). He asks whether underlying the need for stability within life, and that contributes to the preservation of the species, there is not also a 'demand for a forward movement, some remnant of an impulse, a vital impetus' (TSMR 111). Intelligence, says Bergson, is constituted to act mechanically on matter and even postulates a universal mechanism and determinism: 'and conceives virtually a complete science which would make it possible to foresee, at the very instant when the action is launched, everything it is likely to come up against before reaching its goal' (TSMR 139). Intelligence always falls short of this model, however, not only because there is always the discovery of new scientific objects that give science a new impetus, but also because it must confine itself to limited action on a material about which it does not know everything. For Bergson, it would seem, it is not simply the case that we embody the vital impetus, which then works its way through us as some kind of alien life drive, but more that we are to derive inspiration from our reflection on its character within evolution, chiefly that novelty and invention are real features of life, be it biological or ethical. For Bergson all is not given and certainly not everything is given in advance: the time of evolutionary life and of ethical life is a creative one. In the case of ethics his concern is with the obstacles that stand in the way of humanity's moral progress, chiefly, the war-instinct, and to this issue I now turn.

Obstacles to Humanity's Moral Progress

In the long conclusion to his text Bergson asks whether the distinction between the closed and the open is able to help us practically (TSMR 271). The object of the work was to investigate the origins of morality and religion. However, Bergson thinks we cannot simply rest content in our inquiry with developing only certain conclusions, since we still suffer historically from what has been uncovered as constituting the beginnings of human existence, namely the tendencies of the closed society. Bergson insists that the closed mentality still persists, 'ineradicable, in the society that is on the way to becoming an open one' (TSMR 288). Moreover, and this is his key insight: 'since all these instincts of discipline originally converged towards the war-instinct, we are bound to ask to what extent the primitive instinct can be repressed or circumvented' (TSMR 288). I concur with the editors of a recent volume of essays on Bergson's *Two Sources* when they argue that war is, ultimately, the coordinating problem of the book.[36]

What Bergson has shown in his text on morality is that there are strata of human evolution and civilized nations and communities are by no means open societies: they are still largely determined by nature and necessity, and rely for the existence on sentiments that have their basis in earliest humanity. It is thus an error to locate progress naively in a simple transformation from the antique to the modern, from pre-science to science, from unreason to reason and enlightenment. Bergson has sought to show in the book that modern humanity remains as irrational and superstitious as ancient humanity. This does not mean that there has not been progress; rather, there is the need to recognize that genuinely new social and moral inventions are rare and frequently get overtaken again, or subsumed, within the closed. Bergson thinks that it is possible to get back in thought to a fundamental human nature, and this is some original closed society. He holds that the general plan of such a society fitted the pattern of our species as the ant-heap fits the ant, with one crucial difference: the actual detail of the social organization is not given in the case of the human and there is scope for genuine social and moral invention. Now, he acknowledges that a knowledge of nature's plan, which is a way of speaking since nature has not consciously designed anything, would be of 'mere historical interest' (TSMR 272) were it not for the fact that today humanity finds itself 'groaning, half crushed beneath the weight of its own progress' (TSMR 317).

For all his alleged vitalistic optimism Bergson is locating within the heart of civilized humanity a dark past and a terrible secret, namely the war-instinct. He the industrial character of our civilization. The main causes of modern war are: 'increase in population, closing off of markets, cutting off of fuel and raw materials' (TSMR 289). The most serious cause of war today is overpopulation and the need for luxury.

Bergson admits to not believing in the fatality of history since there is no obstacle, he thinks, that cannot be broken down where there are wills sufficiently keyed up to deal with it in time. Thus, he is adamant that, there is 'no unescapable historic law'. There are, however, 'biological laws' that need acknowledging (TSMR 293). This is important if we are to adequately understand the evolution of the human and negotiate the challenges that confront it in its present state. What, then, is the way forward for humanity? Bergson wants to show us what must be given if war is to be abolished. As he says, humanity will change only if it is intent upon changing, but such a change would be dramatic. It would involve, for example, a new ascetic ideal in the form of a commitment to a simpler life, to renouncing the frenzy of consumption that holds us in its grip. As he says, 'should not this very frenzy open our eyes?' Is there not a need for a new frenzy to come into being?: 'humanity must set about simplifying its existence with as much frenzy as it devoted to complicating it' (TSMR 307). Now, Bergson does not think that such an epic transformation means jettisoning either the machine or science. In the first instance, it is a question of coordinating industry and agriculture so that the machine is allotted its 'proper place', that is, the place where it can best serve humanity and where millions do not every year go unfed or are malnourished (TSMR 306); in the second, of recognizing that certain sciences – Bergson mentions physiology and medical science – have the potential to disclose to us the dangers of the multiplication of our needs, including 'all the disappointments which accompany the majority of our satisfactions' (TSMR 300). In short, in addition to mystical intuition, Bergson also calls upon reason, science, and political will and organizations if the necessary transformation is to come about. He gives privilege to moral energy and leadership simply because he thinks we have need of visionaries who serve as exemplars, showing humanity the way forward in the direction of the open and the creation of new ways of feeling and thinking.

Bergson's concluding reflections in *The Two Sources* raise the question of how a divine humanity can come into existence. The obstacle to be overcome is the mode of living that chains the human to the earth as an animal species. One path is to intensify the intellectual work to such an extent, carrying intelligence far beyond what nature may have intended, that the simple tool leads to a vast system of machinery such that human activity is given maximum liberty: this liberation in turn would be stabilized by social and political organization that ensures the application of mechanism to its true object. The danger here is that mechanization may turn against mysticism; in fact, only by reacting against the latter does mechanization reach it highest pitch of development. Bergson allows for a complex development, in which contrary tendencies evolve, struggling against one another. The other path is taken, that of mysticism, and merges with the other development, 'until such time as a profound change in the material conditions imposed on humanity by nature should permit, in spiritual matters, of a radical transformation' (TSMR 236). This means that the mystic soul is destined in the first instance to plant its vital energy on the soil of religion and the founding of religious communities; the ultimate goal, however, is the moral transformation of humanity. The mystic soul waits for humanity to catch up with it and when ready it responds to the call for transformation by bringing its insights into play:

> The task of the great mystic is to effect a radical transformation of humanity by setting an example. The object could be attained only if there existed in the end what should theoretically have existed in the beginning, a divine humanity. (TSMR 239)

Conclusion

Although Bergson appeals to the potentialities of the dynamic impetus of life, and that endeavours to transcend the closed in all its manifestations, he neither

However, it is also clear that humanity today continues to face the decision that Bergson sought to confront it with in his text of 1932, namely whether it wishes to carry on living or not. Bergson's invitation to humanity, it seems to me, remains of vital contemporary relevance: not simply to decide in favour of mere living or survival but to also make the extra effort to fulfil on their refractory planet the function of the universe, which is a machine for the making of gods. As Michael Naas has noted, Bergson is entertaining at the end of his book the terrible hypothesis that humanity may not simply be able to destroy itself but may actually desire to. He is entertaining the idea not simply of the destruction of the enemy but rather the extinction of humanity, in which the thermodynamics of death reaches its limit point.[37] Indeed, according to one commentator, he is anticipating the creation of the atomic bomb.[38] The significance of this it that it means is that Kant's teleology is over: nature does not know better than man what humanity needs and war cannot any longer be said to be a ruse of reason.[39] It is for this reason that Bergson holds that humanity is confronted with the need to make a fundamental decision. The choice Bergson is presenting his readers with at the end of the book is a choice between mere living and all this now entails for us, such as the submission to more and more numerous and vexatious regulations that are designed to provide a means of circumventing the successive obstacles that our nature sets up against our civilization, and making real our potential for going beyond the limits of natural necessity, including a liberation from the compulsion of infinite consumption and its devastating ecological consequences, to say nothing of the shameful injustices and wars this compulsion subjects us all to. This is what it ultimately means for us to become 'gods' and to lead an existence in which pleasure would be eclipsed by joy.

We have seen the extent to which Bergson places the emphasis on creative emotion over reason or intelligence. However, this does not mean a new rational ordering of society is not called for. Bergson thinks we face two grave problems in the present, and both have their roots in the civilization we are creating, which he calls 'aphrodisiacal':[40] (1) The first is war and new kinds of war. Bergson holds that war is natural; humanity is an animal species like any other and so driven by self-preservation. However, the wars of today are new and reflect the industrial character of our civilization. The most serious cause of war today is overpopulation and the need for luxury. So he calls for measures to control population expansion – birth control, for example; and this is eminently rational. (2) The second is sex; or rather, the extent to which we remain animals driven by an instinct to reproduce. This instinct demands that we preserve the species by producing as many individuals as possible. So this is connected to the first problem. However, it is also connected to a different problem, and this is due to the fact for Bergson that sexual pleasure is not an emotion but a sensation, albeit an especially strong sensation. It is something physical, not spiritual by definition. As an especially intense sensation sexual pleasure is based only on differences of degree: its pleasure can vary from one partner to another but as a pleasure it is always essentially the same; there is no difference in kind from one sexual act to another or from one partner to another. The problem is that we are creating a sexualized culture in which the only sound we hear is 'sex': this sound of sex is our obsession, Bergson thinks. We find it pleasurable to love pleasure, and to this end we want conveniences, and we will increasingly find ourselves caught in the grip of the frenzy of consumption. The goal of our activities has become simply pleasure: not a higher or superior ideal (such as 'God' or a new humanity), but only this. So, here Bergson's portrait is not that dissimilar to the one Nietzsche gives in the prologue to *Thus Spoke Zarathustra* concerning the reign of 'the last human' who has discovered happiness and blinks. On the point of reason, John Mullarkey has argued that Bergson can well allow for the love of reason to be a motivating force, but as he points out it is a love first and a love of reason second. In other words, the ends of reason are worth nothing unless there is a desire for them.[41]

In order to appreciate the significance of Bergson's discussion of religion in *The Two Sources of Morality and Religion* it is instructive to bring it into a critical dialogue with arguably the only other comparable attempt in the modern period to articulate a naturalistic account of religion that similarly breaks the confines of a reductive sociobiology, namely Nietzsche's renaturalization of religion. We begin with an exposition of Bergson's conception of static and dynamic religion respectively before turning to a consideration of those aspects of Nietzsche's critical evaluation of religion that seem to complement and challenge Bergson's claims. In the final section, we explore possible points of convergence in Bergson's and Nietzsche's accounts of religion and consider the radical possibility to which their thought often seems to tend – the fusion of the theory of life and religion.

Bergson on Static Religion

We begin by addressing an aspect of Bergson's thinking on religion that finds a rigorous treatment in his analysis. The phenomenon in question is the 'mythmaking function' or 'fabulation' (the fictionalizing of existence or the world through the telling of stories). Where Nietzsche seems to treat this as peculiar to a primitive (religious) mentality, Bergson not only shows its origins here but also argues that it continues to inform and guide the post-religious mind; he claims that it is an element more basic to the operations of the human mind than simply defining it as religious.

Bergson begins his treatment of religion in TSMR by acknowledging that a cursory examination of religions in the past and present provides little more than a farrago of error and folly that is humiliating for human intelligence (TSMR 102). Religion clings to absurdity and error; it enjoins immorality and prescribes crime. Crass superstition has long been a universal fact of human nature. We find societies existing without science and philosophy but never a society existing without religion. *Homo sapiens*, the only creature on earth endowed with reason and intelligence, is also the only creature on earth to pin its existence on unreasonable things. Hence Bergson's initial question: How is it that reasonable beings accept unreasonable beliefs and practices?

He questions the validity of the approach of Levy-Bruhl who sought to show a primitive mentality at work in early evolution, which we can still find today, he holds, among so-called backward peoples. This is not sufficient for Bergson for a number of reasons. The main issue we need to confront is the *psychological origin of superstition*, and this can only be done by examining the general structure of human thought. In fact, it is from an observation of civilized man of the present day that we will find an answer to the question.[1]

What of the approach of Émile Durkheim who lays stress on a 'collective mentality' that can explain the workings of religion? Bergson accepts the idea of a 'social intelligence' that involves collective representations deposited in language, institutions, and customs. But he argues there are deficiencies in the approaches of both sociology and psychology. Sociology takes the social body as the only reality, regarding the individual as an abstraction. Psychology, in contrast, underestimates the extent to which the individual is primarily made for society: abnormal and morbid states, such as listlessness, alienation, isolation, can all be profitably examined once this fact is taken into account. For Bergson, 'our psychical structure originates in the necessity of preserving and developing social and individual life' (TSMR 108). It is a question of focusing on use, or rather both function and structure. The mind is not what it is for the fun of it. Bergson looks for the source of things: mankind has not always had dramas and novels, but it has for most of its history created fictions and myths, and the origins of this lie in religion. How does this myth-making function come about? His answer is on account of a social need.

Fiction, Bergson notes, resembles an incipient hallucination, one that can thwart our judgement and reason. Nature creates intelligent beings but also needs to guard against certain dangers of intellectual activity without compromising the future of intelligence. In a world of facts where nothing can resist their talking of *vital needs* being satisfied and demanding satisfaction, such as having 'confidence in life'. In part, this can explain why religion survives through the ages and survives even in face of the tremendous advances in facts and knowledge of science (Bergson does not offer this as an apology for religion).

Intelligence threatens to break up social cohesion; if society is to continue, there has to be a counterpoise to it. If this counterpoise cannot be created by instinct in the case of the human (intelligence occupies the place it would assume), then the same effect is produced by a virtuality of instinct (or, if one prefers, by the residue of instinct that survives on the fringe of intelligence). It does not exercise direct action but is much more complex than this and involves calling up imaginary representations. These need to hold their own against the representation of reality and aim to counteract the work of intelligence *through* intelligence. This myth-making faculty both plays a (vital) social role and serves the individual's need for creative fancy.

Why is there a problem of intelligence? In the case of the anthill and the beehive the individual lives for the community alone. Here instinct is coextensive with life and social instinct is nothing more than the spirit of subordination and coordination animating the cells and tissues and organs of all living bodies. So there is no problem here. However, where the expansion of intelligence reveals itself as in the case of man, the problem becomes acute. Reflection enables the individual to invent and the society to develop. But how is society to maintain itself in a situation where, through the licence given to individual initiative, social discipline is endangered? What if the individual focuses largely or even solely on himself? The individual cannot work automatically or somnambulistically for the species, but will want to seek individual satisfaction and fulfilment. Of course, training in and exposure to formal reasoning will lead him to recognize that he furthers his own interest by promoting the happiness of others, but then as Bergson notes it takes centuries to produce a John Stuart Mill (who has not convinced all philosophers, let alone the mass of mankind). The fact is that intelligence counsels egoism first. This is its logic, if you like. But the 'virtual instinct' of society makes its demands and places a check on the hyper-individuality of intelligence. This is where religion comes into the picture as a '*defensive reaction of nature against the dissolvent power of intelligence*' (TSMR 122).

The first function of religion, therefore, concerns social preservation. It is a kind of instinct (a defensive reaction), but it is also a spiritual intelligence capable of cultivating individuals. Take, for example, death: animals do not know they are mortal and are destined to die. Such knowledge is the prerogative of the human animal only. This is not just the sheer brute fact of death, though it is this. It is also the knowledge that all that comes into being is fated to pass away, to turn to dust, to come to nothing. Such is the source of the lament, 'all is in vain', and many others too. How can we find the resources for affirming life and for creating new life in the face of such hard knowledge? Bergson argues that religion comes up with the image of life after death, or of the eternal or immortal soul that lives on after the earthly body has perished: '*Religion is a defensive reaction of nature against the representation, by intelligence, of the inevitability of death*' (TSMR 131).

Religion then does not have its origins or roots in fear as Nietzsche supposes in his positivist period (see *Human, all too Human*, chapter 3), but more precisely in a reaction against fear, and in its beginnings it is not a belief in deities (TSMR 153). At first, religion concerns more impersonal forces, and only over time do mythologies grow. Religion exists in order to give man confidence and to support belief: 'In default of power, we must have confidence', Bergson writes, and we do lack this power (TSMR 164); the urge for power as in mastery and human hubris arises from our psychological structure and affliction. Bergson's key insight, then, is that (static) religion works against the dissolvent and depressive power of intelligence.

Bergson on Dynamic Religion

Why does Bergson pass from static religion to dynamic religion? Why not just stop at the static? Bergson has given us a highly interesting account of the 'sources' of that a decision concerning its future is an imperative for humanity (TSMR 317), he envisages this in quite different terms from Nietzsche. Human beings, he suggests, face the task of determining whether they wish to go on living or not: 'Theirs the responsibility, then, for deciding if they want merely to live, or intend to make just the extra effort required for fulfilling, even, on their refractory planet, the essential function of the universe, which is a machine for the making of gods' (TSMR 317). Although this is open to interpretation, Bergson seems to suggest in the final pages of *The Two Sources* that humanity needs to curtail its will to power and restrain its aphrodisiacal nature.

For Bergson, the human is distinguished from the rest of the animal kingdom not only as the rational animal, but also as the sick animal. We are prone to illness and depression, and there are specific reasons why. We know our own mortality and the painful actuality of death, the awareness of perpetually perishing as a law of nature, etc. Only man experiences something like the futility of existence. The rest of nature exists in absolute tranquillity; plants and animals have an unshakeable confidence such is the nature of their instinctive attachment to life (TSMR 204). But this 'attachment to life' is what is so complex in the case of the human animal. The nature of our being wedded to life is of a different kind and order.

Bergson holds religion in its dynamic aspect to be superior to philosophy. This is because Bergson thinks philosophy, which is a species of intelligence, is bound up with contemplation and not action. It is also the case that for Bergson religion, again in its dynamic aspect, is vital, or rather, to be more precise, it carries on the *élan vital* that is the creative force or energy of evolution. In its dynamic form religion expresses a superior vitality and a superior attachment to life. Detaching itself from the closed in all its forms, dynamic religion is able to attach itself in this superior way and show the open tendency of each particular thing. Bergson argues that while static religion is foreshadowed in nature, dynamic religion amounts to a leap beyond nature (TSMR 223). Regards the former, he is largely concerned with identifying its social sources and function; regards the latter, he believes there is something real at stake in genuine mystic states: they herald new ways of feeling, thinking, being, and are of significance to humanity. The former is infra-intellectual, the latter supra-intellectual. To get to the essence of religion and understand the history of mankind, therefore, we need to pass from static to dynamic religion (TSMR 186).

Let us explore further Bergson's idea of attachment to life.[3] The human being's attachment to life slackens with the rise of intelligence (TSMR 210). This is because it no longer lives in the present alone. An intelligent being, such as a human, is one for whom there is no reflection without foreknowledge, and no foreknowledge without what Bergson calls 'inquietude', and this entails 'a momentary slackening of the attachment to life' (TSMR 210). Intelligence is bound up with culture and social and technical development; it is what Nietzsche calls learning to calculate and compute (see also Nietzsche on mnemotechnics in the *Genealogy of Morality*). However, intelligence does not give us full predictive powers. Bergson writes: '*Religion is that element which, in beings endowed with reason, is called upon to make good any deficiency of attachment to life*' (TSMR 210). In static or natural religion the myths counterfeit reality as actually perceived and enables the human animal to recover the confidence it has lost; life is desirable once again.

How does Bergson explain the passage to dynamic religion? The success of religion in giving the human a sense of attachment to life (joy in joy), in the face of the uncertainties and anxieties of intelligence, is the source of this move. In the mystic soul this attachment is felt so deeply that it pervades their whole being as a kind of spirit of life. Bergson's name for this mystic attachment is 'love' (TSMR 38). On this account pure mysticism is rare (this is not by chance but by reason of its very essence), and is not reached in a series of gradual steps from static religion, since a leap is involved. The difference between the two religions is a difference in kind. Of course, impurities empirically exist, and are perhaps the norm:

> When nations at war each declare that they have God on their side, the deity in
> question thus becoming the national god of paganism, whereas the God they

lack or be deficient in. Bergson says that while the creations of the imagination are simply 'ideas', the creations of fabulation are 'ideo-motory' (they literally get into the nervous system). Moreover, they kindle the desire for life, and only the human animal needs to feel this desire. This is owing to its specific conditions of existence as an animal.

This kind of appreciation and analysis is part of Bergson's attempt to show the limitations of reason and intelligence as they are expressed in doctrines of rationalism and intellectualism. Intelligence is practical in a specific sense of responding to specific concrete problems; when it attempts to speculate on a higher plane it enables us to conceive of possibilities, but it does not attain any reality (TSMR 212). If we want to know who or what 'God' is the last person we should consult is a philosopher (TSMR 243; Bergson shows little interest in the proofs of God's existence). Bergson thinks that philosophy, at least in some of its most important manifestations, has allowed the mind to get lost in false problems, such as 'why is there something rather than nothing?' or 'why do I exist?' or 'indeed why does anything exist?' These are problems thrown up by intellectualism for Bergson and are ignored by the mystics. The error lies in the form of the question being asked: it assumes that reality fills a void and that underneath Being there lies nothingness, and so on. But this assumption about absolute nothingness is, says Bergson, a pure illusion and has no more meaning than a square circle (TSMR 251). Bergson notes that when we err like this in our thinking we conceive of our existence as an affair of filling in voids. We consider our lives in terms of passing the time, or killing time, and fail to appreciate that at every moment time is being created (in *Creative Evolution* he seeks to account for this in terms of our existing as creatures of desire and regret, of memory and expectation: 'There is absence only for a being capable of remembering and expecting', CE 180).

In dynamic religion – attained in true mysticism – the confidence in life that static religion gives us is transfigured. Now the attachment to life is not simply of the order of a vital need but of joy, or 'joy in joy, love of that which is all love' (TSMR 212). Bergson devotes several pages to tracing the possible development of genuine mysticism or pure mystic states. This does not reside where we might think, for example, in the Eleusian mysteries and Dionysiac frenzy. Why not? For Bergson it is because they are part of Greek philosophy's elevation of contemplation over action. In some mystical developments of Greek philosophy, such as those of Pythagoras, Plotinus and neo-Platonism, action is held to be a weakening of contemplation, a degradation and degeneration of the perfection attained in the contemplative state. There is an intellectualism endemic to Greek thought and this means that genuine mysticism is never reached or practised by it.

For Bergson genuine mysticism is: 'The establishment of a contact, consequently of a partial coincidence, with the creative effort which life itself manifests' (TSMR 220). Furthermore, 'The great mystic is to be conceived as an individual being, capable of transcending the limitations imposed on the species by its material nature, thus continuing and extending the divine action' (TSMR 220). Bergson's spiritualism is unique since it conceives God as life: the divine force is the creative energy at work in the evolution of life. Life for him is a current of creative energy precipitated into matter that endeavours to wrest from it what it can. This current comes to a halt at specific points, namely species and organisms. On one line of evolution the vital impetus or energy swerves inward and gets locked into a circle of the eternal return of the same: the society of insects where organization is highly perfected and although individuals exist, they do so on the level of complete automatism. However, on the line of evolution that culminates in the human, or something like it, we can conceive of a superhuman or super-life possibility. As Deleuze puts it, this is a capacity for 'scrambling the planes, of going beyond his own plane as his own condition, in order to finally express naturing Nature'[4] (see Bergson TSMR 257). We should not take this to mean that automatism is not a problem for the human animal. For the greater part of its evolutionary history it exists in closed societies and in accordance with the static religion. Moreover, even once we have attained freedom it is automatism that we still need to work against. Freedom for Bergson, in the very movements by which it is affirmed, creates the growing habits that will stifle it if it fails to renew itself by a constant effort.

state of divine rapture that is akin to Dionysian ecstasy (Dionysus becomes in time the God of wine); on the other hand, we find a later development in which a set of practices is devised as a way of inhibiting sensations and deadening mental activity (to induce states similar to hypnosis). These practices are those of yoga. This is not genuine for Bergson on account of the pessimism of Indian religion. For the Hindu the problem is to escape from life, which is seen as unremitting cruelty (suicide offers no solution because of the fact of reincarnation). Life is suffering and therefore the only intelligent goal is to work at the renunciation of desire, to give up on the craving for life (TSMR 225). Nirvana is the state in which we attain the abolition of desire during life. This is mystical but cannot be said to be complete mysticism which is, says Bergson, action, creation, and love. The Hindu or Buddhist does not ignore charity but neither do they believe in action and this is on account of their deep-rooted pessimism.

For Bergson the great Christian mystics achieve complete mysticism: they radiate an extraordinary energy, superabundant activity, in short, accomplishments in the field of action (e.g. St Paul, St Teresa, Joan of Arc). Instead of turning inwards and closing, the soul could now open wide its gates to a universal love. This gives rise to inventions and organizations that are essentially Western. Why has Christianity taken hold in the West? Why has it had effectively no effect in say India that, says Bergson, has gone over to Islamism? Bergson argues that the development or spread of Christianity is linked to the rise and spread of machine civilization and industrialism: this gives us a growing optimism, at least initially, that human beings are not at the mercy of an indifferent and cruel nature but can control and manipulate it and in the service of human betterment and openness. An attitude of hubris towards nature and life takes over. On this point we could compare what Nietzsche says about hubris in the third essay of the *Genealogy of Morality*. Nietzsche holds that it is hubris (what the Greeks understood by overweening pride) that characterizes our whole modern godless existence: it is an awareness of strength or confidence as opposed to weakness or impotence.[5]

Are mystics not crackpots? Should they not be compared to the mentally diseased? We do not know whether Bergson is being deliberately provocative or not, but when he describes these mystics he does so in terms that are decidedly Nietzschean: in them we can locate 'a vast expenditure of energy ... the superabundance of vitality which it demands flows from a spring which is the very source of life' (TSMR 232). In short, what we find in the great mystics is intellectual vigour:

> There is an exceptional, deep-rooted mental healthiness, which is readily recognizable. It is expressed in the bent for action, the faculty of adapting and re-adapting oneself to circumstances, in firmness combined with suppleness, in the prophetic discernment of what is possible and what is not, in the spirit of simplicity which triumphs over combinations. (TSMR 228)

Bergson acknowledges that there are abnormal states at work in mysticism – visions, ecstasies, raptures – and which characterize the mental states of sick people. But he points out that these morbid states can imitate healthy states and prefigure new growth and expansion. There is 'mystic insanity' – for example, the person who thinks he is Jesus or Napoleon and imitates them – but does it follow, he asks, that mysticism is insanity? How do we distinguish between the abnormal and the morbid and sick? Even the great mystics for Bergson warn others against visions (pure hallucinations). They are explicable solely in terms of the *shock* taking place as the soul passes from the static to the dynamic, from the closed to the open, from everyday life to mystic life: 'We cannot upset the regular relation of the conscious to the unconscious without running a risk' (TSMR 229). Bergson concedes that the image may be pure hallucination and the emotion may be meaningless agitation (see TSMR 230–2 on the progress of the mystic soul).

Finally, why is the love of God for all humans proclaimed by the great mystic not the same as the fraternity proclaimed by philosophers in the name of reason from the Stoics to Kant? (TSMR 233) Bergson thinks it is more vital than this: the rational idea of fraternity is one we can admire and respect but not one that we can attach ourselves to with passion. This is the importance of the dynamic mode of religion; it touches and teaches us on a level reason cannot. Does this

Nietzsche on Religion

Nietzsche is deeply suspicious of the figure of the saint and the claim to superior insight derived from alleged mystical experiences. He makes this criticism in a number of texts. In *Dawn*, for example, he argues that the very claim that someone has had visions – a so-called genius or superior soul who has seen things the rest of us do not see – should make us cautious.[6] He is suspicious of a teaching of pure spirituality, locating a 'chronic over-excitability' in virtuous pure spirits who can only gain pleasure from ecstasy, a precursor of madness, which affords them a standard by which to condemn all earthly things.[7] Furthermore, he holds that behind these states of exaltation and ecstasy there lies human, all too human motivations or instincts, such as vengefulness and self-dissatisfaction:

> Mankind owes much that is bad to these wild inebriates: for they are insatiable sowers of the weeds of dissatisfaction with oneself and one's neighbour, of contempt for the age and the world, especially of world-weariness. Perhaps a whole Hell of *criminals* could not produce an affect so oppressive, poisonous to air and land … as does this noble little community of unruly, fantastic, half-crazy people of genius who cannot control themselves and can experience pleasure only when they have lost themselves.[8]

No doubt there is genuine psychological insight here, but Bergson himself insists that it is not ecstasy that is the stopping point or end point of mysticism. If we take a philosopher–saint such as Plotinus, we find that he goes as far as ecstasy, the state in which the souls feels itself in the presence of the divine or creative source, but he does not go beyond it as the genuine mystic should or must – to the state where contemplation is engulfed in action (TSMR 221; see also 230).

But here we must point to a key difference between Nietzsche and Bergson. Nietzsche has a completely different valuation of the different religions, privileging the free-minded Greeks over Christianity, but also Buddhism and Islam over Christianity as well. In essence Nietzsche regards Christianity as a pathological religion; it is a religion ruled by an excess of feeling that leads to a corruption of head and heart. Christianity, he says, wants to stupefy, to intoxicate, to shatter, and as such is devoid of 'measure'.[9] Nietzsche's deity is Dionysos and his commitment is to the teaching of the eternal recurrence of the same. For Nietzsche, the deepest religious faith is a Dionysian one: 'Saying yes to life, even in its strangest and strangest and hardest problems... . In it the most profound instinct of life, the instinct for the future of life.'[10]

Is there anything that resembles dynamic religion in Nietzsche's thought? Perhaps, but for Nietzsche possession or experience of the superior states of the soul is the privilege of the philosopher, not the religious mystic. His definition of the philosopher in *Beyond Good and Evil* resembles Bergson's depiction of the mystic:

> A philosopher: that is the person who is constantly experiencing, seeing, hearing, suspecting, hoping, dreaming extraordinary things; who is struck by his own thoughts as if they came from outside, from above or below ... who may even be himself a thunderstorm, going about pregnant with new lightning.[11]

For Nietzsche philosophy, should we wish to give it a definition, is an affair or activity of 'spiritual perception' entailing the discernment of greatness, significance, importance, of what is rare and extraordinary, and so on. In the chapter on religion in *Beyond Good and Evil* Nietzsche maintains that the religious disposition (piety) – that is, a life with God – is a product of a fear of truth, it is 'the will to untruth' at any price (compare the preface to *The Gay Science* on the youthful madness of the 'will to truth' at any price). Piety has enabled religion to beautify humanity, turning humans 'so completely into art, surface, and kindness that we no longer suffer when we look at them'.[12] In this respect religious humans belong to the class of artists: burnt children or born artists who find their joy in seeking to falsify life's image. The attempt to transcendentalize or idealize the image is a sign of sickness, and Nietzsche does not wish to be uncharitable about it.

However, he attacks non-religious Germans – for example, the free thinkers – for being unable to appreciate the possible use of religion and who and how religions endanger their flourishing. His concern centres on two facts as he sees them: (i) as in the rest of the animal kingdom there is among humans an excess of failures (the sick, the degenerating, the infirm); (ii) the successful among humans are always the exception and their complicated conditions of life can only be calculated with great subtlety and difficulty. For Nietzsche the 'economy of mankind' is ruled over by the accidental and a law of absurdity. Nietzsche then asks the question: what is the attitude of religious beings towards this excess of cases that do not turn out right? His answer is that they seek to, above all, preserve life, 'to preserve alive whatever can possibly be preserved'. While they can receive credit – 'the very highest credit' – for their preserving care, the danger is that such religions, when they exist as sovereign, are among the principal causes that keep the type 'man' on a lower rung of the ladder of life. Or, as Nietzsche perhaps dangerously puts it, 'they have preserved too much of *what ought to perish*'.[14] Nietzsche immediately goes on to express gratitude towards religions, noting what the spiritual human beings of Christianity have achieved in Europe. But he reiterates his main point: this has been at the cost of worsening '*the European race*' and standing all valuations on their head, for example, breaking the strong, casting suspicion on joy in beauty, turning the instincts of the strong, domineering, and turned-out well types into uncertainty, agony of conscience, and self-destruction: 'Invert all love of the earthly and of dominion over the earth into hatred of the earth and the earthly.' Has not an attempt been made to apply 'a single will' over Europe for eighteen centuries, with the aim of turning man into a '*sublime miscarriage*'? Such a 'monster' is interesting and of a higher, refined kind (hence the word 'sublime'), but nevertheless, Nietzsche thinks, it is a miscarriage of what could have been bred and educated. With respect to these tasks, then, Nietzsche holds Christianity to be the most presumptuous religion to date, as well as the most calamitous. What has been bred, and whose hegemony now needs contesting, is man as 'the herd animal'.

As with Nietzsche, Bergson too sees religion as a discipline but only on the level of what he calls 'static religion'; he also argues there is a 'dynamic religion' where great spiritual leaders – Jesus, St Paul, St Theresa, and so on – bring a new emotion into existence that then has the potential to transform humanity. This notion of dynamic religion and what it entails – taking seriously mystical states – are treated suspiciously by Nietzsche. He does not trust mystical experiences and mystical souls (he thinks they are deluded in believing they have what he calls a 'telephone to the beyond'). This raises two issues: (1) how are we to interpret the apparently sublime mystical experiences of Zarathustra?; (2) what of Bergson's insight that religious mystics are not about the beyond but about the transformation of human life? Mystics for Bergson are not simply humans of vision, raptures, and ecstasies, but figures of action. Is there not, he asks, a mystic dormant within each one of us, responding to a call? (TSMR 97)

Natural Religion: Immanence and Affirmation

Another approach is possible in which Bergson and Nietzsche can be profitably conjoined as thinkers of immanence and joyous affirmation. Bergson's assertion in *Two Sources* of the religious pre-eminence of Christianity (and, in particular, its mystical aspect) – conceived as the embodiment of the vital impulse itself – might seem to preclude any fundamental affinity with Nietzsche's essentially hostile evaluation of religion per se but most unequivocally Christianity specifically. However, another, more convergent, configuration of their respective critical discussions of religion can be articulated. We conclude by sketching such an alternative: our focus is on Bergson's and Nietzsche's positive accounts of religion, that is to say, the extent to which both thinkers suggest that religion can be aligned with, and grounded in, their respective (arguably very similar) ontologies of natural life in its most affirmative, primary process.

As we have seen, both Bergson and Nietzsche accord religion a key role in what they regard as secondary or derivative ontological processes of individual and collective self-preservation; but they also suggest that if religion is inappropriately regarded as primordial, it becomes a life-denying impediment obviously in his life-long commitment to identifying the essence of life with the 'Dionysian', the task of sketching and justifying this claim in any detail cannot be undertaken here.[15] The necessary conditions of so conceiving Nietzsche's thought are that (despite his own occasional 'lapses' in this regard) a distinction between religion and Christianity be maintained when reading his texts and that, whatever might be meant by a positive endorsement of religion in Nietzsche's thought, of its identification with the primordial active forces of life itself, this entails a religion of immanence without a personal God and without reference to morality. For Nietzsche religion in this affirmative sense marks the achievement of a complete de-anthropomorphization in which thought divests itself of the personification of life (i.e. 'God') and acknowledges that life lies 'beyond good and evil' and is irreducible to antithetical thinking (i.e. 'morality').

Of course, major textual obstacles seem to exist for such a reading of Nietzsche. In addition to the sober and apparently science-friendly mindset of the texts of his so-called positivist period there are also the late texts in which we find an insistent and rigorous pursuit of a completely de-deified nature.[16] However, it can be plausibly claimed that such a de-deification is not incompatible with, and indeed is a condition of possibility of, the emergence of an impersonal, immanent religion of non-anthropomorphic life and that, furthermore, Nietzsche could not be clearer in his late texts that whatever this de-deification might entail it does not have a scientific or secular trajectory.

Nietzsche contests the claim of scientific atheism to provide the required alternative to the ascetic ideal hitherto embodied by Christianity. Both *The Gay Science* and the *Genealogy of Morality* endeavour to demonstrate the genealogical ties that link Christianity and modern science, the shared constitutive values (masked by their apparent and superficial cultural conflict) that Nietzsche depicts as the mere proprietorial and historical struggle for the custodianship of the 'will to truth'.[17] For Nietzsche, the spirit of scientific atheism is not distinct in kind from Christianity and cannot, therefore, be endorsed as the manifestation of the opposing ideal required in the epoch of nihilism. Genealogical critique indicates that scientific atheism is, 'Christian morality itself ... translated and sublimated into the scientific conscience, into intellectual cleanliness at any price',[18] and as such it resists as much as it promotes the 'de-deification of nature'. As the concealed outwork of Christianity, scientific atheism represents therefore a last desperate expression of a profoundly anthropomorphic religion in its struggle against the indigenous divinity of impersonal life.

Perhaps a productive way of conceiving the confluence of philosophical biology and religion that can be discerned as a shared feature of Bergson's and Nietzsche's thought is to consider both to be undertaking a revival and radical reconfiguration of natural religion. That is to say, both Bergson and Nietzsche urge us to attend to those aspects of nature in which the creative becoming of life is apparent. This, in turn, it is argued is plausibly conceived as religious in that it both exceeds the categories of instrumental thought and occurs in and as an affective state ('joy') phenomenologically identifiable as religious and, furthermore, marks life's own self-affirmation regardless of its relationship to human thought. It hopefully goes without saying that this is a revival of natural religion without reference to the design argument. As a religion of immanence, the point is not to elaborate analogies with purposive and intentional production in order to attempt to justify the positing of a transcendent creator. In addition, the relevant aspects of natural life are those that exceed the explanatory schemas of any evolutionary theory in which adaptation and self-preservation are particularly emphasized or prioritized.

Arguably Nietzsche and Bergson develop the two most significant and sophisticated philosophical biologies elaborated thus far and both promote the claim that natural life is religious in essence. Both insist on the ontological primacy of time (as eternal recurrence and duration, respectively) and affectivity, conceiving the real as first and foremost a differential flow of felt difference not to be confused with the methods by which it is subsequently rendered measurable. On the basis of these shared philosophico–biological principles, both Nietzsche and Bergson reject the presumed primacy of a functional–utilitarian conception of life's inherent tendencies. They challenge the assumed primordiality of source – durational time – which 'ought' to be the affirmatively devotional impersonal reference point of all that it makes possible and sustains. On balance, however, Bergson rejects an explicit appropriation (at least in relation to static religion) of the notion of natural religion due to the burden of its received meaning and historical provenance. Nonetheless, this should not preclude us from recognizing the more profound sense in which Bergson takes forward the project of natural religion on the basis of an ontology of life quite distinct from that of his deist predecessors.

In this vein, it is noteworthy the extent to which Bergson insists throughout *Two Sources* on an essential feature of natural religion, namely the claim that there is a universal origin and source of religion intrinsic to natural life accessible, in principle, to all independently of revealed religion. Bergson's allegiance to this key claim of natural religion is apparent in his reference, in relation to the philosophical interpretation and evaluation of mysticism, to an 'original content, drawn straight from the very well-spring of religion, independent of all that religion owes to tradition, to theology, to the Churches' (TSMR 250). Retrieving mysticism as a natural phenomenon and reclaiming it from its ecclesiastical appropriation, the advocate of natural religion must insist that 'philosophy … must confine itself to experience and inference' (TSMR 250) and forge a partnership with the mystic towards the shared aim of connectedness with the divine process of immanent life. As Bergson states,

> It would suffice to take mysticism unalloyed, apart from the visions, the allegories, the theological language which express it, to make it a powerful helpmate to philosophical research … we must then find out in what measure

mystic experience is a continuation of the experience which led us to the doctrine of the vital impetus. All the information with which it would furnish philosophy, philosophy would repay in the shape of confirmation. (TSMR 250–1)

For Nietzsche, the affirmation of life is identified with an affectivity of bliss and joy. In this regard a proximity to Bergson is clearly discernible. Both thinkers accord affectivity an ontological status such that, in relation to certain emotions, the realm of mere subjective feeling is escaped from and a reconnection is made with life's most primary tendencies. Bergson offers an extended theory of ontological emotion in *Two Sources* in which a further affinity with Nietzsche can be detected. Both thinkers tend towards the identification of the divine with a type of a-subjective qualitative state in and through which the will to power and *élan vital*, respectively, manifest and reaffirm themselves.

Bergson seeks to conceive mysticism in 'relation to the vital impulse ... it is this impulse itself, communicated to exceptional individuals who in turn would fain impart it to all humanity' (TSMR 213). This further underlines his view of the intrinsically religious nature of reality. As he states, 'the ultimate end of mysticism is the establishment of a contact ... a partial coincidence, with the creative effort which life itself manifests. This effort is of God, if it is not God himself' (TSMR 220). Indeed Bergson seems to be of the view in *Two Sources* that mysticism represents a culmination of the critical trajectory of his thought as a whole as it migrates from an original phenomenology of temporal consciousness through to an ontology of life itself. As he states,

> For this intuition was turned inward; and if, in a first intensification, beyond which most of us did not go, it made us realise the continuity of our inner life, a deeper intensification might carry it to the roots of our being, and thus to the principle of life in general. Now is not this the privilege of the mystic soul? (TSMR 250)

As indicated above both Nietzsche and Bergson emphasize the ontological significance of joy. Bergson writes in this regard of 'a boundless joy, an all-absorbing ecstasy ... an enthralling rapture' (TSMR 230). The watchwords in this non-reductive renaturalization of religious affectivity are, for both thinkers, energy and vitality (as apparent in the passage from TSMR, cited above). Religious affectivity, in its non-pathological form (a possibility recognized by both Nietzsche and Bergson), is here identified with and as the creative becoming of life itself.

different religions and aspects thereof). Both thinkers, we suggest, endeavour to identify a becoming-religious of the natural life itself, a self-affirmation that occurs as an ontological affectivity that possesses privileged and exceptional members of one of its creative experiments.

relation to the art of living, as well as with the reformation of education. Bergson insists he has no wish to elaborate a programme of education; rather, he restricts himself to indicating certain habits of mind that he considers unfortunate and that is all too often encouraged by schooling in reality while being repudiated in principle by the same. In this chapter I aim to show the relevance of Bergson's thinking on intelligence and intuition for a thinking of education, and here there are two key insights: first, that education needs to resist the substitution of concepts for things; and second, that it needs to advance the idea that there is not only the *socialization of the truth* (CM 87). His education of philosophy consists in showing that philosophy should be an empiricism in as much as it is focused on realities and here it has an intimate connection with a schooling in the art of living. He is inspired, for example, by the ambition of taking philosophy out of the school, as he puts it, including the disputes between the different schools of philosophy, and bringing into more intimate contact with life (CM 126). Indeed, if we follow the contours of 'intuitive life' with its special kind of knowledge, then the promise is opened up of bringing an end to 'inert states' and 'dead things': 'nothing but the mobility of which the stability of life is made' (CM 127). Such knowledge will do two things: it will enrich philosophical speculation – we see for the sake of seeing and the enrichment that an enlarged perception offers us – and it will nourish and illuminate everyday life (it will enhance our power to act and live, for example). In order to restore our contact with life it is necessary to conquer the deadening world of habit: 'For the world into which our senses and consciousness habitually introduce us is no more than the shadow of itself: and it is as cold as death' (CM 128). In his essay on 'Good Sense and Classical Studies' Bergson contends that the stubborn clinging to habits, when raised to the status of laws of life, is to repudiate change and allow one's vision to be distracted away from the movement that is the condition of life (BKW 424).

Bergson forges a crucial distinction between the provinces of science and philosophy, with the former concerned with well-being, and at most pleasure, and the latter holding out the promise of delivering us over to joy. Bergson does not wish to denigrate the importance of the convenient life, the life of well-being, but it is clear he sees a superior reality in the joyful existence since it is here that we encounter creative life, including the creation of self by self. It is this set of concerns, centred around Bergson's attempt to revitalize philosophy's investment in the art of life, that I wish to explore in this chapter. The task is to galvanize perception, to extend perception, and to effect a conversion of attention. The method for doing this is intuition, and the overriding aim is to become accustomed to seeing all things *sub specie durationis*: in this way what is dead comes back to life, life acquires depth, and we come into account with the original impetus of life that serves to encourage us to create new things. In short, a Bergsonian-inspired philosophy of education restores to the human the vital impetus that lies at the origins of things. The task of education is to become a master in the art of living, and this is something perhaps unique to philosophy.

In what follows I first outline Bergson's fundamental conception of philosophy as the discipline that takes us beyond the human state or condition. I then turn to his specific method, namely intuition, and seek to illuminate this in two sections. In my fourth and final section I explicitly address Bergson on education.

Philosophy

Bergson conceives philosophy as the discipline that 'raises us above the human condition' (*la philosophie nous aura élevés au-dessus de la condition humaine'*) (O 1292; CM 50) and makes the effort to 'surpass' (*dépasser*) the human condition (O 1425; CM 193). As Pierre Hadot notes, Bergsonism offers the promise of a new way of seeing the world and transforming perception, and his thinking on Bergson can help us get a handle on what is involved in this practice of philosophy 'beyond the human condition'.[1] The task is to think beyond our habitual, utilitarian perception, which is necessary for life. Hadot calls it the paradox and scandal of 'the human condition' that we live in the world without perceiving it. He writes:

64). According to Bergson, human intelligence is not what Plato taught us in his allegory of the cave: its function is neither to look at passing shadows nor to turn itself round and contemplate the glaring sun. The function of intelligence is to fulfil the tasks of life, that is, it is to act and to know that we are acting by coming into contact with reality, even living it, but only in the measure in which this concerns the work we seek to accomplish. However, as Bergson asks, does not a 'beneficent fluid' bathe us, 'whence we draw the very force to labour and to live'? (CE 191) Are we not immersed in an 'ocean of life'? Philosophy for Bergson needs to realize its vocation – 'to examine the living without any reservation as to practical utility' (CE 196) – by breaking with the modern (Kantian) view that regards absolute reality as unknowable and that gives us, in its conception of reality, little more than what science has said. In the desire to end the conflict between philosophy and science we sacrifice philosophy without any appreciable gain to science.

The new method of thinking has to work against the most inveterate habits of the mind and consists in an interchange of insights that correct and add to each other. For Bergson, such an enterprise ends by expanding the humanity within us and even allowing humanity to surpass itself by reinserting itself in the whole (CE 192). This is accomplished through philosophy for it is the discipline of philosophy that provides us with the means (methods) for reversing the normal directions of the mind (instrumental, utilitarian), so upsetting its habits. In spite of what one might think, for Bergson this makes philosophy's task a modest one (CE 123).[3] The key insight is the following one: if we suppose that philosophy is an affair of perception,[4] then it cannot simply be a matter of correcting perception but only of extending it. The specific task is to extend the human present, which is the aspect of time in which the human necessarily dwells, a necessity to be explained through the dictates of evolution such as adaptation.

Why should we feel motivated by this endeavour to think beyond our human state? Deleuze provides the essential insight that is required here: we find ourselves born or thrown into a world that is ready-made and that we have not made our own. This world always goes in the direction of the relaxed aspect of duration, Deleuze argues.[5] It is on account of the fact that the human condition is one of relaxation that we have such difficulty in understanding the meaning of creation – precisely the notion that proves essential for artistic invention, for new modes of ethical being, and for philosophical reflection, and that lies at the heart of Bergson's project.

In his writings Bergson advances several conceptions of philosophy, of what it is and its chief tasks. Sometimes he stresses its capacity to enable us to see: philosophy exists to extend our perception of the universe. At other times he also expresses anxiety over philosophy's lapse into contemplation and stresses its ability to enhance our power to act and to live. Philosophy for Bergson is not a rarefied, aristocratic activity, something reserved for the best or the most wise, but a popular activity that all can potentially participate in as a way of being creative. On the one hand, the paradoxical theoretical task of philosophy is, above all, to find some absolute in the moving world of phenomena. On the other hand, it is more dynamic than this and, through this restoration of the absolute we gain a feeling of greater joy and power. Bergson links philosophy and education with the task of becoming masters in the art of living. He writes:

> Greater joy because the reality invented before our eyes will give each one of us, unceasingly, certain of the satisfactions which art at rare intervals procures for the privileged; it will reveal to us, beyond the fixity and monotony which our senses, hypnotized by our constant needs, at first perceived in it, ever-recurring novelty, the moving originality of things. But above all we shall have greater strength, for we shall feel we are participating, creators of ourselves, in the great work of creation which is the origin of all things and which goes on before our eyes. (CM 105)

Typically we exist – both in terms of our species history and our individual development – as slaves of certain natural necessities. Philosophy is a practice and a discipline that can enable us to go beyond the level of necessities and enable us to become 'masters associated with a greater Master' (CM 105–6).

Towards Intuition

Bergson calls intuition the attention that the mind gives to itself 'over and above, while it is fixed upon matter, its object' (CM 78). It is a 'supplementary attention' that can be methodically cultivated and developed.[6] We need to begin by noting the distinction between life and matter that characterizes Bergson's thinking. For the most part he writes of 'inert matter', though he also refers to 'organized matter' and also of matter as made up of vibrations and to which slight durations can be attributed (CE 201). However, marking a distinction between matter and life is a central feature of Bergson's thinking, whether he is attempting to explain the character of evolution or exploring the meaning of the comic.[7] Roughly speaking, it works as a distinction between inertia and vitality, between rigidity and suppleness, between automatism and creative effort, between necessity and freedom, and so on. However, matter and life/consciousness (delay, hesitation, a latitude of choice) are not to be explained apart from one another, and the two have a common source (ME 17, 20). If the determinism of matter were absolute, to the point of admitting no relaxation and showing no elasticity (which Bergson thinks it does), then life would be an impossibility. Life is an insinuating energy, an impetus, that draws matter away from pure mechanism but only by first adopting this mechanism; life installs 'itself in matter which had already acquired some of the characters of life without the work of life' (ME 20). However, if matter were all that there is, then it would have stopped at this point.

This is akin, Bergson thinks, to the work of our scientific laboratories where we seek to manufacture matter that resembles living matter and is an enterprise that one day, he says, may well be successful. However, he adds, 'we shall reproduce, that is to say, some characters of living matter; we shall not obtain the push in virtue of which it reproduces itself and, in the meaning of transformism, evolves' (ME 20).

Bergson draws a clear demarcation between metaphysics (and intuition) and science (intelligence). Both are related to action but the action is different in the two cases. So, Bergson writes:

> To metaphysics, then, we assign, a limited object, principally spirit, and a special method, mainly intuition. In doing this we make a clear distinction between metaphysics and science. But at the same time we attribute an equal value to both. I believe they can both touch the bottom of reality. I reject the arguments advanced by philosophers, and accepted by scholars, on the relativity of knowledge and the impossibility of attaining the absolute. (CM 37)

It is important to appreciate that Bergson posits between science and metaphysics a difference of method and not a difference in value (CM 43–4). The task of metaphysics, as he conceives it, is to concern itself with the actual world in which we live and not with all possible worlds, so philosophy embraces realities (CM 44). Science for Bergson is attached to a specific task, one that he does not wish to negate the importance of, namely the mastery of matter. Positive science relies on sensible observations as way of securing materials and it does this by elaborating, through methods and faculties, abstraction and generalization; in short, it establishes the order of intelligence through judgement and reasoning. Its 'original domain' and its 'preferred domain' is the domain of inert matter, or of matter stripped of the vitality of life: 'it clings to the physico-chemical in vital phenomena rather than to what is really vital in the living' (CM 38). If our intelligence can be construed as the prolongation of our senses, then we can see the force of science and its aid to life, at least life in its aspect of calculability and manipulation. Prior to pure speculation – seeing for the sake of seeing – there is the imperative to live, and so life demands that matter be made use of, and this takes place through our organs (conceived as natural tools) and with tools, properly so-called, as artificial organs. Although science has pushed far the labour of intelligence it has not changed its essential direction, which is to make us masters of matter. Bergson argues that even when it speculates science continues to devote itself to acting, difficulty: is it not, he asks, much more difficult to develop knowledge of oneself than it is knowledge of the external world? He adds:

Outside oneself, the effort to learn is natural; one makes it with increasing facility; one applies rules. Within, attention must remain tense and progress becomes more and more painful; it is as though one were going against the natural bent. Is there not something surprising in this? We are internal to ourselves, and our personality is what we should know best. (CM 41)

Bergson notes, then, a point that is crucial to his own attempt to contribute to how philosophy can aid the art of living, namely that within the field of instrumental action, a certain *ignorance* of self is what is found to be most useful and answers to a necessity of life since here we encounter a being, ourselves, that must exteriorize itself in order to act. Hence his claim that mind finds itself in a strange place when it encounters life, in contrast to its habitual feeling at home in the realm of matter (it knows what it must do when it comes to acting in the world). He does not deny, of course, that when it comes to such effective action that we are distinguished from animals, for example, in having capacities that enable us to reflect on our actions. But, he notes, nature requires that we only take a quick glance at our inner selves: 'We then perceive the mind, but the mind preparing to shape matter, already adapting itself to it, assuming something of the spatial, the geometric, the intellectual' (CM 42). It is in this context of problems that he appeals to intuition as a mode of mental attentiveness: 'This direct vision of the mind by the mind is the chief function of intuition, as I understand it' (CM 42). But we still do not know what this intuition is and how it can amount to a new function of thinking. Part of the difficulty is our reliance on metaphors and ready-made concepts as a way of thinking about reality and reflecting on our experience of the real. This is why Bergson stresses that in order to gain access to intuition – since there is nothing immediate about it as a method – an entire labour of clearing away is required and that this has to be seen as a way of opening up the way to 'inner experience': 'True, the faculty of intuition exists in each one of us, but covered over by functions more useful to life' (CM 47).

In order to gain access to the practice of intuition it is necessary to break with society, in particular with the subdivision and distribution of the real into concepts that society has deposited into language for the sake of the convenience of existence. Society or the social organism cuts out reality according to its needs, and Bergson asks why philosophy ought to accept a division that in all probability does not correspond to the articulations of the real – except, of course, in terms of our mastery of matter. The challenge here for thinking about the art of living is a serious one: it means not accepting the claim, 'that all truth is already virtually known, that its model is patented in the administrative offices of the state, and that philosophy is a jig-saw puzzle where the problem is to construct with pieces society gives us the design it is unwilling to show us' (CM 50). Contra this position, Bergson maintains that in philosophy – and not only in philosophy – it is a question of *finding* the problem and of positing it, rather than of solving it: 'Stating the problem is not simply uncovering, it is inventing' (51). The difference between the two is paramount since in the one case we are uncovering what already exists actually or virtually and in the other case we invent what does not exist and might never have happened: 'Already in mathematics and still more in metaphysics, the effort of invention consists more in raising the problem, in creating the terms in which it will be stated' (51).

Bergson gives an example to illustrate his point, and it serves as a good way of indicating how a Bergsonian-inspired philosophy of education can be developed from the insights I am staging. He imagines the question being set: 'Is pleasure happiness or not?' To answer the question we could examine the conventional meaning of the words involved and take it as a question of vocabulary; alternatively, we could grasp 'realities' and not simply re-examine conventions, and so endeavour to *transform* the problem being posed. Bergson elaborates as follows:

> Suppose that in examining the states grouped under the name of pleasure they are found to have nothing in common except that they are states which man is seeking; humanity will have classified these very different things in one genus because it found them of the same practical interest and reacted toward all

Let me now look in more detail at Bergson on intuition and in particular seek to illuminate its connection with the mode of perception he calls sympathy.

Intuition is said to be a mode of sympathy 'by which one is transported into the interior of an object' (CM 135). The contrast is with the mode of 'analysis', which is an operation that reduces an object to elements already known and that are common to it and other objects. Intuition involves a special kind of attention or attentiveness to life (Bergson speaks of performing an 'auscultation' and in accordance with a 'true empiricism' CM 147). Bergson contends that even the most concrete of the sciences of nature, namely the sciences of life, 'confine themselves to the visible form of living beings, their organs, their anatomical elements' (136). The task at hand is to understand precisely what Bergson means when he says that intuition leads us to the very inwardness of life. Intuition is important to Bergson since he holds that, taken as a mode of sympathy, it will enable us to resolve – indeed, to *dissolve* – many of the problems that are often taken to be the genuine puzzles of metaphysics, such as, 'what is the first cause of existence?' and 'why is there something rather than nothing?' So, he writes: 'To the extent that we distend our will, tend to reabsorb our thought in it and get into greater sympathy with the effort that engenders things, these formidable problem will recede, diminish, disappear' (CM 62).

As Deleuze notes, intuition is the method peculiar to Bergson's philosophy. He rightly stresses that it denotes neither a vague feeling or incommunicable experience nor a disordered sympathy. Rather, it is a fully developed method that aims at precision in philosophy. Where duration and memory denote lived realities and concrete experiences, intuition is the only means we have at our disposal for crafting knowledge of experience and reality. 'We may say, strangely enough', Deleuze notes, 'that duration would remain purely intuitive, in the ordinary sense of the word, if intuition – in the properly Bergsonian sense – were not there as method.'[8] However, intuition is a complex method that cannot be contained in single act. Instead, it has to be seen as involving a plurality of determinations. The first task is to stage and create problems; the second is to locate differences in kind; and the third is to comprehend real time, that is, duration as a heterogeneous and continuous multiplicity. Let me now note some salient aspects of Bergson on intuition and then draw on Deleuze to indicate how intuition aspires to operate as a method of precision in philosophy.

Bergson acknowledges that other philosophers before him, such as Schelling, tried to escape relativism by appealing to intuition. He argues, however, that this was a non-temporal intuition that was being appealed to, and, as such, was largely a return to Spinozism, that is, a deduction of existence from one complete Being. Bergson locates a failure of empiricism in Spinoza. For a system like Spinoza's, Bergson notes, true or genuine being is endowed with a logical existence more than a psychological or even physical one: 'For the nature of a purely logical existence is such that it seems to be self-sufficient and to posit itself by the effect alone of the force immanent in truth' (CE 276). Spinozism is an attempt to make vanish 'the mystery of existence', such as why minds and bodies exist; and instead of making actual observations of nature, the philosopher advances a logical system in which at the base of everything that exists is a self-positing being dwelling in eternity. Bergson's main engagement, however, is with Kant and for obvious reasons. He argues that in order to reach the mode of intuition it is not necessary, as Kant supposed, to transport ourselves outside the domain of the senses: 'After having proved by decisive arguments that no dialectical effort will ever introduce us into the beyond and that an effective metaphysics would necessarily be an intuitive metaphysics, he added that we lack this intuition and that this metaphysics is impossible. It would in fact be so if there were no other time or change than those which Kant perceived' (CM 128). By recovering intuition Bergson hopes to save science from the charge of producing a relativity of knowledge (it is rather to be regarded as approximate) and metaphysics from the charge of indulging in empty and idle speculation. Although Kant himself did not pursue thought in the direction he had opened for it – the direction of a 'revivified Cartesianism' Bergson calls it – it is the prospect of an extra-intellectual matter of knowledge by a higher effort of intellect modelling itself on corporeity, and corporeity on intellect. But this duality of intuition Kant neither would nor could admit. (CE 230)

For Kant to admit this duality of intuition would entail granting to duration an absolute reality and treating the geometry immanent in space as an ideal limit (the direction in which material things develop but never actually attain).

Deleuze thinks we can learn some valuable philosophical lessons from Bergson on intuition, so let me now to turn to his account. He argues that we go wrong when we hold that notions of true and false can only be brought to bear on problems in terms of ready-made solutions. This is a far too pre-emptive strategy that does not take us beyond experience but locks us in it. This negative freedom is the result of manufactured social prejudices wherein, through social institutions such as education and language, we become enslaved by order-words that identify for us ready-made problems that we are forced to solve. True freedom lies in the power to constitute problems themselves. This might involve the freedom to uncover certain truths for oneself, but often discovery is too much involved in uncovering what already exists, an act of discovery that was bound to happen sooner or later and contingent upon circumstances. Invention, however, gives Being to what did not exist and might never have happened since it was not destined to happen, there was no pre-existing programme by which it could be actualized. In mathematics and in metaphysics the effort of invention consists in raising the problem and in creating the terms through which it might be solved but never as something ready-made. As Merleau-Ponty notes in a reading of Bergson, when it is said that well-posed problems are close to being solved, 'this does not mean that we have already *found* what we are looking for, but that we have already invented it.'[9]

Another rule of intuition is to do away with false problems, which are said to be of two kinds: first, those which are caught up in terms that contain a confusion of the more and the less; and, second, questions which are stated badly in the specific sense that their terms represent only badly analysed composites. In the first case the error consists in positing an origin of being and of order from which nonbeing and disorder are then made to appear as primordial. On this schema, order can only appear as the negation of disorder and as the negation of nonbeing (CE 222). Such a way of thinking introduces lack into the heart of Being. Focusing on the more and the less fails to see that there are *kinds* of order and forgets the fact that Being is not homogeneous but fundamentally heterogeneous. Badly analysed composites result from an arbitrary grouping of things that are constituted as differences in kind. Bergson wants to know how it is that we deem certain life forms to be superior to others, even though they are not of the same order, and neither can they be posited in terms of a simple unilinear evolutionism with one life form succeeding another in terms of a progress towards perfection in self-consciousness. Life proceeds neither via lack nor the power of the negative but through internal self-differentiation along lines of divergence. Indeed, Bergson goes so far as to claim that the root cause of the difficulties and errors we are confronted with in thinking about creative evolution resides in the power we ascribe to negation, to the point where we represent it as symmetrical with affirmation (CE 287). When Deleuze says that resemblance or identity bears on difference qua difference, he is being faithful to Bergson's critical insight into the character of negation, chiefly, that it is implicated in a more global power of affirmation.

It is through a focus on badly analysed composites that we are led, in fact, to positing things in terms of the more and the less, so that the idea of disorder only arises from a general idea of order as a badly analysed composite. This amounts to claiming, as Deleuze cognizes, that we are the victims of illusions that have their source in aspects of our intelligence. However, although these illusions refer to Kant's analysis in the *Critique of Pure Reason*, where Reason is shown to generate for itself in exceeding the boundaries of the Understanding inevitable illusions and not simple mistakes, they are not of the same order. There is a natural tendency of the intellect to see only differences in degree and to neglect differences in kind. This is because the fundamental motivation of the intellect is to implement and orientate action in the world.

A simple difference of degree would denote the correct status of things if they could be separated from their tendencies. For Bergson the tendency is primary not simply in relation to its product but rather in relation to the causes of productions in time, 'causes always being retroactively obtained starting from the product itself'.[11] Any composite, therefore, needs to be divided according to qualitative tendencies. Again, this brings Bergson close to Kant's transcendental analysis, going beyond experience as given and constituting its conditions of possibility. However, these are not conditions of all possible experience but of real experience (e.g. the experience of different durations).

Bergson thinks that all the great masters of modern philosophy are thinkers who have assimilated the material of the science of their time. He adds that the partial eclipse of metaphysics in recent times can be explained by the fact that today it is a difficult task to make contact with a science that has become scattered. However, the method of intuition, which is to be attained by means of material knowledge, is something quite different from a summary or synthesis of scientific knowledge. Although metaphysics has nothing in common with the 'generalization of experience', it is possible to define it 'as the whole of experience' (*l'expérience intégrale*).

Intuition is not duration, but rather the movement by which thought emerges from its own duration and gains insight into the difference of other durations within and outside itself. It both presupposes duration, as the reality in which it dwells, but it also seeks to think it: 'To think intuitively is to think in duration' (CM 34). Without intuition as a method, duration would remain for us a merely psychological experience and we would remain prisoners of what is given to us.

Informing Bergson's thinking, therefore, is a philosophical critique of the order of need, action, and society that predetermines us to retain a relationship with things only to the extent that they satisfy our interest, and of the order of general ideas that prevents us from acquiring a superior human nature.

Bergson insists that his method of intuition contains no devaluation of intelligence but only a determination of its specific facility. If intuition transcends intelligence, this is only on account of the fact that it is intelligence that gives it the push to rise beyond. Without it intuition would remain wedded to instinct and riveted to the particular objects of its practical interests. The specific task of philosophy is to introduce us 'into life's own domain, which is reciprocal interpenetration, endlessly continued creation' (CE 115). This is different from what science does when it takes up the utilitarian vantage point of external perception and prolongs individual facts into general laws. The reformed metaphysics Bergson wishes to awaken commits itself to an intellectual expansion of reflection and intuition, which is, in fact, intellectual sympathy.

For Bergson, then, the key move for thought to make lies in the direction of sympathy. By means of science intelligence does its work and delivers to us more and more the secret of life's material or physical operations. But this gives us only a perspectivism that never penetrates the inside, going 'all round life, taking from outside the greatest possible number of views of it' (CE 176). By contrast, metaphysics can follow the path of intuition, which is to be conceived as 'instinct that has become disinterested, self-conscious, capable of reflecting upon its object and enlarging it indefinitely' (ibid.). Bergson has recourse to the example of the aesthetic to develop this insight. It is the aesthetic faculty that gives us something other than what is given for us by normal perception. The eye, he notes, perceives the features of the living in terms of an assembling and not as something involving mutual organization and reciprocal interpenetration: 'The intention of life, the simple movement that runs through the lines, that binds them together and gives them significance, escapes it' (177). It is just this intention that the artist, he says, seeks to regain, 'placing himself back within the object by a kind of sympathy ... by an effort of intuition'. In his essay on Felix Ravaisson, Bergson alludes to the importance of art for metaphysics: 'The whole philosophy of Ravaisson springs from the idea that art is a figured metaphysics, that metaphysics is a reflection on art, and that it is the same intuition, variously applied, which makes the profound philosopher and the great artist' (CM 231).

It needs to be pointed out, however, that Bergson himself does not subscribe to the identification of art with philosophy. He holds that philosophical intuition to us in a palpable form what the discoveries of modern biology have established.

Just what this means is explained well by David Lapoujade in an incisive treatment of intuition and sympathy in Bergson.[12] I will now draw on his inquiry and cover only the essential points. Intuition is a reflection of the mind upon itself and there is no intuition of the material or vital as such. Given this constraint, how can we, with the aid of intuition, open ourselves up to different levels of reality and enlarge our perception of life? This is where sympathy intervenes and assumes an important role. Lapoujade argues that sympathy is not a fusion without distance and so cannot be crudely assimilated to some miraculous intuitive act. Rather, it relies upon reasoning by analogy. The reasoning Bergson has in mind here is not one that appeals to fixed terms but rather to movements. One way to think this is in terms of an analogy between tendencies, in which the 'structure' at work is not one of what is similar but of what is common. So, it does not work through an exterior relation of resemblances, but rather through 'an interior *communication* between tendencies or movements'.[13] Analogy comes into play for us between the movements of our own interior existence and those of the universe, and we uncover ourselves intuitively as material and as vital through a series of explorations into ourselves. Bergson expresses it in just these terms in his lecture of 1911 on 'Philosophical Intuition':

> The matter and life which fill the world are equally within us; the forces which work in all things we feel within ourselves; whatever may be the inner essence of what is and what is done, we are of that essence. Let us then go down into our own inner selves: the deeper the point we touch, the stronger will be the thrust which sends us back to the surface. (BKW 299)

As Lapoujade pithily expresses it, for Bergson, 'We are analogous to the universe (intuition), and inversely, the universe is our analogue (sympathy).'[14] In making the effort, then, to think 'beyond the human state' we come into contact, through intuition, with movements, memories, and non-human consciousnesses deep within us. Deep within the human there is something other than the human. This means that for Bergson the sources of human experience are more obscure and distant than both common sense and science suppose, and these are sources that, Bergson contends, Kant failed to penetrate in his attempt to philosophize about the conditions of the possibility of experience. In essence, this is what Bergson means when he writes of 'dissolving into the whole' and experiencing 'the ocean of life'. Although this dissolving experience may approach the insights of poetry or mysticism, Bergson is after philosophical precision and clarity. He never ceases to emphasize the extent to which intuition requires long and stubborn effort.

As Lapoujade further notes, Bergson accords primacy in reality to alterity: 'It is because the other is within us that we can project it outside us in the form of "consciousness" or "intention".'[15] What we 'project' onto the world is our own alterity. However, it is clear that for Bergson when we experience sympathy it is not merely sympathy for others we subject ourselves to, but equally sympathy for one's self and recognition of the alterity that lies concealed within ourselves: 'One thing is sure: we sympathize with ourselves' (CM 136). Such an insight perhaps allows us to reconfigure the 'in-itself': 'The in-itself no longer designates the way in which things will never be "for us" but the way in which, on the contrary, things will be very much within us.'[16]

To conclude this treatment of intuition: intuition is the primary method of philosophical thinking for Bergson, and from sympathy it gains an extension that enables it to be deployed as a general method. Intuition puts us into contact with other durations and ensures that we do not exist simply or only as internal duration. This constitutes a fundamental part of what it might mean for us to be able to go beyond the human state.

Education Beyond Intelligence

Bergson's thinking provides us with a mode of philosophy that enables us to prize an education that is not based solely or simply on the possession and acquisition of intelligence. Although he holds intelligence in high esteem, which criticize' (CM 83). In teaching someone to be critical the aim is not to get them to work on the thing in question, or on things themselves, but to appraise what others have said. Bergson thus expounds an education in being unreasonable, which is a philosophy of education based on the desire for *searching*, which casts aside ready-made ideas. Only in this way can education disturb society and resist the socialization of truth. In addition, the new education needs to aim well beyond the inculcation of encyclopaedic knowledge. Bergson clarifies his position as follows:

> I value scientific knowledge and technical competence as much as intuitive vision. I believe that it is of man's essence to create materially and morally, to fabricate things and to fabricate himself. *Homo faber* is the definition I propose. *Homo sapiens*, born of the reflection *Homo faber* makes on the subject of his fabrication, seems to me to be just as worthy of esteem as long as he resolves by pure intelligence those problems which depend upon it alone. One philosopher may be mistaken in the choice of these problems, but another philosopher will correct him; both will have worked to the best of their ability; both can merit our gratitude and admiration. *Homo faber, homo sapiens*, I pay my respects to both, for they tend to merge. The only one to which I am antipathetic is *Homo loquax* whose thoughts, when he does think, is only a reflection upon his talk. (CM 84–5)

If education is to centre on the creative needs of the child, then the focus should be on the child as a seeker and an inventor, 'always on the watch for novelty, impatient of rule, in short, closer to nature than is the grown man' (CM 86). Bergson locates a tension between the educator, who is essentially a sociable human being, and the child to be educated who is free of social conventions and expectations. The educator seeks to be encyclopaedic in placing primary importance on the need to impart to children the entire collection of acquired results that make up the social patrimony. Bergson does not doubt for a moment that these results fill us with pride and that each one is precious. But it is not these acquisitions that education needs to be focused on if our interest is in the cultivation of the child and its original being:

> Rather, let us cultivate a child's knowledge in the child, and avoid smothering under an accumulation of dry leaves and branches, products of former vegetations, the new plant which asks for nothing better than to grow. (CM 86)

For Bergson, then, education appears to have two core aspects: socialization and antisocialization. On the one hand, we are to be educated, but not loquaciously, in the domains of intelligence, which is science broadly conceived and which centres on practical truths. On the other hand, we are to be educated in the domain of intuition, which centres on art, literature (including the rhythms of reading), and philosophy, and here there is no pragmatism at work but rather a creative evolution and a style of life or way of life Bergson calls sympathy. The former mode of education provides us with tools of criticism and serves the needs of society; by contrast, the latter mode provides us with superior vision or extended perception and serves only the desires of life for creativity and originality. But in both cases we are dealing with reality, or with different aspects of it, and it is an education in realities that Bergson wants above all. In the case of the higher form of education, it is clear that a Bergsonian philosophy of education seeks to make learning relevant to the tasks of the art of life:

> In this speculation on the relation between the possible and the real, let us guard against seeing a simple game. It can be preparation for the art of living. (CM 106)

Conclusion

Bergson's thinking is highly relevant to the concerns of the philosophy of education since it takes us beyond the idea of a ready-made world in which the child is simply exposed to ready-made ideas and concepts, be it through a scientific education or a philosophical one, with both modelled on intelligence. As he notes, education is needed simply because nature rarely produces in a

4   *The Selected Letters of William James*, ed. Elizabeth Hardwick (New York: Doubleday, 1993), 236.

5   Gilles Deleuze, 'Bergson's Conception of Difference' (1956), trans. Melissa McMahon, in John Mullarkey (ed.), *The New Bergson* (Manchester: Clinamen Press, 1999), 42–66, 46.

6   Emmanuel Levinas, *Time and the Other*, trans. R. A. Cohen (Pittsburgh: Duquesne University Press, 1987), 132.

7   Pierre Hadot, *Philosophy as a Way of Life*, trans. Michael Chase (Oxford: Blackwell, 1995), 278.

8   Nietzsche, *Sämtliche Werke: Kritische Studienausgabe*, ed. G. Colli and M. Montinari (Berlin and New York: Walter de Gruyter, 1987), volume 7, section 21 [6].

9   Maurice Merleau-Ponty, *The Bergsonian Heritage*, ed. with an Introduction by Thomas Hanna (New York & London: Columbia University Press, 1962), 133–50, 139.

10 G. Deleuze, 'Lecture Course on Chapter Three of Bergson's *Creative Evolution*,' trans. Bryn Loban, *Substance*, 36: 3, 2007, 72–91, 76.

11 Deleuze, *Bergsonism,* trans. Hugh Tomlinson and Barbara Habberjam (New York: Zone Books, 1991), 104.

12 Deleuze, 'Lecture Course on Chapter Three of Bergson's *Creative Evolution*,' 86.

13 On the creation of self by self, see Karl Sarafidis, *Bergson. La Création de soi par soi* (Paris: Groupe Eyrolles, 2013).

14 Paola Marrati, 'Time, Life, Concepts: The Newness of Bergson,' *Modern Language Notes*, 120: 5, 2005, 1099–1111, 1100.

15 Marrati, 'Time, Life, Concepts: The Newness of Bergson,'1100.

16 Deleuze, *Bergsonism,* 28.

17 R. Braidotti, *The Posthuman* (Cambridge: Polity Press, 2013), 104.

18 Braidotti, *The Posthuman*, 56.

Chapter 1

1 F. Nietzsche, *Beyond Good and Evil*, trans. Marion Faber (Oxford: Oxford University Press, 1998), section 186.

2 J. Maritain, *Redeeming the Time* (London: The Centenary Press, 1943), 65.

3 See J. Benda, *Sur le success de Bergsonisme* (Paris: Mercure de France, 1954).

4 See R. C. Grogin, *The Bergsonian Controversy in France 1900–1914* (Calgary: The University of Calgary Press, 1988), 73–6; R. Lehan 'Bergson and the Discourse of the Moderns', in *The Crisis in Modernism: Bergson and the Vitalist Controversy*, ed. F. Burwick and P. Douglass (Cambridge: Cambridge University Press, 1992), 306–30, 324–5; on Bergson and irrationalism see H. Höffding, *Modern Philosophers and Lectures on Bergson*, trans. Alfred C. Mason (London: Macmillan, 1915), 232; Maritain, *Redeeming the Time*, 57–61; S. Schwartz, 'Bergson and the politics of vitalism', in *The Crisis in Modernism: Bergson and the Vitalist Controversy*, ed. F. Burwick and P. Douglass (Cambridge: Cambridge University Press, 1992), 277–306, 289–91.

5 G. Gutting, *French Philosophy in the Twentieth Century* (Cambridge: Cambridge University Press, 2001), 73.

6 Nietzsche, *Beyond Good and Evil*, section 230.

7 Nietzsche, *Beyond Good and Evil*, Preface and section 43.

8 Nietzsche, *Human, all too Human, volume II: Mixed Opinions and Maxims*, trans. Gary Handwerk (Stanford: Stanford University Press), section 5.

9 Nietzsche, *Human, all too Human, volume I*, trans. Gary Handwerk (Stanford: Stanford University Press, 1995), sections 10 and 16.

10 Nietzsche, *Human, all too Human volume I*, section 10.

11 Nietzsche, *Beyond Good and Evil*, section 36.

12 Nietzsche, *The Anti-Christ & Other Writings*, trans. Judith Norman (Cambridge: Cambridge University Press, 2005), section 12.

13 For further insight into the affinities and differences between Bergson and Nietzsche on some core issues, see Arnaud François, 'Life and Will in Nietzsche and Bergson', *Substance*, 36: 3, 2007, 100–15; and Messay Kebede, 'Beyond Dualism and Monism: Bergson's Slanted Being', *Journal of French and Francophone Philosophy*, XXIV: 2, 2016, 106–30, especially 123–8.

14 On biologism see Martin Heidegger, *Nietzsche volume three: The Will to Power as Knowledge and Metaphysics*, trans. J. Stambaugh, D. F. Krell and F. A. Capuzzi (San Francisco: Harper. 1987), 39–48.

21 See Deleuze, *Bergsonism*, 26–7.

22 Deleuze, *Bergsonism*, 33.

23 Kant, *Critique of Pure Reason,* trans. Paul Guyer and Allen W. Wood (Cambridge: Cambridge University Press, 1997), B 72.

24 Kant, *Critique of Pure Reason,* A 277/B 333.

25 Kant, *Critique of Pure Reason,* A 278/ B 334.

26 Ibid.

27 Kant, *Critique of Pure Reason,* A 288/B 344.

28 For Descartes on intuition, which he conceives in terms of 'an unclouded and attentive mind', see Descartes, 'Rules for the Direction of the Mind', in *Descartes. Philosophical Writings*, trans. and ed. Elizabeth Anscombe and Peter Thomas Geach (London: Nelson and Sons, 1954), 155.

29 Deleuze, *Bergsonism*, 14.

30 Merleau-Ponty, 'Bergson', 9–33, 14.

31 G. Deleuze, 'Bergson's Conception of Difference', trans. M. McMahon, in *The New Bergson*, ed. J. Mullarkey (Edinburgh: Edinburgh University Press, 1999), 42–66, 25.

32 Nietzsche, *Beyond Good and Evil*, section 186.

33 Nietzsche, 'Of Old and New Tablets', *Thus Spoke Zarathustra*, trans. Graham Parkes (Oxford: Oxford World Classics, 2005).

34 See F. Amrine, '"The triumph of life": Nietzsche's verbicide', in *The Crisis in Modernism: Bergson and the Vitalist Controversy*, ed. F. Burwick and P. Douglass (Cambridge: Cambridge University Press, 1992), 131–53, 135–8. On Bergson's alleged reduction of the spiritual to the biological, see J. Maritain, *Redeeming the Time*, 79. This issue is explored in more detail in Chapter 6 of this book.

Chapter 2

1 Karl Marx, 'Difference Between the Democritean and Epicurean Philosophy of Nature', in *Collected Works: Volume One 183*–43, ed. K. Marx and F. Engels (London: Lawrence & Wishart, 1975), 73.

2 Jean-Marie Guyau, *La Morale D'Epicure* (Paris: Librairie Gemer Baillière, 1878), 280.

3 F. Nietzsche, *The Wanderer and His Shadow*, trans. Gary Handwerk (Stanford: Stanford University Press, 2013), section 295.

4 See P. Hadot, 'Philosophy as a Way of Life', in *Philosophy as a Way of Life*, trans. Michael Chase (Oxford: Blackwell, 1995), 264–77.

5 Henri Bergson, *Extraits de Lucrèce avec un commentaire, des notes et une etude sur la poésie, la physique, le texte et la langue de Lucrèce* (Paris: C. Delagrave, 1884), Introduction 1, p. II and *The Philosophy of Poetry. The Genius of Lucretius*, trans. W. Baskin (New York: Philosophical Library, 1959), 44; hereafter *Philosophy of Poetry*.

6 Lucretius, *On the Nature of the Universe*, trans. R. E. Latham, revised by John Godwin (London: Penguin, 1994), book II, lines 1–19.

7 Lucretius, *On the Nature of the Universe*, V: 10.

8 Ibid., V: 1119.

9 Ibid., IV: 22.

10 Ibid., II: 59–62; see also III: 91–4.

11 Ibid., V: 186–90.

12 Ibid., V: 1203.

13 Ryan J. Johnson, 'Another Use of the Concept of the Simulacrum: Deleuze, Lucretius and the Practical Critique of Demystification', *Deleuze Studies*, 8: 1, 2014, 73.

14 Lucretius, *On the Nature of the Universe*, II: 181.

15 Ibid., V: 81.

16 Ibid., II: 1058–66.

17 For Nietzsche on Lucretius and Epicureanism on mortality see, *Dawn*, trans. Brittain Smith (Stanford: Stanford University Press, 2011), section 72, and *The Anti-Christ & Other Writings*, trans. Judith Norman (Cambridge: Cambridge University Press, 2005), section 58.

18 Lucretius, *On the Nature of the Universe*, III: 868–71.

19 Lucretius, *On the Nature of the Universe*, III: 1023–4.

20 Bergson, *Philosophy of Poetry*, 14.

21 Ibid., 14–15.

22 Ibid., 15.

23 Ibid., 65.

24 Ibid., 69.

Cambridge University Press, 2007), 306–24, 309. Schopenhauer was, of course, a key intellectual influence on Hardy. For insight into the history of reading Lucretius's poem in terms of the theme of melancholy see Monica R. Gale, 'Introduction', in *Lucretius,* ed. R. Gale (Oxford: Oxford University Press, 2007), 1–18.

35 Ibid., 46.
36 Ibid., 47.
37 Ibid., 50.
38 Ibid., 51–2.
39 Ibid., 55–6.
40 Ibid., 56–7.
41 Ibid., 63.
42 Ibid., 75.
43 Ibid., 74. Lucretius himself writes: 'We who are now are not concerned with ourselves in any previous existence: the sufferings of those selves do not touch us. When you look at the immeasurable extent of time gone by and the multiform movements of matter, you will readily credit that these same atoms that compose us now must many a time before have entered into the selfsame combinations as now. But our mind cannot recall this to remembrance. For between then and now is interposed a break in life, and all the atomic motions have been wandering far astray from sentience' (III: 852–62).
44 Bergson, *Philosophy of Poetry*, 80.
45 Ibid, 80–1.
46 For insight into the sublime in Lucretius, see James I. Porter, 'Lucretius and the Sublime', *The Cambridge Companion to Lucretius* (Cambridge: Cambridge University Press, 2007), 167–85.

47 Bergson, *Philosophy of Poetry*, 82.
48 See David Sedley, *Lucretius and the Transformation of Greek Wisdom* (Cambridge: Cambridge University Press, 1998), 160–5..

Chapter 3

1 Benedict de Spinoza, *Ethics*, ed. and trans. Edwin Curley (London: Penguin Books, 1996), Book II, 35.
2 On the doer and the deed and the positing of a fiction of a free willing subject see Nietzsche, *On the Genealogy of Morality*, trans. Carol Diethe (Cambridge: Cambridge University Press, 2017, third edition), Essay One, section 13. Nietzsche puts forward a number of conceptions of freedom of the will in his writings, both negatively conceived and positively conceived. For further insight see Ken Gemes and Simon May (eds), *Nietzsche on Freedom and Autonomy* (Oxford: Oxford University Press, 2009).
3 Jacques Chevalier, *Henri Bergson*, authorized trans. Lilian A. Clare (London: Rider & Co., 1928), 123.
4 Christophe Bouton, *Time and Freedom*, trans. Christopher Macann (Evanston: Northwestern University Press, 2014), 193.
5 See the appreciation in Ian W. Alexander, *Bergson. Philosopher of Reflection* (London: Bowes & Bowes, 1957), 20.
6 As Moore points out Bergson does not approach the issue of sensations and their recognition from the point of view of a 'private language argument': 'Bergson is as strong an opponent of the old empiricist view of sensations as Wittgenstein – not because of their supposed *privacy*, but because of their supposed *distinctness*.' F. C. T. Moore, *Bergson. Thinking Backwards* (Cambridge: Cambridge University Press, 1996), 44–5.
7 Deleuze, *Bergsonism*, trans. Hugh Tomlinson and Barbara Habberjam (New York: Zone Books, 1991), 19.
8 On plurality and numerical difference as given by space compare Kant, *Critique of Pure Reason*, trans. and ed. Paul Guyer and Allen W. Wood (Cambridge: Cambridge University Press, 1997), 'Identity and Difference', A 264/B 320.
9 Compare Kant, *Critique of Pure Reason* A 143/B 182: 'The pure *schema* of magnitude (*quantitatis*), as a concept of the understanding, is *number*, a representation which comprises the successive addition of homogeneous units. Number is therefore simply the unity of the synthesis of the manifold of a homogeneous intuition in general, a unity due to my generating time itself in the apprehension of the intuition.' Kant draws our attention not to the act of counting and what it implies but rather to what is implied in things being numerable. Over

(London: J. M. Dent, 1911), 131ff, and from whose account I shall draw upon.

11 Lindsay, *Philosophy of Bergson*, 133.

12 Ibid., 134.

13 Ibid.

14 Bouton, *Time and Freedom*, 194.

15 Ibid., 197.

16 Ibid.

17 Suzanne Guerlac, *Thinking in Time: An Introduction to Henri* Bergson (Ithaca and London: Cornell University Press, 2006), 77, 79–80.

18 Guerlac, *Thinking in Time*, 42.

19 Bouton, *Time and Freedom*, 196.

20 For an attempt to illuminate issues of the self in Bergson's philosophy of duration see Elena Fell, *Duration, Temporality, Self: Prospects for the Future of Bergsonism* (Bern: Peter Lang, 2012), especially chapters seven and eight. Fell does not, however, focus on the issues I draw attention to in this chapter. See also the instructive analysis in Mark S. Muldoon, *Tricks of Time: Bergson, Merleau-Ponty and Ricoeur in Search of Time, Self and Meaning* (Pittsburgh: Duquesne University Press, 2006), especially 96–102, 107–15.

21 Guerlac, *Thinking in Time*, 105.

22 Bouton, *Time and Freedom*, 196.

23 Ibid.

Chapter 4

1 See S. Freud, *The Interpretation of Dreams*, ed. James Strachey (Middlesex: Penguin, 1976), 770ff. In an essay of 1922 Bergson writes: ' My idea of integral conservation of the past more and more found its empirical verification in the vast collection of experiments instituted by the disciples of Freud' (Bergson CM 75).

2 See G. Deleuze, *Bergsonism*, trans. Hugh Tomlinson and Barbara Habberjam (New York: Zone Books, 1991), chapter 3.

3 Sebastian Gardner, 'The Unconscious Mind', in *The Cambridge History of Philosophy 1870-1945*, ed. Thomas Baldwin (Cambridge: Cambridge University Press, 2003), 112.

4 See J. Hyppolite, 'Various Aspects of Memory in Bergson' (1949), trans. Athena V. Colman, in Leonard Lawlor, *The Challenge of Bergsonism* (London: Continuum Press, 2003), 112–28.

5 This is very much in line with how neuroscientists frame consciousness today: 'Consciousness reflects the ability to make distinctions or discriminations among huge sets of alternatives,' Gerald Edelman, *Wider than the Sky: The Phenomenal Gift of Consciousness* (London: Allen Lane, 2004), 141. For a treatment of Bergson's text in relation to strands in the philosophy of mind, see Frédéric Worms, *Introduction à Matière et mémoire de Bergson* (Paris: Presses Universitaires de France, 1997).

6 Hyppolite, 'Various Aspects of Memory in Bergson', 113–14.

7 See Edward S. Casey, *Remembering* (Bloomington: Indiana University Press, 2000), 310.

8 For insight into Bergson's theory of images, see Jean-Paul Sartre, *Imagination*, trans. Forrest Williams (Ann Arbor: University of Michigan Press, 1962), and more recently, F. C. T. Moore, *Bergson. Thinking Backwards* (Cambridge: Cambridge University Press, 1996), and Edward S. Casey, 'Image and Memory in Bachelard and Bergson', in *Spirit and Soul: Essays in Philosophical Psychology*, second and expanded edition (Putnam, CT: Spring Publications, 2004), 101–17.

9 Patrick McNamara, *Mind and Variability: Mental Darwinism, Memory, and Self* (London: Praeger, 1999), 37.

10 McNamara, *Mind and Variability*, 38.

11 For a critique of Hume's early associationist account of memory, see H. O. Mounce, *Hume's Naturalism* (London and New York, Routledge), 30, and compare Deleuze, *Bergsonism*, 93ff., and John Biro, 'Hume's new science of the mind', in *The Cambridge Companion to Hume*, ed. David Fate Norton (Cambridge and New York: Cambridge University Press, 1993), 33–64, 50.

12 Deleuze, *Bergsonism*, 54.

13 Ibid.

Ontology, trans. Hazel E. Barnes (London and New York: Routledge, 1989).

18 See Merleau-Ponty, *The Incarnate Subject*, 89–90 and Sartre, *Imagination*, 39–40.

19 Jean-Francois Lyotard, *Phenomenology*, trans. Brian Beakley (New York: SUNY Press, 1991), 78.

20 See, for example, Ann Game, *Undoing the Social: Towards a Deconstructive Sociology* (Milton Keynes: Open University Press, 1991).

21 This move is prefigured in the work of Levinas, 'Beyond Intentionality', in *Philosophy in France Today*, ed. Alan Montefiore (Cambridge: Cambridge University Press, 1983).

22 Levinas, *Time and the Other*, 132.

23 Walter Benjamin, 'On Some Motifs in Baudelaire', *Illuminations*, trans. H. Zohn (London: Collins, 1973), 157–202, 159.

24 For further instructive insight see Claire Blencowe, 'Destroying Duration: The Critical Situation of Bergsonism in Benjamin's Analysis of Modern Experience', *Theory, Culture, and Society*, 25: 4, 2008, 139–58.

25 Benjamin, *Illuminations*, 186.

26 Max Horkheimer, 'On Bergson's Metaphysics of Time', trans. Peter Thomas, *Radical Philosophy* 131, 2005, 9–20 (originally published as 'Zu Bergsons Metaphysik der Zeit', *Zeitschrift fr Sozialforschung*, Heft 3, 1934, 321–43). For insight into the affinities between Adorno and Bergson see Roger Foster, *Adorno. The Recovery of Experience* (New York: SUNY Press, 2007), 113–20.

27 G. Deleuze, *Cinema 2: The Time-Image*, trans. Hugh Tomlinson and Robert Galeta (London and New York: Continuum Press, 1989), 82–3.

28 Oliver Sacks, *A Leg to Stand On* (London: Picador, 1991), 178.

29 Israel Rosenfield, *The Invention of Memory* (New York: Basic Books, 1988).

30 McNamara, *Mind and Variability*, 23.

31 Paul Ricoeur, *Memory, History, Forgetting*, trans. Kathleen Blamey and David Pellauer (Chicago and London: University of Chicago Press, 2004), 430–1.

32 Ricoeur, *Memory, History, Forgetting* 440. On the role of forgetting in Bergson's account, see also the excellent insights developed by Messay Kebede, 'Action and Forgetting: Bergson's Theory of Memory', *Philosophy Today*, 60: 2, Spring 2016, 347–70.

33 Ricoeur, *Memory, History, Forgetting* 440.

Chapter 5

1 Bergson's work did figure in books of the time on the philosophy of biology. See, from 1914, James Johnstone, *The Philosophy of Biology*, and that Cambridge University published in a new edition in 2014.

2 A. N. Whitehead, *Nature and Life* (Cambridge University Press, 1934), 9.

3 It is the only text, for example, that Leonard Lawlor does not treat in his *The Challenge of Bergsonism* (London and New York: Continuum Press, 2003). In her book on Bergson, *Thinking in Time. An Introduction to Bergson* (Ithaca and London: Cornell University Press, 2006), Suzanne Guerlac attends only to *Time and Free Will* and *Matter and Memory*. An exception is the work of Elisabeth Grosz, though she has not attended to *Creative Evolution* as a book that attempts to reform the practice of philosophy. See Grosz, *Becoming Undone: Darwinian Reflections on Life, Politics, and Art* (Durham and London: Duke University Press, 2011).

4 This reception continues today in France. See important studies of the text: Yvette Conry, *L'Évolution Créatrice D'Henri Bergson: Investigations critiques* (Paris: L'Harmattan, 2000); A. Francois (ed.), *L'Évolution créatrice de Bergson* (Paris: Vrin, 2010).

5 Collingwood's claim that Bergson's cosmology eliminates matter from it is fundamentally misguided. It is clear that for Bergson we are both matter and life and both must be attended to and given their due. See R. G. Collingwood, *The Idea of Nature* (Oxford at the Clarendon Press, 1945), 137–8.

6 Compare Bernard, 'Systems and doctrines in medicine are hypothetical or theoretic ideas transformed into immutable principles. This sort of method belongs essentially to scholasticism and differs radically from the experimental method,' in Claude Bernard, *An Introduction to the Study of Experimental Medicine*, trans. Henry Copley Greene (New York: Dover, 1957), 220. For further insight into Bergson's relation to Bernard, see Marie Cariou, *Lectures Bergsoniennes* (Paris: Presses Universitaires de France, 1999), 84–112.

14 Weissman's theory of the germ plasm theory states that organisms consist of germ cells that contain and transmit heritable information, and somatic cells that carry out ordinary bodily functions. In the theory inheritance only takes place by means of the germ cells, such as egg cells and sperm cells. Other cells of the body do not function as agents of heredity. The effect is also one way: germ cells produce somatic cells, and more germ cells; the germ cells are not affected by anything the somatic cells learn or any ability the body acquires during its life. Genetic information cannot pass from soma to germ plasm and on to the next generation.

15 See, for example, Norm Hirst (who draws on Whitehead, not Bergson), 'Towards a Science of Life as Creative Organisms', *Cosmos and History: The Journal of Natural and Social Philosophy*, volume 4, no's 1–2, 2008, 78–98.

16 Robert Rosen, *Life Itself* (New York: Columbia University Press, 2005), 12.

17 Rosen, *Life Itself*, 12.

18 Ibid., 17.

19 Ibid., 254.

20 Ibid., xvii.

21 Ibid.

22 Ibid., 14. Rosen's approach to biology is in part inspired by the work of the geophysicist Walter Elsasser and Elsasser's insistence on this need for a holistic approach. Elsasser published an article on Bergson on memory in *Philosophy of Science* in 1953 (not noted by Rosen).

23 Rosen, *Life Itself*, 18.

24 See Brian Goodwin, *Nature's Due. Healing our Fragmented Culture* (Edinburgh: Floris Books, 2007); Mae-Wan Ho, *The Rainbow and the Worm: The Physics of Organisms* (London: World Scientific, 1998). See also the study by David Kreps, *Bergson and Complexity* (Basingstoke: Palgrave Macmillan, 2015).

Chapter 6

1 John Mullarkey, *Bergson and Philosophy* (Edinburgh: Edinburgh University Press, 1999), 89.

2 Peter J. Richerson and Robert Boyd, 'Darwinian Evolutionary Ethics. Between Patriotism and Sympathy', in *Evolution and Ethics: Human Morality in Biological and Religious Perspective,* ed. Philip Clayton and Jeffrey Schloss (Grand Rapids, MIand Cambridge: William P. Eerdmans Publishing Company, 2004), 50–78, 71.

3 Paola Marrati, 'Mysticism and the Foundations of the Open Society', in *Political Theologies: Public Religions in a Post-Secular World,* ed. Hent de Vries and Lawrence E. Sullivan (New York: Fordham University Press, 2006), 501–601, 597.

4 Marrati, 'Mysticism and the Foundations of the Open Society', 597.

5 Ibid.

6 See Jean-Marie Guyau, *A Sketch of Morality Independent of Obligation or Sanction,* trans. Gertrude Kapteyn (London: Watts & Co., 1898).

7 Marrati, 'Mysticism and the Foundations of the Open Society', 594.

8 Ibid., 595.

9 For one such attempt see the study by Una Bernard Sait, *The Ethical Implications of Bergson's Philosophy* (New York: The Science Press, 1914).

10 A. R. Lacey, *Bergson* (London: Routledge, 1989), 197.

11 Jacques Maritain, *Redeeming the Time*, trans. Harry Lorin Binsse (London: The Centenary Press, 1943), 76.

12 Maritain, *Redeeming the Time*, 80.

13 Frederic Worms, 'Is Life the Double Source of Ethics? Bergson's Ethical Philosophy Between Immanence and Transcendence', *Journal of the British Society for Phenomenology*, 35: 1, 2004, 82–9, 84.

14 See Marrati, 'Mysticism and the Foundation of the Open Society', 595.

15 Although the issue of biologism is associated with Heidegger and his 'confrontation' with Nietzsche in the 1930s, it is a prominent feature of Vladimir Jankélévitch's interpretation of Guyau and Bergson as philosophers of life in the 1920s. See V. Jankélévitch, 'Deux philosophes de la vie: Bergson, Guyau', in *Premières et Dernières Pages* (Paris: Seuil, 1994), 13–62, 17 and 22.

16 Marrati, 'Mysticism and the Foundation of the Open Society', 596.

17 Ibid.

18 For excellent insight into Bergson on this point see Alexandre Lefebvre, *Human Rights as a Way of Life. On Bergson's Political Philosophy* (Stanford: Stanford University Press, 2013), especially chapter 2.

19 See Peter Singer, *The Expanding Circle: Ethics and Sociobiology* (Oxford: Clarendon Press, 1981).

34 Bergson argues: 'if there were really a pre-existent direction along which man had simply to advance, moral renovation would be foreseeable; there would be no need, on each occasion, for a creative effort' (TSMR 267).

35 Dorothy Emmet makes this criticism of Bergson. See Emmet, '"Open" and "Closed" Morality', in *Function, Purpose, and Powers,* (London and Basingstoke: Macmillan, 1972, second edition), 137–68, 151.

36 See Alexandre Lefebvre and Melanie White (eds), *Bergson, Politics, and Religion* (Durham and London: Duke University Press, 2012), 5.

37 Michael Naas, *Miracle and Machine. Jacques Derrida and the Two Sources of Religion, Science, and the Media* (New York: Fordham University Press, 2011), 316.

38 Philippe Soulez, 'Bergson as Philosopher of War and Theorist of the Political', in Lefebvre and White, *Bergson, Politics, and Religion,* 99–126, 110.

39 On this point see Soulez, 'Bergson as Philosopher of War and Theorist of the Political', 110–11.

40 I owe the insights that follow to the superb analysis in L. Lawlor, *The Challenge of Bergsonism* (London and New York: Continuum, 2003), especially Appendix I, 85–111.

41 John Mullarkey, *Bergson and Philosophy* (Edinburgh: Edinburgh University Press, 1999), 99.

Chapter 7

1 Here Bergson means something much broader than the analysis Nietzsche undertakes, for example, in the second essay of the *Genealogy of Morality* and in the context of tracing developments of bad conscience. In pre-history, argues Nietzsche,

the basic creditor–debtor relationship that informs human social and economic activity also finds expression in religious rites and worship, for example, the way a tribal community expresses thanks to earlier generations. Over time the ancestor is turned into a god and associated with the feeling of fear, and this is the birth of superstition (see also *The Gay Science* 23 for a different treatment of superstition).

2 Nietzsche, *Beyond Good and Evil*, trans. Marion Faber (Oxford: Oxford University Press, 1998), section 203.

3 For a novel account of Bergson's conception of our 'attachment to life', see David Lapoujade, 'L'Attachement à la vie: Bergson médecin de la civilisation', in *Puissance du temps: Versions de Bergson,* (Paris: Les Editions de Minuit, 2010), 77–99.

4 Deleuze, *Bergsonism*, 107.

5 F. Nietzsche, *On the Genealogy of Morality,* trans. Carol Diethe (Cambridge: Cambridge University Press, 2017, third edition), Essay III: section 9.

6 F. Nietzsche, *Dawn: Thoughts on the Presumptions of Morality*, trans. Brittain Smith (Stanford: Stanford University Press, 2011), section 66.

7 Nietzsche, *Dawn*, 39.

8 Nietzsche, *Dawn,* section 50.

9 Nietzsche, *Human, all too Human*, trans. Gary Handwerk (Stanford: Stanford University Press, 1995), section 114; see also section 117 and *Dawn* section 78.

10 Nietzsche, *Twilight of the Idols*, trans. Duncan Large (Oxford: Oxford University Press, 1998), 'What I Owe the Ancients.'

11 Nietzsche, *Beyond Good and Evil*, section 292.

12 Ibid., section 59.

13 Ibid., section 58.

14 Ibid., section 62.

15 For an attempt to offer such a reading, see Jim Urpeth, '"Health" and "Sickness" in Religious Affectivity: Nietzsche, Otto and Bataille', in *Nietzsche and the Divine,* ed. J. Lippitt and J. Urpeth (Manchester: Clinamen Press, 2000), 226–51. For a more extended discussion of the relationship between Bergson's and Nietzsche's conceptions of religion that takes account of all of Bergson's major works (particularly *Creative Evolution*), see Jim Urpeth: 'Reviving "Natural Religion": Nietzsche and Bergson on Religious Life', in *Nietzsche and Phenomenology,* ed. A. Rehberg (Newcastle upon Tyne: Cambridge Scholars Publ., 2011).

16 Nietzsche, *The Gay Science,* trans. Walter Kaufmann (New York; Random House, 1974), section 109.

17 See Nietzsche, *The Gay Science* sections 344, 347, 357; and *On the Genealogy of Morality*, Essay III, sections 23–5, 27.

18 Nietzsche, *The Gay Science,* section 357. Cited in the *Genealogy*, III; section 27.

7   For Bergson the comic does not exist outside what is human and is to be explained in terms of the mechanical being encrusted on the living. He writes: 'The comic is side of a person which reveals his likeness to a thing, that aspect of human events which, through its peculiar inelasticity, conveys the impression of pure mechanism, automatism, of movement without life', H. Bergson, *Laughter: an essay on the meaning of the comic*, trans. Cloudeseley Brereton and Fred Rothwell (Kobenhavn and Los Angeles: Green Integer, 1999), 82. For further insight into Bergson on the comic, see the following: George McFadden, *Discovering the Comic* (Princeton: Princeton University Press, 1982), chapter 5; Russell Ford, 'On the Advantages and Disadvantages of Comedy for Life', *Journal of the British Society for Phenomenology*, 35: 1, 2004, 89–106; Stephen Crocker, 'Man Falls Down: Art, Life, and Finitude in Bergson's Essay on Laughter', in *Bergson and Phenomenology*, ed. Michael R. Kelly (Basingstoke: Palgrave Macmillan, 2010), 78–101.

8   G. Deleuze, *Bergsonism*, trans. Hugh Tomlinson and Barbara Habberjam (New York: Zone Books, 1991), 14.

9   Merleau-Ponty, 'Bergson', 14.

10 G. Deleuze, 'Bergson's Conception of Difference' (1956), trans. Melissa McMahon, in John Mullarkey (ed.), *The New Bergson* (Manchester: Clinamen Press, 1999), 42–66, 45.

11 Deleuze, 'Bergson's Conception of Difference', 45.

12 David Lapoujade, 'Intuition and Sympathy in Bergson', *Pli: The Warwick Journal of Philosophy*, volume 15, 2004, 1–18. See also Lapoujade, *Puissance de temps*, 53–77.

13 Lapoujade, 'Intuition and Sympathy in Bergson', 8.

14 Ibid., 9.

15 Ibid., 11.

16 Ibid., 12.

Index

"*Educational Eye Exam* is a wonderfully penned metaphor that paints a clear picture and provides attainable strategies for refining our vision of education—no matter your role. Alicia's ability to interweave her personality, her sweet southern accent, and her valuable life lessons brings clarity to the topic's poignancy. Alicia's book will leave you focused to make a difference in your educational setting! During this eye exam, you will not need to make the tough decision of 'Which is better, one or two?' What are you waiting for? This book is for *you*!"

—**Tara Martin, educator, keynote speaker, and author of *Be REAL*, DBC, Inc. director of media and communications**

"Stories are powerful. In *Educational Eye Exam*, Alicia Ray tells her story in a way that causes the reader to reflect on his or her own story as well. What's your *why* as an educator? What's your vision? What's most important to you? It's powerful when you develop a strong educator identity. It's powerful to better know who you are and what you stand for. And as the stories unfold, you'll also find lots of examples and ideas to inspire you to make a bigger impact in your classroom and school. Schedule your exam today. Build on your strengths. You'll appreciate the new clarity you'll enjoy."

—**David Geurin, author of *Future Driven*, award-winning principal, and international keynote speaker**

"Alicia Ray lays it all out in *Educational Eye Exam* and absolutely keeps it real with the reader as she shares her story and motivates others to be the best educators they can be. Alicia gives ideas that can be implemented in your classroom right away and brings it all back together with personal stories from her own teaching experience. The passion and mojo for innovation, excitement, collaboration, and never stopping until she's achieved her goals are evident as you turn each page. *Educational Eye Exam* is a must-read and will be for years to come!"

—**Adam Welcome, author, speaker, and educator**

"*Educational Eye Exam* will challenge, inspire, and motivate you to bring your EDUvision into full focus! Alicia brilliantly weaves in metaphors of a visit to the optometrist and personal experiences to help define and refine your *why* as an educator and develop an educational plan to be the best educator you can be! As you read each chapter, you'll find your educational vision getting clearer, and by the end you'll be seeing 20/20! This book is a must-read for any educator!!!"

—Tisha Richmond, tech integration specialist
and author of *Make Learning Magical*

"Alicia Ray is a reflective and relatable educator, and you just might feel like she is your best friend after reading her book, *Educational Eye Exam*. The stories she shares are entertaining and full of important lessons that will cause readers to reflect on their own stories. Alicia asks important questions as we re-examine our *why* and our practices. She offers ideas that can be implemented right away, and the creativity she shares sparks the imagination. This book is a gift to educators and will translate into meaningful and important changes in our practices."

—Allyson Apsey, elementary principal
and author of *Through the Lens of Serendipity*

"In *Educational Eye Exam*, Alicia offers a refreshing outlook on her growth as an educator. She shares the personal journey, struggles and all, that led her to become the passionate, inspiring, and connected educator she is today. Using the analogy of a visit to the optometrist, Alicia provides a different way to think about education and our roles as educators. Her passion for her work and doing what is best for students shines throughout the book. *Educational Eye Exam* will encourage educators to build on their own strengths, take the next steps, and not be afraid to be wrong or to show vulnerability."

—Rachelle Dene Poth, educator, author, and consultant

"Packed with practical advice, thought-provoking questions, and a realness that is palpable from page one, *Educational Eye Exam* will keep you turning pages and keep your thoughts churning about education and life. This book wanders through the intersection of family life and teaching while delivering the valuable lessons learned along the way. It is delivered in a folksy, funny, and funky way, telling the story through the lens of an eye exam. When you decide to administer your own educational eye exam, you will find the beauty of our profession, the simple joy of teaching kids, the marvels of ingenuity in classroom design, and the impact of self-reflection. Turn inward and then look out. Let Alicia Ray show you how!"

—Andrew Sharos, author, educator, and consultant

to help everything make sense. Alicia's ability to connect her story to our need to reflect on our work and practices will inspire you and remind you how important the work we do is to the future of our world! So . . . schedule your Educational Eye Exam and then make a yearly commitment to come back for a check-up."

—Jay Billy, author of *Lead with Culture*

"*Who am I? What do I believe? How will I incorporate those beliefs professionally?* Alicia asks us to revisit these questions through a different lens. This book for educators takes a fresh look at how we can view what we're already doing in our classrooms and shows us how to make plans for our current vision of what we'd like at our schools. Any time is a great time for an update to our vision plan, so grab this book if you feel you need a new prescription in order to continue teaching with focus."

—Joy Kirr, seventh-grade ELA teacher and author of *Word Shift* and *Shift This!*

"If you've ever wanted to establish or refine your *why* as an educator, you will not want to miss the encouragement and inspiration packed inside this book. Through genuine stories and thought-provoking questions, Alicia Ray's *Educational Eye Exam* will push educators to reflect and see our work differently."

—Aaron Hogan, author of *Shattering the Perfect Teacher Myth*

"Using the powerful art of storytelling, Alicia Ray walks us through the steps necessary to help us determine our beliefs and philosophy in education. Her book is practical and relatable, and will help you learn and grow as an educator no matter your role or who you serve. As I read her book, I felt like I was talking with a close friend, and those kinds of conversations are always uplifting, validating, and good for the soul."

—Annick Rauch, French immersion educator, learner, and mom

"Alicia makes the case for great teaching by providing authentic stories, ideas, and action plans that can be implemented in everyone's daily life. She articulates her philosophies by using her educational experience and recounting events, and her stories leave me feeling like I am a part of the family. Relatable, authentic, generous, and kind, Alicia speaks from her heart and will definitely leave an impact on yours!"

—**Brian Aspinall, educator, author, and speaker**

"Jim Henson said, 'Kids don't remember what you try to teach them. They remember what you *are*.' After reading Alicia Ray's book, you will not only come away inspired but also feeling like you know Alicia personally. She is generous with her stories and honest about her failures, and her optimism, creativity, and faith in education will leave you wishing she taught in the room next to yours."

—**Julie N. Smith, professor, Webster University, and author of *Master the Media***

"I've heard it said that reading is breathing in and writing is breathing out. Over the course of a single summer, Alicia Ray inhaled teaching strategies with cover-to-cover reads of fifty different books about education, and in *Educational Eye Exam*, she exhales the very best of what she's learned along the way to offer teachers some truly eye-opening insights. Heartfelt, humorous, and loaded with practical strategies for any classroom, Alicia's book offers teachers a welcome tune-up and helps us focus on the stuff that's really important."

—**John Meehan, author of *EDrenaline Rush***

Eye Exam

Creating **YOUR** Vision for Education

Alicia Ray

Educational Eye Exam
© 2019 by Alicia Ray

This book is available at special discounts when purchased in quantity for use as premiums, promotions, fundraisers, or for educational use. For inquiries and details, contact the publisher at books@daveburgessconsulting.com.

Published by Dave Burgess Consulting, Inc.
San Diego, CA
daveburgessconsulting.com

Cover Design by Genesis Kohler
Editing and Interior Design by My Writers' Connection

Library of Congress Control Number: 2019944563
Paperback ISBN: 978-1-949595-60-4
Ebook ISBN: 978-1-949595-61-1

First Printing: September 2019

CONTENTS

DEDICATION

To my Mama:
When given the choice to sit it out or dance, I danced.

To Bailey & Sophie:
Never sit out a single dance! Always dance,
my loves, even if no one else hears the music!
I believe you will blow us all away!

To all of "my kids":
Thank you for allowing me to be part of your lives beyond
the classroom and for being such a special part of mine.
Each one of you has changed me for the better.

FOREWORD

by Dave Burgess

I stared in stunned silence at the prescription bottle as she repeated the question, "What is the Rx number on the label?" I stammered an embarrassing excuse about needing to call back and hung up, even though it had taken me a seemingly endless amount of time and frustration fighting through a phone tree to get to an actual human being. I could not read the number. A similar incident had occurred on a plane a week or so earlier as I tried unsuccessfully to buy Wi-Fi because I could not make out the numbers on my credit card. I had chalked it up to the plane being too dark and thought little of it. There in the bright lights of the kitchen, however, I couldn't escape the truth; my eyesight had deteriorated to the point that I needed reading glasses in addition to my contacts. Apparently, this is why I had found it increasingly hard to focus on books, blogs, and articles of late. The problem is it came on slow. If it had happened all at once, I would have done something immediately, but it crept up on me.

The same thing happens to us all the time in life, whether it is in relationships, fitness and health, or our occupations.

How did I end up this out of shape?

Is this what I would have chosen for my life?

Did I ever see myself teaching like this?

It happens one day at a time, and you never see it coming. Gradually you become more frustrated and a little less satisfied with your life.

. . . a little less likely to make healthy decisions.

. . . a little more complacent at work.

. . . a little less self-reflective.

. . . a little too comfortable with the status quo.

And then, in one moment, it can all change. Decades of descent down a dastardly steep slope into despair and darkness can be reversed, and you can walk away with a purpose and passion that are rekindled and restored and return to a path of promise and progress. Sometimes all you need is that precipitating event, that fortuitous encounter, that perfect prompt from a partner—or even a protagonist—that jars you just enough to knock you out of your comfort zone and into a state of heightened and enlightened awareness.

I have incredible news: Your decision to pick up and read this book is exactly that precipitating event, that fortuitous encounter, and your all-access pass to an #EduEyeExam chock-full of prompts that will shift your paradigm, sharpen your edu-vision, and propel you forward into your career with a renewed commitment to being the best possible version of yourself. Don't let the folksy stories and the southern drawl fool you—Alicia Ray is sneaky in the best way and will have you marveling at the courage of her vulnerability, transfixed by her storytelling, and just when you let your guard down— *BOOM*—she will have led you by the hand to an all-new clarity of purpose and intriguing new insights, and you will walk away with a wonderfully revitalized and radiant outlook on education.

It's time for your appointment; "Dr." Ray is awaiting you inside the coming pages.

FROM MY PERSPECTIVE

Some people fear the dentist. Me? I dread the optometrist. I've never had a "bad experience" per se; I just hate having my eyes dilated. I hate for anything to be near my eyes. It took me forever to get used to applying eyeliner and mascara. (On any given day, if you look closely enough, you'll notice that my eye makeup is wretched. This is why.)

I share this personal quirk so you'll understand why I dodged the eye doctor for something like sixteen years before my most recent appointment. I just don't want you to judge me too much yet. (There will be plenty of time for that later on!)

I had put off visiting the DMV to renew my driver's license until the very last day. When it was finally my turn to read the signs—which I had studied, just in case—I was shocked to hear the lady behind the desk ask me to press my head against the activation bar above the screen and read the letters along the top line on the screen. I panicked. It was one blur followed by a space and another blur. Changes in vision are often subtle, and I hadn't realized how much my eyesight had changed over time.

I gave it my all. Noting all the curves and straight lines, I offered up my best educated guess. I have no idea how many I got correct, but it was enough to renew my license. That's when I knew: it was time to visit the optometrist.

After making the appointment, I anxiously arrived at the requested fifteen minutes before appointment time to fill out paperwork. After I got in the exam room, however, I realized that all my nervousness was unwarranted. My eye doctor didn't even dilate my eyes! That "puff of air" has been replaced by a light—an insanely bright light, but still, just a light. Minutes later I was seated in a chair, listening to the familiar drone of, "Which view is better, one or two?" It took several iterations to find the right combination. After "Which is better, eleven or twelve?" the optometrist started with letters. Bless her heart.

"Which is better, A or B?"

After a few of the letter options, she made one final click. Y'all! The lines came together in the most perfect way. Like magic. I. Could. See.

The letters on the screen were crystal clear! It was as if my eyesight had been reversed by ten years!

How many times have you experienced a moment of clarity like that in other parts of your life? Things seem blurry, fuzzy, unfocused, and then, *BOOM*—you find one piece of information to add to the puzzle, and suddenly you gain a new, crystal-clear perspective. Hindsight. You can then apply that crystal-clear perspective to everything you do from that moment forward.

These discoveries are what propel us to move through iteration after iteration to create the best successes, not only in the classroom but also in our lives. The lessons we learn through our setbacks allow us to react differently in similar situations in the future, giving us small victories until we achieve grand success. Everything we do inches us toward success if we just continue to tweak our perspective. In every setback, we can learn something if we take the time to stop and reflect. All it takes is that one *click* to change everything!

Are you ready for your Educational Eye Exam?

EDUCATIONAL "I" EXAM

Throughout this book, you will be taken on a trip to the optometrist. Don't worry; it won't be as painful as you might be expecting. Or maybe it will be. That all depends on how willing you are to deeply consider yourself and your teaching practices.

I have been an educator in a tremendous school system in rural northwest North Carolina for thirteen years. After a transition from the elementary classroom to a middle school instructional coaching position, I realized I had grown a bit stagnant in my career. I was signing in, teaching students and teachers all day, and signing out. I had lost the passion and enthusiasm I once had for education and traded them in for compliance and complacency. I had read *Teach Like a PIRATE* by Dave Burgess years ago and knew my half-hearted attitude was a disservice to the students and teachers I served. It was after I came to this realization that I scheduled my own Educational "I" Exam.

In June 2018, Dave Burgess Consulting, Inc. celebrated the publishing of its fiftieth book, and I got this crazy idea that I should read all fifty of those books, starting with the first, *Teach Like a PIRATE*, and continuing through the fiftieth, *The EduNinja Mindset* by Jennifer Burdis. Not only did I want to read all of those books, but I also planned to finish them during the summer months of June–September, and I wanted to share my reflections and thoughts with others once I was finished. I chose to use the hashtag #DBC50Summer on Twitter to share the journey with my professional learning network and make it quickly searchable. I would read each book and write a blog post highlighting quotes from the book, sharing my own reflections, and choosing one thing from each book to implement in the following school year. I decided to choose something to implement because, as Dave Burgess says in *Teach Like a PIRATE*, "Inspiration without implementation is a waste." I did not want the time spent reading these books to be a waste.

I had 101 days to complete the task and wasn't sure I'd ever finish once I started. I'll be honest: I am notorious for having ideas and failing to follow through (anyone else out there?). I published the first blog post, titled "#DBC50Summer Explained," more for accountability than anything else. I knew that if I didn't put myself out there and tell readers of my blog about this adventure, I might not ever finish.

I had no idea what was in store for me when I began the journey of reading fifty professional books in such a condensed time period. What I do know is that, upon finishing all fifty books, I was a different educator. I grew more as a professional in those one hundred days than I did in all my years in the classroom, and it has taken a while for me to realize why the growth was so exponential. Why do I feel like my summer journey of professional development on steroids was so valuable? What was it that reignited my passion for my profession? What was it that empowered me to even consider writing this book? My experience was more than I ever anticipated. But why?

The authors were incredible and the messages sensational. The love for our profession within the pages of those books was contagious and filled my heart with pride. I've often said to my peers that *Teach Like a PIRATE* is like a church revival for the educational soul. (Here in the South, they really understand that.) And if that's the case, you can only imagine what that revival multiplied by fifty would be like. But that energy wasn't what made the experience so moving; it was a catalyst but not the linchpin.

What made the difference was taking an introspective look at my own beliefs. It was mining my own professional life and connecting the stories from those amazing authors to my own personal stories. It was substituting the names of the phenomenal educators in those books with the names of the extraordinary educators I have worked with in the past thirteen years. It was taking the time to dive, and I mean *really* dive, heart first, into my own educational philosophies on everything from classroom management and feedback to grading and lesson planning. It was rediscovering my passions and remembering my *why*.

This process, in my opinion, is about more than reflection; it's about establishing your beliefs. It is my hope that this book will push you, that it will stretch you, and that you will grapple with what you believe and how your own beliefs can come to life in your own classroom, school, and community. Reading this book will be something like a visit to the eye doctor, but you won't just peer at letters and numbers on the surface—you'll be asked to look deep within yourself. I'm not going to tell you what to believe. I will share my own beliefs, and you don't have to agree with them. The aim is to get you believing *something* and believing it so strongly and so passionately that it oozes from you. It is said that the eyes are the windows to the soul. What are your eyes telling others? When you speak of education and this noble profession we have devoted ourselves to, do you speak with conviction? Do your eyes light up? Can you stand up for your beliefs when they are challenged? Do you really know what you believe?

I thought I did, until I encountered the first critics. Their logic made so much sense to me, and I found myself wavering in my "beliefs." I have joked for years that I am a parrot—I am good at repeating what smarter, more accomplished educators have said. The problem is that when a parrot hears conflicting information, she repeats it with no regard for her own thoughts. Upon reading the personal stories from the authors of Dave Burgess Consulting, Inc. and taking the time to remember my experiences and learn from my own stories through blogging, I realized that I have my own thoughts and beliefs about education. I am no longer a parrot. I don't repeat the beliefs of others; I share my own beliefs. I hear conviction and passion in my own voice when I speak because what I'm saying are my own beliefs.

Reading those first fifty books and sharing the #DBC50Summer blog posts was like an educational eye exam. It turned into something so much more than a quick fix for compliance and complacency; it became an educational "I" exam. I gathered the courage to ask vital questions: *Who am I? What do I believe? How will I incorporate those beliefs professionally?* I also realized that when I know my own educational philosophies, my students are the ones who reap the greatest benefits because they no longer have a parrot for a teacher. They have an educator with convictions and passions. They have an educator who believes in *them* and advocates for *them*. How powerful it is for a student to see a teacher who is on fire for teaching! You can't help but spark a love of learning and self-discovery when you are excited about what you are teaching. There is nothing more inspiring than a student who is lighting their world on fire, and behind that student, there is often an educator who has had an "I" exam.

I'm not suggesting that it's a requirement to read every professional book written about education in order to find your voice; however, if you'd like suggestions for books to read, I can give at least fifty! This book is the culmination of the transformation I experienced by doing this. It is my hope that you can reach the same epiphany I had about my own beliefs through reading this book. If you are struggling through the trenches, this can be your lifeline, if you will allow it to be. If you are fortunate enough to be in a good place professionally, are you ready for the critics? They are coming and they will have questions. Are you ready to share why you do what you do? Are you prepared to defend your beliefs? This book will equip you with what you need to stand up for your own educational philosophy. Free yourself from being a parrot and find your own voice through scheduling your first Educational Eye Exam.

As you develop and refine your educational philosophy, I would be most honored if you would share your vision with me! It doesn't matter if you blog, sketchnote, write poetry, create a video response, or use any other format— please share it with others around you, face-to-face and online! Share your thoughts on social media using the hashtag #EduEyeExam!

You've arrived at the doctor the standard fifteen minutes early and have checked in. Your mountain of paperwork is completed, and you're anxiously waiting to be called. The nurse comes to the door, takes a second look at the file in her hand, and calls your name. It's go time!

CHAPTER 1

The Paperwork

At every doctor visit I've ever had, the first thing we do is go over my demographics and my history. I fill in my address, phone number, birthdate, full name, insurance information, and so on. At follow-up visits, I review this information, updating old information, making corrections as necessary, or initialing to confirm the information is still accurate. Why is this always the first step? Because the doctors need to know that you are who you say you are, and they need a full family history to provide you with appropriate medical care.

It is important to know who we are before starting the Educational Eye Exam. Take a moment and ask yourself who you are. Where do you come from? What is your background? Share your history. Here's mine:

Throughout my entire life, my mom has always told me, "Alicia, it doesn't matter what happens to you in life. Those things don't define you. What defines you is how you react to them, how you choose to learn from those moments and apply what you've learned to your future." This has resonated with me when I have experienced setbacks and gotten back up again to turn them into successes.

I grew up in rural North Carolina in one of those towns where it seems that everyone knows everyone, a town where news travels fast, and gossip travels even faster. Even before the days of social media, my parents typically knew what I had done in school before I even got home. I love the small-town life. In fact, my husband and our two daughters still live in the same town I was born in, and I teach in the same county.

Teaching was not passed down from generation to generation in my family. I am, in fact, a first-generation college graduate. My father dropped out of school when he was in eleventh grade and later earned his GED. My paternal grandfather had to quit school in the seventh grade to work at the family sawmill while my paternal grandmother completed high school. My mother graduated from high school and attended some college before entering the workforce. Her mother finished seventh grade and her father finished fifth grade before they had to give up formal schooling to support their families.

My mom and dad split up when I was ten years old, and the divorce was finalized a year later. To this day, it is still awkward for me to have both my mom and my dad in the same room together, and it rarely ever happens. The one thing they both always agreed on was the importance of getting an education. Going to college was a nonnegotiable, and I believe it's because they both wanted more for their kids than a high school diploma or GED was going to give. They knew the financial struggle that comes with the lack of a college education. At one point, after the divorce, my younger brother and I were some of the Salvation Army angel-tree kids at Christmas. There just wasn't a way for our parents to stretch the money to buy food, pay the bills, and purchase minimal gifts, so we relied on the kindness of strangers to serve as Santa that year. My brother and I never knew until we were much older that this was part of our story.

I never really enjoyed school even though I excelled at it. I just went through the motions, playing the game. Luckily for me, I played the game well. I jumped through all the hoops and finished high school ranked seventh in a class of sixty-seven, which placed me just out of the top ten percent. At some point in high school, we took an aptitude test that revealed I had a gift for teaching others, and I fell in love with the idea and never looked back. At seventeen years old, I walked across the stage to get my high school diploma with an early acceptance to a college that, according to popular opinion, was the very best for educators in North Carolina.

I was on a self-imposed fast track through college. I finished my coursework in two and a half years, then completed my student teaching to graduate with a Bachelor of Science in elementary education at only twenty years old. I was shocked when I landed my first job as a fifth-grade math teacher at an elementary school only minutes from my home. A little more than six weeks after my first open house for a new school year, I turned twenty-one. I was not only an inexperienced teacher but was also what some would call inexperienced at life.

I married young, just a few months after turning twenty-one. My husband and I had our "first" (another story for later) child when I was twenty-three and our second when I was twenty-seven years old. Throughout this time, I taught fifth-grade students—math for two years, math and science for two years, and then all subjects in a self-contained setting for three and a half years.

I am rarely satisfied with the status quo and am constantly setting goals for myself and pushing myself to meet them. With a one-year-old, I went back to school to complete a Master of Arts in education with a focus in instructional technology. Just earning the degree wasn't enough for me—nope, I went ahead and completed the thirty-nine-hour coursework requirement in eighteen months. (I might be slightly crazy.)

A conversation with my human resources department, during which I found out that an instructional technology job would not be an option in my district, led to the decision to return to graduate school to earn a second master's degree. (Probably crazy.)

I found out I was accepted into the cohort in late May and that we were expecting our second child in early June. I chose to go to grad school anyway. (OK, definitely crazy.) I earned a Master of Library Science when our second child was four months old.

To add just a bit more insanity, I also changed jobs, leaving the only school I'd ever worked at midyear to begin a new experience as a media coordinator at a high-poverty elementary school in the same district. And my commute jumped from twenty minutes one way to forty-five minutes one way. If you're keeping score, that means I was juggling two children in child-care (cha-ching), driving an hour and a half each day, teaching grade levels I'd never taught, tackling a library curriculum that I didn't quite understand, working with people I didn't know (but who quickly became like family), and completing the final courses of a graduate degree that I wasn't sure I wanted.

Against all odds, I survived it. Two and a half years later, I was offered an incredible opportunity to pilot a new position in my district that formally merged the roles of instructional technologist, digital learning coach, and media coordinator. The only catch to this seemingly perfect scenario was that I had to move to a middle school. To save a lot of your time, I will just say that after a lot of fear and anxiety and a long, long discussion, I accepted the offer.

Here we are three years later and I'm loving what I get to do every day. I work with teachers to incorporate STEM (Science, Technology, Engineering, and Math), digital learning, and best practices through professional development workshops and a co-teaching coaching model, *and* I get to hang out with some of the world's coolest middle schoolers (yes, I'm a bit biased). I have also led professional development for media coordinators and administrators in my district and serve as a mentor to educators throughout my state.

That's my history and should get you up to speed, for the most part. You have your own story. Take a minute and look back. Reflect on your overall journey. Where you've been is as important as where you're going! What has molded you into the person you are today? When filling out the paperwork for your Educational Eye Exam, what will you share?

CORRECTIVE MEASURES

- 👁 Knowing where you've been keeps you grounded. What is your story?

- 👁 How has your history shaped who you are as an educator?

- 👁 What major slowdowns or setbacks have cleared your vision or steered you in a better direction?

- 👁 Share your thoughts on social media using the hashtag #EduEyeExam.

EDUCATIONAL HINDSIGHT

Surviving Setbacks

Have you ever had the perfect lesson set up, only to have it become the perfect disaster?

I had worked for weeks to prepare an end-of-year activity. Students were going on a StoryWalk. This is an opportunity to be active and promote literacy. I purchased two copies of *Rosie Revere, Engineer* by Andrea Beaty, took off the binding, and laminated page spreads. I nailed each page spread of the story to surveyor's stakes and set them along the nature trail at our school. I had prepared questions and an activity promoting inquiry and iterations for the students when they returned from their walk. I had factored in every possible scenario, including rain, and was prepared for success.

I had not anticipated wind, however. The wind blew in and ripped the beautifully laminated pages off the stakes in the middle of my first class of the day. We spent so much time collecting the pages that the activity and questions didn't happen. What's worse is that I was so sure of the success of this StoryWalk experience that I had every class in the school signed up to do it over the next week.

How did I survive? Two words: duct tape. I hustled out to the trail between classes, cleaned the dust and dirt off the laminated page spreads, and used duct tape along the back to adhere them to the stakes. After the next class, I realized I still wouldn't have time for the inquiry activity, so I built that into a discussion after the experience. I collected answers to the original questions using a digital formative assessment tool. By the end of the week, the StoryWalk was the huge success I'd intended it to be! It was just a bit bumpier than I had anticipated along the way. The most important thing is that I didn't let the setback ruin the success. I survived the setback.

I experience setbacks every day. That's not an exaggeration. Every. Single. Day. I constantly have moments that I look back on, longingly wishing for a redo. I prefer to call these events setbacks and not failures. Failures occur when you quit. To fail is to stop trying. A setback is simply a bump in the road, an opportunity to learn a lesson and move forward with newfound knowledge.

I don't claim to have all the answers. When we feel as though we have all the answers and we're done learning, we need to step away from education. How can we model lifelong learning for students when we feel like we have no more room for growth? While I don't have all the answers, I do have the ability to own and learn from my mistakes. But let me pose an important question: Can you still learn from those moments of hindsight—your reflections—if they are not related to a mistake??

I hope your immediate reaction was a resounding *yes*. If not, hang with me. I'm going to share several success stories that I learned from as well. Those victories are still moments that inspire meaningful reflection. We can still experience hindsight, the act of understanding a situation or event only after it has happened or developed, with success!

Throughout this book you will get a few more glimpses into these moments of hindsight. These are lessons that I learned through looking back at various areas of my life and how the understandings from those events inspired success. Think of them as cross-curricular, where a piece of science content fits perfectly in your English Language Arts (ELA) class, or when a moment in history lends itself perfectly to the math concept you've been studying. I may have experienced the setbacks or successes in my role as a parent and then applied the lesson as a coach, or it may have been a moment of hindsight in my role as an educator that benefited me as a wife. Moments of hindsight are everywhere, which is why I share them throughout the book. Through these experiences, my blurry vision has been transformed into crystal-clear vision, and what we do with the lessons learned through the understanding of our successes and setbacks will determine whether we grow and improve in the future.

CHAPTER 2

The Big E

You know exactly what this is, right? The big E on the classic eye chart. What's the process for determining if you have a deficit in your vision? You stand twenty feet away from the Snellen eye chart (yes, that's the real name) and call out the letters you are able to comfortably read from left to right.

If you struggle to read the big E, you're in trouble. In the United States, being legally blind means you have a vision of at least 20/200, which is the value of the big E. I became very interested in these seemingly arbitrary numbers—20/200, 20/100, 20/15, and so on. Did you know that the twenty in the numerator refers to the twenty feet you are standing away from the chart? The denominator refers to the distance from the chart that an *average* person can accurately read the letters.

Think about that. Those 20/20 people are only *average*. If you have 20/20 vision, you can see at twenty feet what the average person sees at twenty feet. Perfect sight is not 20/20. People with 20/15 vision have better-than-average sight because they can see at twenty feet what the average person can only see standing fifteen feet away.

Here's the thing. The Snellen eye chart is a quick measurement, the first step to diagnosing a problem. Even after all these years and all the advancements in technology, this is still the triage area, if you will. It lets us know the severity of the problem before we begin trying to fix it. Time and time again, the attention comes back to this eye chart. It's the starting point.

What happens in education when we're having a bad day? A bad week? Heck, I've had bad years before. If you've been in education for long, you know what I'm talking about, those years that push you to the very brink of insanity. When you're in the midst of those years, it's hard to catch your breath, much less tread water. This might be due to the dynamics of your students, a change in educational assignment, a change in curriculum, or it might be the perfect storm of all three. (Bless your heart.)

You know what got me through those rough years? Do you know why I'm still loving this career? Because I can look back at the end of those years and see the unbelievable growth in myself, not only as an educator but as a human being as well. You may be thinking, *Sure, looking back you can see it, but what kept you there at the end of those bad weeks? Why did you go back morning after morning?* Maybe you're thinking right now, *I'm done. I can't do this any longer. You just don't understand how much I've been through.* You would be correct. I don't understand. I have no way of knowing what you've been through. For just a minute, though, I'd like you to walk with me. Like a good optometrist, I'm going to bring you to the big E and find out what we might be dealing with here. What got me through those rough years was remembering why I was there to begin with! I went back to the beginning, that moment I chose to enter this amazing profession. I remembered the impact I wanted to make on the lives of those students in my classroom every year. I pictured each and every student, even the ones who challenged me every day, and then I tried to imagine what those same students would offer the world. I thought of the ripple effect of my being at work every day, and I also considered the ripple effect of my *not* being at work. This helped me refocus and change my perspective. What did we say we do when we first discover a deficit in our vision? We go to the eye chart, the big E.

When it comes to the Educational Eye Chart, I believe the big E represents our *why* and our passions. It's big and bold and readily apparent to most people right off the bat. The big E is the reason you got into education.

Many people say education is a calling, and I wholeheartedly agree. I'm at home when I'm in front of a group of students. My face, my eyes, everything about me lights up when I have that privilege. You can't hide that excitement, and you certainly can't fake it. In *Teach Like a PIRATE*, Dave Burgess says you can fake enthusiasm but you cannot fake passion, and in my opinion, our passion stems from our calling.

When we have trouble seeing our big E, it's a sign our vision—our educational vision—has become impaired. We have lost sight of our *why* and our passions. There is a multitude of reasons why this could happen. Perhaps the stress of high-stakes standardized testing has impaired your vision. Maybe change isn't moving fast enough for you. Or perhaps it's moving *too* fast, and you feel a lack of control. This career is hard, my friends. It's not for the faint of heart. And sometimes, it's difficult to remember what your big E is!

Vision doesn't just bounce back. It's usually only regained with some kind of corrective lens or procedure. In this case, that corrective measure is to go back in your mind to that pivotal moment when you knew education was where you were meant to be. Remember that feeling, the feeling of pride, intense responsibility, and the impact you wish to make on others. Ah . . . there it is. Now let's discuss our *why* and our passions.

Your *Why*

Taking inventory of our *why* is paramount in making it through setbacks in education so we can reach the moments of success. Take a moment and consider what your *why* is. Why did you choose this profession? Or, rather, how did it choose you? Was education a generational legacy in your family? Were you inspired by a particular teacher you loved, or maybe one you didn't love? Was it a family member with special needs? Think through your own *why* as I share mine with you.

As I said earlier, I did not come from a family of teachers. I was the first in my family to attend and graduate from college. Getting an education was important in my family, but working in education was not. After my mom and dad divorced, my younger brother, Jacob, and I lived with my mom. While my mom worked late nights, I was responsible for ensuring that my brother had dinner, took a shower, got his homework completed, and went to bed at a reasonable time. When I had my license, I would take him to school in the mornings and pick him up in the afternoons.

My brother is one of the smartest people I know. Like my dad, he can listen to a car engine whine, tell you exactly what part needs to be fixed, and have it repaired in no time. My brother has an insane artistic ability as well. He has always had a steady hand and could sketch images that would blow me away. His artistic ability also spilled over into dancing. We would move the coffee table in the living room and have dance-offs while rocking out to MTV in the days of music videos. He would always beat me, hearing the rhythms that I could never detect and making his moves look fluid like they were meant to be a part of a song that only he could hear. (I am so sorry for sharing our little secret, Jacob.)

Doing homework with Jacob was a struggle. He would do all he could to get out of his spelling, reading, and math worksheets until I threatened to call our mom. He'd finally go to the dining room table, huffing and puffing while he started his work. Two hours later, he'd finally put it all back up. I always felt it was unfair that he struggled to complete the small amount of homework he had. I had easily double the homework and finished in less than half the time. School always came easily to me. I didn't enjoy it, but I was good at it. I was good at playing the game; Jacob was not.

We discovered that Jacob had an Auditory Processing Disorder and Attention Deficit Disorder. He struggled with processing information, which led to his struggling throughout school. Like my dad, there were days he was ready to walk out the door and never return. With a *lot* of hard work, he graduated with his class and went to the local community college to study automotive repair. In the shop, he excelled. He was happy there. He would take apart an engine, clean it, and put it back together so that the car was running smoothly again. Today he uses his artistic talents to paint and repair cars and has worked his way to managerial positions.

Jacob is a big part of why I became a teacher. He had so many talents that were never appreciated in school because the focus was on his academic skill, and as a result, he never enjoyed school. I wanted school to be a place where people enjoy learning. I wanted my students to come in every day happy to be there and ready to take on anything because they knew I'd be there to support them. I wanted my students to see that "smart" is more than being able to meet academic standards. There are many ways to be "smart," and all of those should be celebrated. My brother never felt celebrated in school, never felt "smart," and he's one of the smartest people I know.

I'm not saying that I didn't get frustrated with my brother, because I did! There were many nights that I'd just tell him the answers for his math work so he could get finished with it. There were nights that I wrote the papers and he copied them in his own handwriting. The nights that we just quit and went to bed are innumerable! I thought that surely it didn't have to be that way. I excelled in school, but that didn't make me any smarter than my brother. We were forced to play the same game and follow the same rules but with different sets of cards. I worked hard to be the teacher who appreciates the talents that traditional school often fails to acknowledge. I wanted not only to acknowledge those skills but also to highlight and showcase them as often as possible!

There are other parts of my story that give me my *why* as well. When my mom and dad divorced, life was difficult. The custody battle was ugly, and we struggled financially. There were many times when the money ran out before the month did. Many of the students I serve also come from families facing similar situations and much worse. At home they deal with all manner of social ills including physical abuse, drug abuse, mental abuse, and sexual abuse. So many families in my small town in rural North Carolina are living in poverty. College, for many of my students, seems like a far-away dream. Poverty becomes a cycle, and generation after generation suffers through it. Over time my *why* became breaking the cycle of poverty by empowering children to value their education and take control of their futures. My desire is to show children that poverty isn't an immovable barrier; it's an obstacle they can crush on their way to achieving their dreams.

My students are typically shocked to hear my story for the first time. I believe they imagine that we, as teachers, were raised in idyllic conditions with perfect families, that we know nothing of struggle and sacrifice. (I also suspect they believe we went to teacher school and after we graduated moved into the school building and now sleep on a cot that's stored in the closet.) The story of my childhood shatters their ideas of me growing up in idyllic conditions. On the very first day, when I share a getting-to-know-you slideshow, students meet my daughters and my husband, and I share the story of my childhood. Once they realize that I was very much like they are now, I have their undivided attention. I tell them that I believe in them, that they can provide for their own families one day, and that they don't have to live in poverty. They can have more, they can dream big, and with hard work and dedication, they can achieve those big dreams.

Have you shared your *why* with your students? Do they know what gets you out of bed in the mornings? Do they know why you *chose* to be in this noble profession? Do they know how much you believe in them? If your answer is, *I hope so*, then you need to tell them, out loud. Let them know by using your words and your actions. Make it undeniable to any learner that you are there for a reason and that reason is them. Share your story. Share your *why* with your students.

Your Passions

Your *why* gets you out of bed, but what gets you moving? Have you ever reached the point where you are just going through the motions? Have you found your safe zone and let yourself get stuck in it? Are you b-o-r-e-d?

Last spring, I realized that I had gotten bored. I kept wondering what was next. My students were already experiencing high-end virtual reality, maker-spaces had made their appearance in my district six or seven years ago, and coding had become a course all on its own at our schools. These were topics that used to light me on fire. They were once my passions in education.

I realized, however, that my passions could not be focused on the technologies available around me. Technology changes so fast that by the time I got excited about a particular tool, the next one would be available. This realization led me to focus on the many possibilities each tool or app or piece of technology made available to my students. Even that, however, wasn't enough to cure this recent boredom and get me moving. The problem was that part of my "big E" was missing. I wasn't enjoying my job anymore; it had become *work*.

It wasn't long after this that I met Dave Burgess face to face for the first time. He was giving the keynote at a conference where I was also presenting a session. I had read *Teach Like a PIRATE* a few times and had even facilitated Edcamp sessions on the philosophy behind it. Hearing him speak lit me on fire. It was life-changing! That's when I vowed to read the first fifty books that Dave and Shelley had published and learned more about myself than I ever imagined possible as a result. It was during that time that I really zeroed in on my passions.

While reading Quinn Rollins' *Play Like a PIRATE*, I realized that he knew exactly what his passions outside of education were—toys, games, and comics—and brought those into his classroom with great success. Rollins' book helped me see that I dabble in a bit of everything within educational technology and other educational trends, but that I was unsure of my true educational passions. I wasn't even halfway finished with my career in education, and I wanted to discover what my passions were, what could sustain my enthusiasm for teaching through the next sixteen years. As I reached the eighteenth book in my pile, *The Writing on the Classroom Wall* by Steve Wyborney, I worried about not having those passions nailed down. *How could I post my passions if I didn't even know what they were?* As I read the next few books in the line-up, I came upon a section about discovering your passion. (Seriously, I'm not making this up!) In *LAUNCH*, John Spencer and A.J. Juliani discuss the use of brackets to force a decision between two topics, and I used this idea to find my #EDUpassions.

Do you know your #EDUpassions? If you don't, get ready, because we're going to figure them out together!

The Process

The process works much like March Madness. During March Madness, college basketball teams compete against one another in a large-scale tournament. Fans follow along with the teams and track who remains in the tournament through the use of brackets. In each game, one team is eliminated while the other advances to play against the winning team of another game. Sixty-four teams dwindles to thirty-two teams, then to sixteen teams, and so on until only one team remains.

The first thing I did to set up my passion brackets was brainstorm any and all concepts, tools, big ideas, and lessons that get me excited about teaching. I started by thinking of tech tools, such as Google Apps for Education and BreakoutEDU, and their functions. Then I dove deeper into the coaching I do with teachers and the authentic relationships I forge with my colleagues. I simply wrote these down on a sheet of paper in no particular order. I numbered each topic one to sixty-four, and by using an online number generator so it was completely random, I was able to pit two ideas against each other in brackets, like in March Madness. I considered my passion level for each and went with my gut when choosing which idea should advance in the brackets. In a couple of the brackets, both of the passions I had listed moved forward because I honestly couldn't eliminate one or the other, or because I realized the two passions were similar and could be consolidated into one.

I narrowed them down, eliminating one of the two options at a time, until I was left with only four passions. (My brackets are available in Google Sheets at bit.ly/EduEyeExamPassionBrackets. The cells highlighted in teal blue are my original sixty-four educational passions that get me excited. You can save a copy and then create your own #EDUpassion brackets as suggested in *LAUNCH*. Just replace my passions with yours!)

My final four are:

- Making a difference in students' and teachers' lives through coaching
- Lifelong learning through being a connected educator
- Being a catalyst for change
- "Those" stories (the ones that make you tear up when you share them with others) and creating a welcoming, inclusive culture for everyone who enters the school building

I enjoy coaching teachers. I love to see the impact made on the teacher, the classroom, and, most importantly, the students through a successful coaching cycle. When the teacher and I have co-planned a lesson, co-taught it, and reflected on it together, it is easy to see the overall growth.

As a lifelong learner, I am rarely satisfied with the amount of knowledge I have. I always crave more, and I have found that one way to satisfy that craving is to be a connected educator. Being a connected educator—one who is active on a variety of social media platforms—is one of the main reasons I committed to reading those fifty DBC books in the summer of 2018. Thanks to Twitter, in particular, I had other educators cheering me on and holding me accountable, and I was able to share #DBC50Summer with so many more people. Since that summer, several educators have joined in on the fun and are strengthening their own skill sets. Being a connected educator allows me not only to learn and grow on my own but also to connect with other educators from across the country who have an affinity for DBC books and have begun their own versions of #DBC50Summer. Almost every one of the authors from the first fifty books has reached out to me with kind words after reading the #DBC50Summer posts. This blew me away and strengthened my connection with the books, and it made me adore these authors even more! Being connected has brought me and my students opportunities we likely would not have had otherwise. Because I am a connected educator and have forged relationships with so many of the authors, I continue to read, reflect, and blog about every book released by Dave Burgess Consulting, Inc.

Being a catalyst for change comes by working at my school, local, state, and national levels to revolutionize education. I greatly enjoy the work I do mentoring coaches throughout my state and serving on the North Carolina Technology in Education Society's board of directors. Being asked to share my thoughts on the national framework for Future Ready Instructional Coaches™ with Future Ready educational leaders across the nation is incredible. I was selected to spend two weeks facilitating professional development with teachers across the western half of North Carolina. I found that I was in my element, with passion oozing from every pore, while the educators in the sessions and I discussed leading change in our profession together.

My fourth and final passion is "those" students and "those" stories—the ones that touch our hearts and stay with us for years to come. These stories, often as heartbreaking as they are heartwarming, have become part of my story. Year after year, my students and I cry together and celebrate together, and their stories of overcoming adversity inspire me to continue my educational career.

"Those" stories are the ones that sustain me and many other educators across the world! They are what compel me to play an integral role in establishing an inclusive culture at my school. I want every student and staff member to feel valued. I want my administration to know they are appreciated (and that I would never EVER want to walk a day in their shoes). I want parents and community partners to know that they are always welcome. When a school has this kind of culture, there is no stopping the growth.

It took a while to nail them all down, but I feel confident that these are my #EDUpassions. These passions are what get me moving after I get out of bed in the morning. They are what excites me and makes me look forward to the new school year. It always comes back to the students for me. *They* are my *why*. *They* are my number one priority.

Once we have our focus set on the big E, no matter what the problem is, we can always put it back into perspective. We can always come back to our *why* and our passions and look forward with a renewed energy. Without the big E, we are simply spinning our wheels and wandering aimlessly.

CORRECTIVE MEASURES

- 👁 What does your "big E" represent? What's your *why*? What are your #EDUpassions?

- 👁 Go to eyechartmaker.com and create your own eye chart. Enter a word or two that represent your *why* and your passions! Share your chart using #EduEyeExam.

- 👁 How will you share your "big E" with your students?

EDUCATIONAL HINDSIGHT

Communication with Parents

Starting my career in education at twenty years old was a blessing and a curse. Parents were a bit hesitant coming into open house that first year because I looked more like someone they'd hire as a babysitter than their child's fifth-grade teacher. Several of the parents could easily have been *my* parents! I could see them speculating about my age in their heads. I knew I had to develop relationships, not only with my students but also with their parents.

A bit into my career, I had a parent who was known for being disagreeable and spent quite a lot of time complaining about their child's teacher to the principal and the community. Let's just call this parent Robin. Robin's child was not the most well-behaved student in the school. He struggled academically and was known for instigating drama behind the scenes. Knowing Robin would likely continue the same pattern of complaints, I decided to open the lines of communication a mile wide! During open house, I gave out my cell phone number . . . yes, my cell phone number. I assured the parents that if they needed me between the hours of 7 a.m. and 7 p.m., I would be happy to help with homework and discuss any concerns they had. Basically, I was available to them if they needed me.

You're probably thinking I'm absolutely insane for giving out my phone number to all of those parents. You might be right; however, do you know how many parents actually called? Not many, maybe four or five throughout the entire year. The parents who called needed help with homework or clarification regarding an item on my parent newsletter. There were a couple of calls about grades. And then there was Robin. Robin called me weekly. Robin called me to check in on her son. Robin called me to vent when she was angry with me for separating her son from the group when he was misbehaving. Robin called me to complain. But do you know what also happened? I listened. I stopped what I was doing when Robin called, and I listened. I separated my emotions and shared my side of the story with her if she was upset. I helped her son with homework. I explained mnemonics I used in class to her so she could teach her son at night. The calls became less frequent throughout the year. Robin just needed to be heard. She needed to know that she was an important part of her son's education. See, he was her world. He was her son, and she felt left out. When I busted open the doors of communication that she thought were closed and locked for so long, she stopped sharing her complaints with the community and with our administration. In fact, she stopped having complaints. I wish I could say that her son magically started academically performing on grade level that year or that he stopped instigating drama among his peers. That didn't happen. He eventually moved, but I still keep tabs on him (and many of my former students). He is now a grown man and is doing quite well. Robin and I still chat from time to time, and I always ask about her son. She never ends a conversation without thanking me for her son's fifth-grade year.

Now, I'm not telling you to give out your cell phone number to your students or their parents. The valuable hindsight I gained is how helpful it can be to open the door of communication. Let nothing hold you back from having open and honest conversations with the parents of your students. They are your number one ally! I have yet to meet a parent who doesn't want what's best for their child. Sometimes our methods may not align, but as long as our focus is on their child, we are both moving in the right direction. Let parents know from the very beginning that you are accessible to them. Set office hours, make answering emails and phone calls from parents a priority, and give various contact points—email, school phone, fax (yes, those still exist). There are now apps and learning management systems that allow for parent communication without giving out personal phone numbers. Use them.

*Note: If you choose to have office hours when you are available by phone outside of the school day, I would recommend communicating that with your administration, checking your district policies, and keeping detailed notes on what is said during those conversations.

CHAPTER 3

Dilated Eyes

I t was time for my least favorite part of the eye exam. The nurse walked in and asked if I would rather have the eye drops or the puff of air.

Neither, please.

Considering it had been sixteen years or so since my last exam, that wasn't an option. With nervous laughter, I said it would have to be the drops because there was no way that puff of air was ever going to hit my eye. (I always anticipate the worst and close my eyes milliseconds before the puff!)

Let's hit the pause button for a second. How often in education do we assume the worst of a situation? We immediately close ourselves off to the possibilities because we are afraid, self-conscious, or have too much on our plates? Let that simmer for a minute. Back to my eye exam.

The nurse proceeded to tell me about a new piece of equipment that provides even more information than a dilation or puff of air but is more expensive because insurance won't pay for it. She went on to explain that the machine captures an image of the internal structure of your eye from a flash of light, and I immediately said, "Yes, please!"

We moved into another room, she dimmed the lights, and less than three minutes later, I was done! It was kind of like having a camera flash go off right beside your eye. There was the initial blindness followed by the orbs of light dancing in front of my eyes, but that was nothing compared to the effects from the other options. There was no blurry (well, blurrier than normal) vision from dilation and no watery eyes from a puff of air! This quick test also provided my doctor with more thorough and updated information about the health of my eyes, and I was able to view an image of my optic nerve on a computer screen. Wow!

Technology in education has grown exponentially in my thirteen years in the profession. In 2006, my classroom was in a mobile unit due to an overcrowded school. In that mobile classroom, the only technology to speak of was two big, white computers with floppy disk drives and an overhead projector. Our parent-teacher organization was purchasing interactive whiteboards for classrooms. We had to write a grant proposal for our principal, explaining how students would use the board and how it would enhance learning in our classroom. I received one of the interactive whiteboards during my second year of teaching and immediately fell into the trap that so many do. I went back to what I knew. I'd only known overhead projectors, so I used the interactive whiteboard as a whiteboard, minus the interactive. It became a really expensive overhead projector, and that's all. There was no interactivity unless I was the one interacting, and that was usually limited to switching slides and erasing my pen marks as I taught my three classes of math per day.

Soon after this, iPods made their way into our school. I remember our media coordinator doing a workshop on them one day, and she made it sound like they were the next big thing! They terrified me. No way was I going to put those in my classroom and have students watch math videos in small groups. Absolutely not. I could show videos on my interactive(ish) whiteboard to the entire class, all at once.

I was *that* teacher. I was terrified of what I didn't know, so I wanted no part of anything new. Somewhere along the way, however, something changed. I would love the ability to pinpoint the exact moment that I began to let my guard down and take risks. If I could determine what caused that shift in my mindset, I would happily share the secret with each and every one of you. Rather than feeling attacked and feeling like others thought I needed more tools to be successful, I began to embrace technology. I've got to be honest, though—it was really never about fearing the technology; it was a fear about losing the control. Without the technology, I felt as though I still had full control over my class. Today, as a digital learning coach, I can empathize with the teachers who are fearful, resistant, or hesitant to use technology.

That doesn't mean I allow those hesitant teachers to be stagnant. I spend time co-planning and co-teaching lessons with them. I am their back-up, their safety net, if something in the world of technology goes wrong. As long as we are taking steps forward, even if they are baby steps, we are making progress. Because the teachers I serve teach the same subject area multiple times per day, I am able to scaffold for them. During the first lesson, I will take the lead implementing the technology while still validating the teacher as the content knowledge expert. In the second lesson, the teacher becomes more involved in the technology after hearing me troubleshoot problems as they arise. By the end of the day, the third lesson, the classroom teacher is running the show and I'm there to observe and step in, only if asked. Watching teachers feel more empowered in their use of technology throughout the day is one of the most satisfying parts of my current position. I feel like a proud mama every time!

I love looking back on these early days in the classroom because the transformation and growth, especially in regard to technology, is phenomenal. The tools have evolved to include augmented and virtual reality and artificial intelligence, and the availability of devices allows many schools to employ 1:1 initiatives or bring-your-own-device policies. I am amazed by this changing landscape because technology was the area where I struggled most as a beginning teacher. Five years later, I began a graduate program to earn a degree in instructional technology. Today, seamlessly incorporating technology into the classroom and helping others do the same is a deep passion of mine.

What fascinates me are not the tools themselves; it's what those tools do to simplify a process and how they enhance the learning environment. It's about creation and publishing. As Dave Burgess has said from the stage many times, "We want creators, not consumers; makers not memorizers." The technology tools of today and tomorrow allow us another access point into creation and making. Anytime I am co-planning with a teacher or planning my own media lessons and we are using technology, I ask, "What are the students creating?" If students are using the tool as a glorified worksheet, we're doing them a disservice. Our students are already creating YouTube videos, publishing content through various mediums, and sharing their thoughts with the world in their free time. Why are we not using this to our advantage? Why are we not helping students navigate this digital world they live in? If we don't teach them, who will?

I challenge you to develop your own opinions about technology use in the classroom. What do you say to those who are hesitant? Do you allow others to remain stagnant, or do you help move them forward with baby steps or even giant leaps of faith? Are you enabling the use of worksheets and the regurgitation of content, or are you empowering students and teachers to create products using the technologies available to them? Have you reached that place where digital learning is simply learning?

Are your educational eyes still being dilated? Are you stuck relying on that terrible puff of air? Or are you ready to teach your students with the most advanced technology possible? My hope is that you will ponder these questions and challenge yourself to move out of your technological comfort zone.

CORRECTIVE MEASURES

- Examine your beliefs about technology. What do you like? Dislike? What excites you? What intimidates you?

- How are you currently using technology in your classroom or school?

- What framework or model for technology and digital learning do you enjoy or find most helpful?

- How can we reach a place where digital learning is just learning?

- Think of one lesson you are currently teaching. How can you enhance it by allowing students to create a product using the technologies available to them?

- Share your thoughts using the hashtag #EduEyeExam!

CHAPTER 4

Cover Your Right Eye

While at the optometrist for the aforementioned dreaded eye exam, the doctor gave me a small black paddle-like contraption and had me hold it over my left eye. I was to read the eye chart in front of me to the best of my ability (which wasn't very good, by the way), then do the same with my right eye.

Our eyes apparently work in tandem, and by testing our eyes one at a time, the doctor can see which eye is preventing us from seeing clearly. One evening I was on a Twitter chat when someone (I wish I could remember who it was so I could give this person credit) pointed out that teaching is two-fold—to be an expert teacher, we must have both pieces of the puzzle working in tandem, just like our eyes.

There is the *science* of teaching, and there is the *art* of teaching. The science of teaching is the content. It's the research-based pedagogy, the psychology, and the taxonomies we learn throughout our education courses. The art of teaching is what brings all of that to life. It's the presentation of the content and the relationships formed with the students and teachers you serve. The art of teaching is what makes you *you* in the classroom. Anyone can learn the science of teaching, but only you can bring your unique artistry into the classroom, and both of these must be at work in our classrooms if we want to teach effectively.

Mastering the art of teaching isn't enough to make us excellent teachers. If our artistry is all we are bringing to the table, we are nothing more than babysitters, entertainers, showmen. On the flip side, if we focus only on the science of teaching, we are equally ineffective at what we do. Students might be learning (emphasis on *might*), but I can just about guarantee that they aren't enjoying the class; they certainly aren't falling in love with learning.

When we cover and examine each aspect one at a time, like with our eyes during an exam, and we're honest with ourselves in reflection, we can see where our problem lies. Only when both aspects of teaching are working together can we excel at educating others and inspire a lifelong love of learning.

Are you more focused on the science or the art? Is your left eye or your right eye causing the deficit in vision? Let's go back to a few moments along my journey when I was focused on one or the other.

Science of Teaching

My first year teaching, I was a robot. Not really, but close. I had an incredible mentor teacher who helped me every step of the way. She gave me lessons, worksheets, quizzes, tests, and projects. She freely and openly gave me everything I needed to successfully teach math—like her. I had all the tools and resources I needed to make my math class a carbon copy of hers.

I still appreciate her efforts because she was doing what she believed was best. Her lessons were fantastic! Students were learning and enjoying their time in her class. She had phenomenal test scores year after year after year. Administration loved her, parents loved her, and, most importantly, the students loved her. She was an amazing teacher, and to be like her would have been a dream come true. But I was not her! No matter how many terrific lessons she handed me on a silver platter, those lessons were *her* lessons. I was not a carbon copy of her or anyone else. So, even though her heart was in the right place, this approach was akin to the disservice we do our students when we don't allow them to engage in productive struggle.

I'm not saying her method wasn't effective, because it was. I had terrific test scores my first year of teaching. They were pretty incredible, if I'm being honest. It makes sense, if you think about it. I taught the exact same lessons, worded in the same way, as a master teacher. I was "teaching to the test" and didn't even know that was a *thing* yet. I never would have understood that saying then, and I certainly didn't have the awareness to incorporate my own passions and my own voice into my first classroom. The science of teaching was all I was focused on. I was building relationships outside of the classroom, but I wasn't bringing those relationships into the classroom. I was a robot. My students were robots. They did worksheet after worksheet, page after page in the workbook, and packet after packet of "fun and festive" holiday activities (a.k.a., worksheets). Let's be honest for a moment: putting a snowman on a worksheet doesn't make it fun, nor does it make it festive. It's a worksheet for crying out loud. They. Are. Not. Fun.

My students didn't know who I was. I was twenty years old teaching nine-to eleven-year-olds. It was the perfect opportunity to form bonds that would last a lifetime, and I missed it. I was so focused on making sure they were ready for that test that I didn't take the time to get to know their hopes and dreams and weave them into the class content.

Art of Teaching

I am not one who gets into the creation of bulletin boards. Never have been. I put up one bulletin board and leave it there all year. It is asking too much for me to come up with creative themes month after month. My one enjoyment each month is changing the calendar. Anyone who works with me knows that changing the calendar is my jam. I take intense pleasure in taking off the Velcro numbers, stapling the new month at the top of the board, and highlighting birthdays, holidays, and special occasions. What joy to know that one month is completed and new opportunities are on the horizon. When I was on maternity leave with my youngest daughter, my assistant and substitute teacher sent me a message letting me know that they had—gasp—changed my calendar. I was out for eight weeks, so it had to be done; it did break my heart a bit. To this day, I still love switching the calendars at my house.

I love telling stories while I teach. There is power in a well-told story and in the age-old practice of storytelling. Storytelling has been around as long as humans, with generation after generation sharing tales of life, love, daring adventures, mystery, heartbreak, and victory both verbally and through images and written words. I love to hear a good story. I get pulled in and captivated by a great story. This is perhaps why my fourth-grade teacher is one of my very favorites. She taught in story frequently and always had my undivided attention.

When I failed at bringing myself to the classroom, I realized one of the elements that I was missing was the art of storytelling. I began to tell stories and weave them into my content. There were times, however, that I'd get so into telling a story that I'd forget the content. Those are the times that I totally forgot the science of teaching. I forgot that, ultimately, my students need to understand the content, not just to pass a test but also to be successful.

Every year, I would share a story about my wedding to teach students how to factor. I would hook them by sharing pictures of my wedding and telling funny stories about that crazy day. The big moment of the church doors opening and the bride walking through was a disaster for me! The door swung back and hit me square in the face. My brother, Jacob, was walking me down the aisle and couldn't stop laughing. I was furious. The food didn't make it to the reception, so our extended family was frantically transporting food from the restaurant next door to our reception venue. They were doing all they could to make the food presentation beautiful for our guests while the bridal party was taking pictures for over an hour after the ceremony because of other circumstances before the ceremony even began.

Although my stories about my wedding were super fun for me to tell, we had a blast laughing together, and I loved showing off the pictures, sometimes it would be nearly time for class to be over before I even got to the part about the wedding cake and how it related to finding factor pairs. It was important that the students created memorable connections, but it was even more important that the students be able to find the greatest common factor so they could simplify fractions the following week.

I had to find a way to stop the pendulum from swinging to the extremes. I needed to combine the science of teaching and the art of teaching to create a memorable experience for my students that was authentically me and still connected to curriculum. It took a few years, a few iterations, and several

"Which is better, one or two?" moments to make it happen, but when it did, wow, it was good stuff!

Roprah and Quadrilateralville

When I was growing up, *The Oprah Winfrey Show* (eventually shortened to just *Oprah*) would come on every day at 4:00 p.m. This was about the time my grandmother would start making dinner for my grandfather (and sometimes my brother and me if my mom was working late), and the television would just stay on that channel after she had watched her daily soap operas.

Oprah was so captivating. She would interview guests on her show, tell stories, and give away prizes to her audience members. Oprah was so full of life and enthusiasm. I would watch her and not even realize an hour had gone by when the show ended. Her ability to tell stories and ask thought-provoking questions, and the way she would have you laughing one moment and crying the next, was everything that made a talk show wonderful.

Every year, my fifth-grade students would struggle with geometry.

Lines and angles? No problem.

Types of polygons? Check!

Identifying various quadrilaterals and their properties? Not. Happening.

It was the same story year after year. Since that first year of teaching to the test and being unhappy as a copycat teacher, I consciously looked for ways to implement storytelling into the classroom. There would be days that I would have a well-planned lesson and literally change my plans mid-sentence because of something I heard a student say or something that crossed my mind or caught my eye. Those were the days that magic happened in our classroom.

On one of those days, in the middle of class, "Roprah" was born.

I told the kids that we had a guest speaker coming to class and I expected their best behavior and full participation. I rarely did the guest speaker thing at the time, so they were instantly intrigued. Glancing up at the door, I told them our guest had arrived. I would go "greet our guest" just outside the door, and when I walked back in, I had transformed the way I walked, the way I talked, my mannerisms, everything. Full of energy and flamboyance, I strutted into the classroom saying, "Hello, boys and girls, welcome to our show! I'm so glad you could be here. Today we have a few guests that need your help! Do you think you can help them?"

I had them. A fire drill could have happened at that very moment, and those kids would not have moved until they heard more of the story. One student shot a hand into the air and, before being called on (of course), shouted, "What's your name?"

I hadn't even considered that. Oops. It was a spur-of-the-moment lesson change. Where did I turn? Back to those afternoons at my grandmother's house. I told them my name was Roprah—Ray + Oprah. (I never thought I'd write about this in a book, ever.) Looking back now, I wish I had come up with a more creative name, but it stuck, so here we are (apologies, Oprah!).

The talk show continued, complete with commercial breaks where Roprah would need to go powder her nose and Mrs. Ray would reappear and discuss what had happened on the show. I would explain the mathematical connections and have the students capture the talk show in their notebook and then hustle off when "hearing" that the show was about to go live again.

Without further ado, I give you *Roprah and Quadrilateralville*.

Quadrilateralville was situated between Triangleville and Pentagonville. General Quadrilateral ran the town, and he was a pretty strict fellow, as you can imagine. He required that anyone taking up residence in Quadrilateralville have four sides and four angles. It didn't matter if their sides were perpendicular or parallel as long as they met the requirements of four sides and four angles. Once upon a time, General Quadrilateral required the sum of the interior angles of each citizen to be 360 degrees, but then he realized that as long as citizens met the first two rules, they would automatically meet the 360-degree rule as well. He let that rule go in the name of compromise.

One day a troublesome young man by the name of Tricky Trapezoid showed up at the town's gates. He looked quite different from the others, but he met the requirements of four sides and four angles, so he was allowed inside. He gained quite the reputation and gave General Quadrilateral a really hard time. Tricky Trapezoid was constantly being bullied by others.

There was a young lady in one of his classes who took pity on him. Everyone liked her; she was positive and perky and pretty, and her name was Popular Parallelogram. She realized that just because he looked different from most of the townsfolk, he shouldn't be treated differently. One day, she noticed that Tricky Trapezoid was sitting alone and went over to strike up a conversation. She wanted to learn his story, but Tricky Trapezoid felt trapped and terrified. He refused to talk to Popular Parallelogram, which is why they are appearing on Roprah today.

At this point, I paused for a commercial break and we discussed the storyline so far, creating notes for a general quadrilateral, trapezoid, and parallelogram.

Popular Parallelogram is a guest on our show today and brought Tricky Trapezoid to see if we could ask the right questions to bring him out of his shell. After lots of prying and coaxing, Tricky Trapezoid finally confided—and this may be a bit much for many audience members, so beware if you are younger than nine years old—that he had been wrongly accused of some crime while residing in Triangleville. The only punishment that was appropriate for him was banishment from his country. How was he banished from Triangleville? They cut off the top of his head and sent him away.

(I showed my class a graphic of a triangle with the top section removed.)

Because of this, Tricky Trapezoid felt unloved and unwanted. Popular Parallelogram, with tears in her eyes, hugged Tricky Trapezoid and assured him that even though he looked different, as he only had one pair of parallel sides and she had two, they would be friends forever.

During the next commercial break, we captured all we learned about a parallelogram and a trapezoid.

Popular Parallelogram is seen visibly upset after the commercial break. After inquiring, Roprah discovers that Parallelogram wishes everything was that easy to solve and requests that Roprah speak to her friends Rowdy Rhombus, Romantic Rectangle, and Sassy Square. Roprah, of course, complies and brings on the new guests.

> *Sassy Square and Popular Parallelogram are best friends, but lately Sassy has been spending a lot of time lamenting over her boy troubles, and Popular Parallelogram is just tired of hearing about it.*

(In fifth grade, this is a hot-button issue.)

> *Both Romantic Rectangle and Rowdy Rhombus believe Sassy Square should be his girlfriend, but she doesn't know which shape to choose. She and Romantic Rectangle both have four right angles, four sides, and opposite sides that are parallel, but she and Rowdy Rhombus are alike in that all their sides are congruent. Sassy Square is so torn. Roprah suggests they take a commercial break to have an off-the-air discussion.*

At this point I, as Mrs. Ray, asked students to capture their thoughts and debate which shape Sassy Square should choose. Now picture this: we have had an entire production, I'm talking foreign accents, sashaying, and the like. The kids are hooked, but it's time for math class to end, so they will have to tune in to *Roprah* the next day to see what Sassy Square decides. The students' groans were my favorite part!

To discover who Sassy Square will end up "dating," I passed out index cards and square sticky notes the next day. We folded the index cards along the diagonal (from corner to corner) and saw that an index card has only two lines of symmetry. The sticky note, however, has four lines because both diagonals are lines of symmetry. There was discussion about a rhombus being a square tilted on one vertex and the lines of symmetry for that.

Sassy Square ends up choosing Rowdy Rhombus, but the good guy doesn't finish last. As it turns out, Romantic Rectangle sees how much he and Popular Parallelogram have in common, so they all decide to double date.

After sharing this two-day story and documenting the details from *Roprah*, students showed incredible knowledge of the properties of quadrilaterals and how to identify them, as evidenced by tremendous gains on the standardized tests in these areas. I had a winner!

In the following years (and changing objectives), *Roprah's* cast also included a Kite who spent so much time in the clouds that we didn't get to chat with her much. We did get a few elusive photos of her and used that to document her existence. She became like the Loch Ness Monster of Quadrilateralville.

Quadrilateralville developed more and more with every passing year. Students began creating emojis of what the characters looked like in their minds. They crafted fake social media profiles using platforms like fakebook and twister from classtools.net. In the end-of-year letters that the current class would write to the next class, Roprah was mentioned nine out of ten times! "Just wait until you meet Roprah!" they would say. Thanks to some incredible student teachers and fellow teachers in my professional learning community (PLC) during that time who went on to become administrators, Quadrilateralville has reached new heights in my district. Even my own daughter came home and told me about Quadrilateralville one afternoon. I couldn't help but smile and remember those incredible times with my students.

One night I was at a basketball game at the middle school I currently serve, and a young man with a full beard approached me and asked, "Wait a minute, are you Mrs. Ray?" After a quick, "Yes, what's your name?" I discovered that the bearded fellow had been in my fifth-grade class eight years ago. He immediately, without any hesitation at all, mentioned Roprah—complete with a finger snap and everything. (That was indeed a piece of the puzzle. It was a production, I'm telling you!) I could not believe that he remembered Roprah that well and asked him why it was so fresh on his mind. He told me he would never forget Roprah as long as he lived. I quickly quizzed him on the attributes of a quadrilateral (because I could), and he could still tell me every single one.

Moments like that always fill me with happiness because they are proof that I was able to combine the science of teaching and the art of teaching with incredible success in the classroom. I want to replicate that experience for as many students as I possibly can.

CORRECTIVE MEASURES

- What is the difference between the science of teaching and the art of teaching? How do you see those differences play out in your teaching?

- Which one do you do better?

- How can you strengthen your other "eye" so that you can see and teach more clearly?

- What is a successful lesson from your bag of teacher tricks that you can replicate and tweak with each new iteration?

- Share your thoughts using #EduEyeExam.

EDUCATIONAL HINDSIGHT

Teacher and Mother

All parents really want what's best for their child. They want them to be happy. They send us their most precious asset, their child, and sometimes they are as lost as we are when behavior concerns creep up. At a parent conference for one particular student, I was discussing some concerns I had regarding the behavior of this child in class. We discussed possible rewards and consequences, none of which had worked thus far. Both of the parents looked at each other and asked me a question I'll never forget, one that shattered my heart. The parents looked up at me and innocently asked, "Mrs. Ray, do you have any children?"

I need to explain why this question was so devastating. It broke my heart because by this point in my life, my husband and I had endured not one, not two, but three miscarriages. We desperately wanted a child to love.

Now it was my turn to have tears in my eyes as I told them that no, I did not have children of my own. They said something next that still echoes in my mind and my heart: "Then you can't possibly understand."

See, they were implying that until I became a parent, I wouldn't be able to understand their struggles with their child. And in some respects, they were right; however, what they couldn't possibly know, because I was a very private person in regard to my personal life, was that their child, along with the others in the class, kept me going every day. Helping their child make good choices was as important to me as the teacher as it was to them as the parents, and coming to work every day and teaching these students, including their child, busied my mind so I wasn't thinking about my infertility every moment of the day.

My husband and I now have two beautiful daughters. They are so very different. Our oldest daughter, Bailey (and I still struggle to say *oldest* because our three babies that we lost are still very much in our hearts), is a people pleaser; she wants to make the world smile. She does well in school because she wants her teachers and her father and me to be proud of her. She plays the game of school well, like I did. She has the kindest, most gentle spirit and amazes me every single day. Our youngest daughter, Sophie, is a rebellious spirit. She tells the most hilarious jokes and has the cutest, most contagious laugh. She has wit that is unmatched by any child her age. (I may be a bit biased.) She is currently struggling in school with appropriate behavior and social skills. We jokingly refer to her as our Sour Patch Kid—sour, then sweet. She was recently diagnosed with Type 1 Diabetes and is one of the strongest and bravest kids I've ever known. When we went on a family vacation and our daughters got to have a little boutique makeover, Bailey chose a tiara, and her "makeup" was comprised of pastels, the romantic color palette. She walked around the rest of the day like a delicate princess. Sophie got hot pink hair extensions, bright red lipstick, and told us she wasn't a princess—she was the queen. One day after their bus had dropped the girls off at my school, Sophie, who was in kindergarten at the time, ran down the hall, so very proud of herself, yelling, "Mama, I didn't slap anybody today," while Bailey just buried her head in her hands. *That's our girls!*

I learn lessons every day as a parent that give me tools and experiences that make me a better teacher, but do I believe you have to be a parent to be a good teacher? Absolutely not!!!

The lessons I learned in hindsight actually affect me more as a parent than as a teacher. As a parent, I do my best not to judge my children's teachers. I try to remember that they have their own trials outside of school. They may be struggling to make ends meet financially or have broken relationships. They may be enduring their own struggles with infertility or have a sickness in their family I will never know about. I am on my children's teachers' team! I treat them with the utmost respect and never question them in front of my children. I want my daughters to see their teachers, their father, and me as a united front working together to help them be successful, productive citizens.

I don't believe the parents in the conference ever meant any harm when they asked if I had children; I believe they were just at their wits' end and searching for answers. That question is one I will never forget, though. It taught me a valuable lesson about teachers, judgment, and our roles in life. I continue to use this lesson to remind myself that everyone has a story—the students I serve, their parents, the teachers and administrators I am blessed to work with, and you. You have a story. Every plot line has a conflict. Many of us have several. It's what makes us who we are and what makes us effective in the classroom.

CHAPTER 5

Which Is Better: One or Two?

How many of you knew exactly what this was referring to when you read it? How many of you read it in a monotone voice? (My voice sounded suspiciously like Ferris Bueller's teacher calling the roll, in case you were wondering.)

Most of us associate this saying with the eye doctor. I'd be willing to bet this question is asked at every single optometry appointment. All of them. Everywhere. Every appointment I can remember has included the same series of questions. In my case, it went something like this (paraphrasing of course):

> Doctor: I need you to sit up straight, press your forehead against the bar, and look through the lens at the mirror ahead to read the letters behind you. When you're ready, begin.

Me: (Correctly reads a line of letters)

Doctor: Okay, great! Now, looking at the same line of letters, I'd like for you to tell me which is better: One (click, click) or two (click)?

Me: What am I looking for?

Doctor: When do the letters become more focused? Sharper?

Me: Oh, okay.

Doctor: Again, which is better: One (click, click) or two (click)?

Me: Two.

Doctor: Okay, terrific. Again, which looks better: Three or four?

Me: Hmmm . . . four.

Doctor: And now: Five or six?

Me: Um . . .

Doctor: Five (click) or six (click)?

Me: I think five.

Doctor: Okay, so how about now? Which makes the letters look as if they're jumping off the page: Seven (click, click) or eight (click)?

Me: Hmmm, may I see seven again?

This went on for about ten minutes. We ventured into the world of letters after reaching "Eleven or twelve?"

There are two main parallels between what the optometrist was doing and how we can evaluate our own educational eyes. Both are equally important and worth discussing.

Attitude

At no point did my optometrist seem aggravated with me. She wasn't bothered by my need to see number seven again. She was patient, thoughtful, caring, and willing to continue working until I could see to the best of my eyes' ability. Can you imagine if my doctor had huffed and puffed her way through the exam, if she had exhibited body language that made me feel as though she had other things to do? She didn't seem to worry at all about the patient in the next room. Her devotion, at that moment, was to me.

I'm the type of person who will shut down when I think I'm a nuisance to someone else. If I had sensed that my eye doctor was annoyed or frustrated with me, our conversation would have gone very differently, and my prescription for glasses would have been completely wrong, likely damaging my eyes even further. My doctor's attitude was one of service and kindness.

How many times have I failed to have that kind of attitude? How many times have I mumbled under my breath or exhibited dismissive body language when working with a student who needed extra help to understand a new, or even a not-so-new, concept? We often do this without even realizing it. How demeaning it must be to that student who needs us!

Would we act that way toward a child learning to walk for the first time? My niece is eleven months old. She loves to stand up and will walk while holding onto something, but she hesitates to walk on her own. She will hold my finger and walk all around the house, but the second I try to free my finger to allow her to walk on her own, she drops to the floor and starts crawling. When she does this, I don't walk back to my sister-in-law and say, "She refuses to do it alone, so just forget it. Just let her crawl for the rest of her life. She'll never be able to walk, so I suggest we just stop trying!" Even writing it seems insane! She just isn't able to walk alone *yet*. What might help her walk on her own faster? Allowing her to build her confidence by holding on to our fingers, the wall, the coffee table, her walker—anything she can. When she is ready, when she feels confident, she will take off, and we will not be able to stop her!

Apply that same thought process to a student in your class who is struggling. You've been working with her for a month on adding and subtracting fractions with unlike denominators. She can do it beautifully while you sit with her and coach her through the steps, but the second you walk away, her hand is in the air and she asks the same question for the 618th time. What do you do? You answer it, for the 618th time. You do whatever it takes to support her until she has built up the courage and confidence to do it on her own. Because when she is ready, when she feels confident, she will take off, and you will not be able to stop her! Maybe it's the 619th time that it clicks. Maybe it's the 718th time. Who knows?

What we do know is that our attitudes play a role in building our students' confidence. If we absolutely cannot contain our frustration, we must find more creative ways to help them. Try recording a screencast of you working a problem, then allow that student to watch it as many times as needed. Make a flowchart that shows the steps. Assign a peer tutor, and when that student gets frustrated, assign another peer tutor. Do not give up. Do all you can to maintain a positive attitude, much like my optometrist did throughout my eye exam.

Iterations

That eye doctor went through iteration after iteration until she found the prescription I needed to allow me to see better. She could have stopped at iteration ten. But she didn't, thankfully.

When I was in high school, I was a cheerleader. During football season, our marching band would create a CD of their songs for us to practice our dances to. We would spend practices creating dances to new songs and count out the steps as we danced. Once the dances were created, we would devote hours of time, both during practice and individually in front of our mirrors at home, doing the steps again and again and again. We would eventually feel good enough about the routine to perform it during a Friday night football game. This would never happen unless we completed all the practice hours and revisited the routine again and again.

Whenever we made an error with the dance moves, we would review the correct step, then try again. Sometimes we would even decide that a particular move was just too difficult for the whole squad to perfect, so we would change the dance to something everyone was able to master.

In the classroom, we don't have direct control over our standards; in most cases, however, we do have control over how we teach them. When something doesn't work quite right the first time, don't throw it out; change it up. When something works great, don't assume it will work as well the next year; you will have a different audience with different needs, and it might not work as flawlessly as it did the year before!

An iteration is simply the repetition of a process, and we should be willing to rethink and adjust our lessons every time we repeat them. When I created Roprah and Quadrilateralville, the character of Popular Parallelogram didn't exist until the second or third iteration. The kite was added because of a change in the standards during my final year of teaching fifth grade. Even though it was an extremely successful lesson, every iteration was slightly different from the one before. And just because a lesson doesn't work once doesn't mean that it won't work again with some tweaks. When the lesson doesn't work time and time again, however, it's definitely time to find something new. As they say, "Back to the drawing board."

When I was teaching math three times a day, I was presenting the same content, activities, and experiences, but I *never* taught the same lesson. In his book, *Pure Genius*, Don Wettrick shares some valuable advice from his dad. His dad, Chuck, told him during his second year of teaching, "Son, I don't care if you teach for the next twenty years, but promise me you won't teach one year twenty times." An iteration is not a carbon copy. No lesson will ever be good enough to repeat year after year. Even the best lessons lose relevance over time. Teaching a lesson using fidget spinners now won't have the same impact it did a few years ago. We need to change it up.

With that in mind, I'm now going to upset some people, so if you are easily offended, simply skip over the next couple of pages and continue reading from there. For the rest of you, you know that filing cabinet in your classroom? That closet with file folders in carts organized by standard? The binders full of worksheets in sheet protectors? Be like Elsa, and let it go! You cannot convince me that the outstanding lesson that was passed down to you from the teacher who had the room before you ten years ago is going to be effective for your students today. Have a purge party! Grab some of your educator friends, pull the carts of file folders into a room together, bring your favorite snacks, and purge, purge, purge! At a minimum, at the end of each year, go through your files and decide what's worth salvaging, what can be tweaked and improved, and what needs to be discarded.

Next to librarians, teachers are some of the worst packrats. (Trust me, I know—I am both.) We keep e-v-e-r-y-t-h-i-n-g. That bulletin board border from sixteen years ago? Yeah, I might need that! The dried-up glue stick? I can use that to show students what happens when they don't put the lid on properly. The electric pencil sharpener that no longer sharpens pencils? That's a terrific maker project!

No, no, no. Let it go! The white snowflakes on that bulletin board border are now yellow, and everyone knows not to go near yellow snow! The dried-up glue stick will be replaced with another example of a dried-up glue stick in less than a week. Give it time. Those electric pencil sharpeners are expensive and sharp—don't give them to a child to try to repair! They are SHARPeners. But I digress . . .

What I'm saying is that you need to give yourself permission to do a deep clean. Allow yourself to keep only the best of the best. It will force you to discover new ideas year after year, keeping you fresh and relevant. It also helps you stay interesting and will likely rejuvenate you as well. Unless you truly believe it's going to make an impact on students in the next 365 days, pass it on to someone else or throw it away.

CORRECTIVE MEASURES

- Examine your attitude. What does your body language say to the student who needs you?

- What classroom activities or experiences can you tweak to make them more relevant?

- What lessons and resources can you purge from your educational repertoire?

- What do you have that is pure gold that you can share with others? Are you sharing it? If not, why not? Go share it now using #EduEyeExam!

CHAPTER 6

Tunnel Vision

Have you ever experienced tunnel vision? It's that sensation of only being able to see that which is directly in front of you. There are some instances when tunnel vision is a good thing, like when horses wear blinders to keep them focused on what's ahead of them, but it's usually a disadvantage when we can't use our peripheral vision as well. Of course, there are cases of extreme peripheral vision—we call it having "eyes in the back of our head." Only kidding.

Let me paint you a picture. Every Thursday night my daughters have back-to-back, hour-long basketball practices. The youngest starts at 6:00 p.m., and the oldest wraps up between 8:00 p.m. and 8:30 p.m., so every week I spend roughly two and a half hours at the gym. I'm going to be perfectly honest—these practices are painful to watch. Practice is for growth, and though I know it's good for my girls to engage in productive struggle, the mama bear in me wants to cuddle them up and encourage them when they make a mistake. Any coach would tell you that practice isn't the time or place for cuddles, so I do everything I can to remain busy throughout practice.

During one particular practice, I was sitting on a rather uncomfortable folding chair in a chilly gymnasium during the second hour of practice. Siblings of those practicing were shooting the basketball at the side goals. The aforementioned uncomfortable chairs are under the side goals. Can you see where this is going?

I experienced this phenomenon of tunnel vision while typing frantically on my computer, doing everything but paying attention to what was going on around me. I didn't even see the ball coming after it bounced off the rim. Luckily, no one (and no laptop) was hurt. If I had been aware of my surroundings and attentive to those kids shooting at the basket rather than checking social media, I would have put a hand out to stop the ball before it hit me.

How often does this happen in our educational careers? How many times do we get so focused on what we're doing that we fail to experience what's going on around us? Let me put it another way. How many times are we so focused on teaching the history content that we miss the perfect opportunity to pull in reading strategies? How often are we pushing to get through graphs in math class that we neglect to discuss why the population of a particular animal is declining at a rapid pace as shown in a graph? How many learning opportunities, how many teachable moments, do we miss with our students because we have tunnel vision?

Spiral Curriculum

Having peripheral vision in education is about seeing what is around us and asking how many different content areas we can integrate into one activity. Spiraling curriculum is one of the key instructional strategies for great teachers. They find ways to make connections and revisit content throughout the year in a meaningful and purposeful manner.

Think through the experiences you have prepared for students in the coming week. Where are the opportunities to incorporate something you've already covered this year? It is amazing what can happen in learning when we take just two minutes to reinforce a skill that was covered weeks before.

It's like my daughters' basketball practice. They dribble, shoot, guard, pass, run, rebound, and then do it all again. They isolate problem areas, and the coach watches to see how they apply the knowledge in a simulated game-like experience. The players hit every skill multiple times, and at their next practice, the coaches won't just assume that they remember those plays and the skills from the last practice; they will incorporate those skills again and again.

What does this model look like in a classroom? A teacher observes a problem area in her classroom—students are struggling with rules for plural nouns. A poor teacher will ignore the area or, worse, blame the students and think, *I've taught it, so they should have learned it.* A good teacher will acknowledge the problem and create a mini-lesson covering the rules of plural nouns, complete with a two-column chart. A great teacher will complete that mini-lesson and revisit plural nouns when it pops up in reading. An excellent teacher, however, will intentionally create opportunities for plural nouns to be in all content areas over and over again, spiraling consistently until every student has mastered that skill.

Sharing Ideas

Another example of tunnel vision is when we are so focused on what's going on within our own classroom or school that we fail to look around us and see what others are doing. I was guilty, at least once or twice, of leaving a professional development session with the full intention of closing my classroom door and continuing to do what I've always done with no regard for the incredible strategy I had just learned. Why are we not tapping into the strengths of the educators around us?

I was part of a professional learning community that excelled at tapping into its members' individual strengths. After discovering our strengths of reading strategies, technology use in math centers, and math and science instruction, we were unstoppable. We began utilizing those strengths at every meeting we held. All of that preparation would have been pointless if we had not committed to one key action: we shared. Our students were the sole beneficiaries of this act of sharing. We tweaked and adapted the lessons to meet the needs of the respective students in our classrooms, but the bones of the lessons stayed in place, and they were strong. We trusted one another to create exceptional experiences for all of our students. There was no "my students" and "your students." We truly operated under the belief that all of the students were *our* students.

With the fierce competition created through test scores and assigning report card grades, it's easy to forget that we are all on the same team. It doesn't matter if we are responsible for educating the kids in our classroom or down the hall, in the next district or on the other side of the world, we are all responsible for educating our future. The students sitting in our classrooms right now will be the difference-makers in our world. The world doesn't ask students if they were in Mrs. Ray's fifth-grade class or Mr. So-and-So's fifth-grade class! Let's stop competing with one another and start sharing ideas!

Connect

Last year, my community group from my church studied the book *My One Word* by Mike Ashcraft and Rachel Olsen. It was the first time I'd ever heard of using one word to define the year, and I loved it! I rarely made New Year's resolutions because I knew I wouldn't keep them, no matter how good my intentions were, but the idea of needing to remember only one word was intriguing to me.

My word was *moderation*. My reason for choosing that word was that it applied to many aspects of my life: financial moderation, moderation in eating unhealthy foods, moderation at work, and so on. I'm a bit obsessive when I put my mind to something. My focus is laser-like, often to a fault, when it comes to achieving my goals. If I want something, I will push and push until I get it or until I've exhausted all options. I laugh every time I think of that being my word because last year reflected anything but moderation.

This year, my word is *connect*. Not only do I want to connect with others through social media and face-to-face conversations to share ideas, but I'm also looking to connect my students to others across the globe. This year, my students have had the pleasure of editing Allyson Apsey's (@AllysonApsey) novel for middle school students and connecting with Karen Caswell's class in Australia. (You should follow her on social media @kcasw1.) This has been an eye-opener for my students as they have seen that the interests of students in Australia are similar to their own here in the United States. They have been exposed to other cultures, and their minds were blown when they first heard the accent of the students in Australia (as I'm sure the Australians were shocked at our southern American accents.) For my students, this was a first step toward developing empathy for others. They have seen that students who are "different" from them actually aren't so different after all. Eliminating cultural tunnel vision and insisting on facilitating global connections is vital to creating a generation of empathetic and respectful citizens.

We continued building on these relationships through a Global Kindness Read Aloud created by Karen, as well as collaborations with other classrooms across the world. These opportunities are incredible and memorable for everyone involved.

CORRECTIVE MEASURES

- 👁 In which areas would you diagnose yourself with tunnel vision?

- 👁 Does your PLC believe that students are "your/my" students or "our" students? How can you shift responsibilities to educate all students as "our" students?

- 👁 What are your philosophies on connecting yourself and your students to others?

- 👁 How can you help eliminate cultural tunnel vision?

CHAPTER 7

Seek Help Immediately

When I leaned my forehead against the bar to light up the road signs at the DMV and the attendant asked me to read the *letters* rather than the signs, I knew I was in trouble. Squinting and praying I had the letters correct when I read them aloud was a horrible and familiar feeling. It wasn't the first time I had waited too long to seek help.

When I was twenty years old and a senior in college, I had the privilege of interning in a fourth-grade classroom. It was there that I first noticed a pain in the heel of my right foot. It felt like a mild cramp, but it was enough to make me favor my left leg as I walked to my car to drive the forty-five minutes back up the mountain to my townhouse. When I arrived there, my roommate and I cooked dinner and settled in for the night. I mentioned that my heel had been hurting and asked for her advice. She was an avid biker, hiker, and runner, so

I suspected she would know more about my ailments than I would. We put ice on it and elevated it. She wrapped it for me the next morning, and I drove down the mountain for another day of fourth-grade excitement. During recess I jumped into a competitive game of kickball. When it was my turn to kick, I managed to connect with the ball and began my run to first base. My calf muscle cramped up and I went down on the base. An eager student took my place, and I proceeded to walk it off. When I got home, it was still aching, so I took a hot bath to relax the muscles.

This became my routine for the next three days. When I went home for the weekend to work, as I did every weekend, I shared my odd leg cramps with my mom, and she asked if I needed to see a doctor. I waved it off, thinking I had just overexerted myself and needed rest. That night I woke up in a cold sweat in the worst pain of my life. My leg was throbbing and cramps were shooting up and down my leg, from my lower back to my toes. My mom took me to the emergency room, where they gave me pain medicine and suggested that I had torn a ligament and needed see an orthopedic surgeon as soon as possible. They put an orthopedic leg brace on my leg which restricted all movement from my thigh to just above my ankle, and sent me on my way. I was lucky to get an appointment with an orthopedic surgeon on Monday morning, and it was there that I found out just how much danger I was really in.

That surgeon likely saved my life, and I do not say that for dramatic effect. After asking me a handful of questions about my symptoms, he had me stretch my toes upward. I immediately burst into tears as I experienced the most horrible explosion of pain from directly behind my knee all the way down to my toes. He looked up at my mother, who had come with me since I couldn't drive with the stabilization brace, and told her that I was not to move. He had an ambulance on the way to take me to the hospital, which was a two-minute drive from his office. I knew then that it was something very serious.

After arriving at the hospital, I was rushed to the ultrasound room where the sweetest technician tried to keep me calm as she completed an extensive ultrasound on my right leg. Pressing on my thigh, behind my leg, and on my calf was excruciating. The doctor came in and confirmed that I, at twenty years old, had an enormous blood clot lodged behind my right knee. Later we were told that it had likely formed around my heel and that the cramping was the clot slowly moving up my leg. The hematologist could not believe that I had survived for a week with this clot moving as it had. He was blown away at the size of the clot, and due to its location and size, did not feel comfortable risking a surgery that could cause pieces of the clot to move to my heart or brain and result in a heart attack or a stroke. I was placed on a high dosage of anticoagulants to thin my blood and stayed in the hospital for six days.

Six months later I was taken off the blood thinners and was told to return to the hematologist in two weeks for follow-up bloodwork. I didn't make it two weeks before needing more bloodwork, though. Within ten days, I had developed a second blood clot, this time in my left thigh. I learned that day that I have a protein S deficiency and will need to be on anticoagulants (blood thinners) for the rest of my life.

This part of my story is one that I don't share often. I'll be honest—some days I don't even think about it; I just take a pill before bed and continue my routine. But some days it scares me to my core. A normal cramp can send me into a panic attack. My condition is suspected to be the reason for my three miscarriages. I have had six iron infusions to correct anemia. I bruise easily due to the medication, and I regularly monitor my arms and legs for changes that indicate any new clots. My right leg swells noticeably, as the veins are permanently damaged. I visit my hematologist at least twice a year for a checkup, and as this is a hereditary condition, my daughters will have to be tested when they are older, as there are no physical symptoms until a clot occurs.

My diagnosis was nearly fourteen years ago, and I frequently look back on that time as a turning point in my life. It was a wake-up call. Many of us think we are invincible, but I was shown just how quickly that can change. I had also just met this wonderful guy and talked to him every day that I was in the hospital. We went on our first date a week after I was released, and less than a year later, we got married. We will celebrate thirteen years of marriage shortly after the release of this book.

I hesitated to share this story, as I don't want sympathy. Many people I work with on a daily basis don't even know this story. The lesson, however, is so important that I felt the book would be incomplete without it.

Seek help. In every aspect of your life, remember to seek help immediately when you need it.

Educators tend to feel they can do it all alone. I know because I am one of those educators. And we're wrong. We cannot do it all alone. The good news? We don't have to! As the first person in my district to be given the opportunity to formally merge instructional/digital coach and media coordinator, I felt utterly alone. Other media coordinators were afraid that we'd push too much of the technology and neglect libraries, and digital coaches did not even exist in my district, so I had to seek help from outside of my district. This help came in the form of social media. While on social media, I was digitally introduced to Nancy Mangum, associate director at the Friday Institute on the campus of N.C. State University. A few months later, Nancy reached out to share about an opportunity to apply for a new program through the Friday Institute in which educators from throughout the state would be brought together four times a year to grow professionally, connect with others, and lead within our districts. I knew this was exactly what I needed, applied, was accepted, and spent a year with the North Carolina Digital Leaders Coaching Network (#ncdlcn). After completing the program as a participant, I returned for the following three years as a mentor to new participants throughout the state and continued to soak in all the wisdom I could from those around me. I sought help and was provided with a wealth of knowledge and a professional learning network that has expanded over the past five years.

Listen to your body. When your brain is muddled, it's telling you that it needs a reboot. Put down those papers that need to be graded and get the rest you need. You'll be much more productive after a power nap. When your body is sore, listen to what it's trying to tell you. Do you need to get up and get active? Or are you pushing your body too much and need to give it a day or two to rest and heal? You know your body better than anyone. Don't ignore the aches and pains. I should have known that a cramp that lasted more than a few minutes was out of the ordinary, but I was too busy to think about it and refused to stop long enough to do anything about it.

Here's one that we all need to listen to—when your body says it's hungry, eat. Keep a bottle of water with you and drink water throughout the day. Your body needs hydration constantly. When it says it's time to go to the restroom, go! Don't put it off until lunch, or worse, the end of the day. Develop a buddy system with a neighbor educator in which you watch each other's classrooms when you need to make a pit stop!

When volunteers come in, I am usually at a loss for what to have them do, because by the time I give them instructions, I could have done it myself. I struggle to ask for help. One way to utilize them, however, is to create a folder for volunteers with some of those tedious tasks that need to be done, complete with explanations so everything's ready when they walk in. Maybe it's cutting out freshly laminated name tags or cleaning those dry erase boards that have become almost illegible with use. Have them organize your classroom library or ask them to read with students in your class. Friday Folders went home every week in my classroom. If you send home weekly folders, have volunteers place any graded papers, tests, and projects into your students' folders for parents to sign. Give them a questionnaire asking about their strengths and areas of skill and use those to benefit your students! If you're like me and struggle with bulletin boards and being creative during the door decorating contests, show them where the supplies are and let them dream something up for you.

I'm just going to put this out there: some of us are just too proud to ask for help or too controlling to accept it when offered. We need to put those feelings on the back burner. None of us can do this job alone, at least not with all of our sanity intact. We need one another, not just in our buildings but also in life. I needed my doctor to figure out what was wrong with my leg. I need my husband to help keep our household running from day to day, making sure there are clean clothes, meals on the table, and kids taken to ball games and practices. I need help from grandparents when one of our children is sick and my husband and I just cannot miss that day of work. I need fellow educators to inspire, encourage, and motivate me every single day because this career is not an easy one.

We need one another. We need to feel a sense of comfort in the deep connections that most educators share. We want to leave the world better than we found it. We want to inspire young people to continue learning even after they leave us, which will allow them to do amazing things with their lives. We want to leave a legacy, and we need to seek and accept help in order to do that. It's not about me, and it's not about you; it's about them. The best way to help them be successful is to seek help immediately when we need it.

CORRECTIVE MEASURES

- 👁 Think of a time you needed help. Did you ask for it? If you did, what happened? If you didn't, why not? Share using the hashtag #EduEyeExam.

- 👁 Could you use some help right now? Who can you ask for help? Go. Get help now.

- 👁 Do you know of someone else who needs help? Look around you. How can you lend a hand to someone who could use a bit of help?

EDUCATIONAL HINDSIGHT

Administrators Are Educators Too

My first administrator was a no-nonsense kind of principal. She expected excellence from everyone on her staff and every single student in the school.

Every day I would hear the cadence of her footsteps coming down the hall, and I'd immediately feel guilty, even if I was doing exactly what I was supposed to be doing. The staff and students at the school knew little about her personal life. When she walked through the school doors, she left behind anything outside of work that might have been on her mind. She was *always* at work. The term "larger than life" immediately comes to mind when I think of her. I'll admit it; I was scared of her.

Earlier I mentioned that my husband and I lost three babies to miscarriages before we were blessed with our two daughters. Losing our second child (on my birthday no less) contributed heavily to a particularly tough year at work. I was struggling. I will never forget the day, months later, that she visited my classroom and left me a note saying she "missed the enthusiastic Mrs. Ray" and to "come see her after school." I had been called to the principal's office—as a teacher—and I worried all day about the impending meeting.

With shaky knees, I approached her office, where I was instructed to sit down in the chair across from her desk. She shut the door to her office and took her place behind her desk. All it took was a look of genuine concern followed by, "Tell me what's going on," for me to begin to ugly-cry. I opened up to her about everything and how it was impacting me as a teacher.

The moment she realized that I had not taken time off work to grieve our lost child, to focus on self-care, she insisted that I take a few days off to begin to heal and assured me my lesson plans would be taken care of.

Through that experience, I learned that administrators are not to be feared. If I had simply shared my story with her months before, I would have saved myself, as well as my students, from many difficult days in our classroom. The administrators I've worked for genuinely care about the students and teachers they serve. I now make it a point to get to know every one of my administrators, as educators and as people. I allow them to get to know me as well. I remember that we are on the same team. Every administrator I know was a classroom teacher first. We are cut from the same cloth, and I've yet to meet an educator who doesn't ultimately want to change the lives of the children in their school. I now realize that when the vision of administration and teachers aligns, we can move mountains together.

It wasn't until I moved out of the classroom and into a school-based role that I realized just how lonely being an administrator can be. It can be very lonely as a coach as well. And there are many other "singletons" at your school. These are the people there are only one of on your campus. We can't comprehend what their professional lives are like. Just like the teachers I serve can never fully understand what it's like to be in my role, I will never fully understand the life of an administrator.

My administrators used to scare me. They are my superiors, and I was afraid to troubleshoot ideas and brainstorm together. However, I now realize that administrators light up when they get the opportunity to troubleshoot and brainstorm with their staff! My most recent administrator was amazing. I could go to her and say, "I have an idea," and we'd get to work on it! She and I would come up with a final product that was ten times better than anything either of us could have created on our own. Administrators are educators who are changing the lives not only of students but also of teachers. I highly recommend sharing space with administration and taking advantage of their knowledge to increase your own!

I challenge you to determine which leadership traits are most important to you. Determine which of those traits your administration exudes and learn from that. Form a relationship with your administration team, and thank your administrators at every opportunity.

CHAPTER 8

Diagnosis

After all the exams were finished, the optometrist rolled her chair beside me and pulled up the image of my eyeball on her computer. She proceeded to point out my optic nerve and confirmed that she saw no malformations there. She mentioned that since this was my first image, we would know more about degeneration after taking my images at my exam the following year. Then we'd have two images of the same eye side-by-side and would be better able to spot any changes.

She then went into the diagnosis phase of the appointment. I did, in fact, need glasses, and she suggested that I wear them all the time, especially when reading, working on the computer, or driving at night. I was diagnosed as being farsighted with astigmatism in both eyes, and she recommended progressive, non-glare, non-reflective, transition lenses.

What? I had no idea what she was talking about!

But I have an incredible optometrist, and she took the time to explain my diagnosis in detail. Being farsighted means that I see objects better at a distance than I do up close. Astigmatism means that I have difficulty focusing on objects. She said this could be why I often see shadows when I'm driving at night that make me think something is jumping in front of the car (deer are a real problem here in North Carolina) and why my eyes grow tired and dry after hours of reading or working on my computer. She even explained that the curvature of my eyes occurs at different places. When I left her office, I was excited to finally understand why I needed glasses and to choose glasses that would "turn back time" on my vision.

Let's take a moment and relate that experience to our jobs as educators.

The Right Kind of Feedback Is Essential

My optometrist could have easily handed me a prescription with some seemingly meaningless numbers on it and sent me on my way. How often do we do the same thing to our students? How many times have we passed back an assessment or worksheet with some arbitrary number on it between 0 and 100 (or more if you're the "extra credit" type) and expected our students to know exactly what went right and what went wrong? I'll admit it—I am guilty of this! What's worse is that there were times when I'd stand in front of the room and, with my words, tell them to let me know if they had questions, but my body language said, "You'd better not ask questions, because I went over this content weeks ago!" Now that I know better, I do better.

I am thankful that I now work in a position where I do not have to grade. There is no space on the report card with my name on it. Because of that, I've really paused to consider how I feel about grading. I have developed my own philosophy on grading and feedback that has been shaped by some incredible educators, including Rick Wormeli, Cindi Rigsbee, Carol Ann Tomlinson, Robert Marzano, and John Hattie. Oh, how I wish I had stopped to consider how I felt about grading and feedback when I was in the classroom!

I have frequently stated that grades are for parents and feedback is for students. We, as parents, understand grades because we grew up with that same scale. With a quick glance at my daughter's report cards, I know she's excelling in one particular area while struggling a bit more in another. Those grades are for me, the parent.

When her teacher takes the time to share verbal or written feedback based on a rubric or ongoing conversation, that feedback is meaningful to my daughter. Here's my question: Who is doing the learning? Who needs to know where she stands in regard to her education? She does, right? I hear a lot of talk about empowering students, but grades aren't empowering anyone. Traditional grades are, in my opinion, further evidence that our educational system is stuck in black and white while the rest of the world has moved on to more vibrant colors.

My daughter Bailey can do her very best on an assessment, stretch her thinking, give 110 percent to the task at hand, and then either be crushed or uplifted by what her teacher puts on that paper. Think about that. Every student you have is like my Bailey. We can crush their spirits—even those who appear not to care—simply with what we write on a returned paper. When they see red Xs or red circles all over the paper with a big numerical or letter grade, it's disheartening. Any review you might do of missed problems is for naught at that point because they have tuned you out. They no longer have any interest in the subject matter. They're just trying to figure out how to deal with that less-than-stellar score, even though that score often doesn't show the amount of effort that student put in. How about we ditch the red pen (please, please ditch the red pen) and acknowledge our students' efforts with meaningful feedback instead!

I consider our ability to provide good feedback to be the equivalent of a doctor's bedside manner. Some doctors, optometrists included, are incredibly brilliant but leave you feeling cold and unwanted. Maybe you've experienced this. It might have been that time that you felt more like a puzzle than a human, a mystery to be solved rather than a living, breathing being. I don't know about you, but I want a doctor who makes me feel valued, important, and cared for. Isn't that what we should give our students as well?

What's the best way to have good "bedside manner" as an educator? By giving feedback! Meaningful and encouraging feedback!

We all have those students who, despite all their hard work, still miss almost every question on your assessment. Fifteen total questions? They miss thirteen. Think of how demoralizing it must be for those students to see a "-13/15" or "13/F" written at the top of the paper!

Rather than focusing on what the student missed, why not place the emphasis on what they got right? What if we bought green pens, purple pens, or blue pens and placed a check mark beside the questions that student answered correctly? What if we put a +2 on top of the paper? What if we found pieces of correct information within the answer and bragged on that! It might take a few additional minutes on each assignment, but, hey, they spent the time taking the assessment, and we should take time grading it and giving feedback!

Remove "Good Job" from your feedback toolkit. "Good job" means nothing. Good job on what? Try some of the following instead:

- 👓 I am so proud of you for showing your thinking!
- 👓 I appreciate that you took the time to use your strategies!
- 👓 What a creative answer!
- 👓 Can you tell me more about your answer to this problem?
- 👓 It is obvious that you worked hard today!
- 👓 Keep up the hard work!
- 👓 I can tell you're determined to get this right!
- 👓 You are so close! Let's work together to finish this one!
- 👓 I'd love for you to show the class how you did _____.
- 👓 You're on the right track! Almost there!
- 👓 Helpful hint: _____.

These are just a few ways that we can respond quickly with feedback to our students! Though these are not all responses for correct answers, none of them make us feel defeated. Each response has a positive spin. Would you rather receive a paper with a +2, a couple of helpful hints, and a promise to work on it together, or a paper that has *13/F* slapped on the top with red circles everywhere? If you're a parent, what would you rather see on *your* child's paper?

The way we give feedback speaks volumes about us as educators! What does your feedback say about you?

Here's one more thought to ponder as you consider the diagnoses we give our children in the form of feedback. Did my optometrist wait a week to discuss my exam with me? Did she share her diagnosis "when she got around to it"? No! She gave me feedback immediately after the exam. I believe the educational connection is quite obvious here. Give that meaningful and encouraging feedback as quickly as possible! Once the moment has passed, it's in the past! Your feedback becomes more and more irrelevant with every passing day. Any assessment students take should drive the learning in the next lesson. Well-written assessments give us valuable information about what our students know and what they don't know. We can all agree that if students don't understand a necessary piece of content, we need to reteach that content. I believe we can also agree that if our students "have got it," we should, as shared earlier in the book, spiral the curriculum and revisit that same content as authentic applications. If assessments drive the learning, what good does it do anyone to hold on to those assessments without giving students feedback in a timely manner? If it's not important enough for you to check and respond to quickly, perhaps it wasn't important enough to take up the class time they spent doing the assessment.

Here are a few ways to check work while still giving valuable feedback and without focusing on the numerical grade:

- 👓 Digital quizzes, when used as a learning tool, can immediately give valuable feedback to students! Create a Google Form with feedback for correct and incorrect responses. Link those incorrect responses to a terrific YouTube video to show how to answer correctly!

- 👓 Have peers review one another's work! Allow students to coach one another through the incorrect answer! Be sure to model appropriate feedback with students.

- 👓 Use a rubric and have students score themselves before turning in the assignment. Verify their score through your own feedback.

- 👓 Allow students to be creative in showcasing their mastery of content! If students are presenting their content to the class, you can become the student and give feedback in written form during their presentation.

- 👓 Use digital video tools like Flipgrid or Screencastify to record your feedback verbally and share the link with the student.

There are many options for giving meaningful, encouraging, and timely feedback to students. I was given meaningful, encouraging, timely feedback by my optometrist and was immediately able to select and order my glasses so my vision was corrected as quickly as possible!

CORRECTIVE MEASURES

- 👁 Examine the feedback you gave on the last assignment. Did it resonate with your learners upon returning it? What would you do differently to make it more timely, encouraging, or relevant?

- 👁 If you could choose only one adjective to describe the feedback you give (meaningful, encouraging, timely), which would you choose and why?

- 👁 What is your personal philosophy about grading and feedback? What experiences shaped this philosophy?

- 👁 Share your thoughts using the hashtag #EduEyeExam.

CHAPTER 9

Nearsighted or Farsighted?

Discovering that I was farsighted with astigmatism let me know I needed vision correction. I chose to get glasses and spent quite some time scouring the wall for the perfect frames. This corrective eyewear allows me to see objects both near and far, and the blurry vision has been cleared.

What about our "eyesight" as educators? Do we need corrective eyewear for our nearsightedness? Or are we too farsighted? Let's explore what that means metaphorically.

Nearsighted

Being nearsighted means that we see things up close better than we see objects at a distance. Nearsighted teachers are the ones who are so focused on the here and now that they lose sight of what comes later. There have been times in my personal life where I am so overwhelmed that I can't think past the day at hand. It drives Chris, my husband, crazy when he is trying to plan something and I tell him that I can't think about that event just yet.

Just this year, we took our family on a much-needed vacation. We spent a week aboard the *Fantasy*, a ship in the Disney Cruise Line fleet. This trip was scheduled for the week before Thanksgiving, and upon our return, we had two district-wide events at my school. My workspace is the media center, and if there is an event in the school, it typically involves the media center. My calendar was full. I was scheduled to facilitate virtual reality experiences for multiple students as well as plan for our annual STEMposium, an event that brought in future students and their families. When Chris asked me at the beginning of November what time we were available to go to his mom and dad's to celebrate Thanksgiving, I told him that I didn't care and couldn't think that far ahead right then. As we were waiting in the airport to fly to Orlando, he asked again. My answer hadn't changed. On our return, while waiting to fly back to Charlotte (the Saturday before Thanksgiving), he asked again. By that point, I was exhausted, and my focus was making sure we were at the correct terminal. I was also trying to write, answer the hundreds of emails I had missed, and ensure that I was ready for the events at school that coming week, so my answer was the same: "Babe, I can't think past right now." On Monday evening, he asked again. When my answer remained the same, he was visibly frustrated with me. On Tuesday afternoon, I was finally ready to have a conversation about when we were available for Thanksgiving to see his parents. It was too late; the decision had already been made.

He had to make that decision without me because I had been so near-sighted. I tend to get that way when my plate is full. If I can just get through a day at a time, I am able to be more productive and more successful at what I'm doing at that moment. What are you nearsighted about? Are there times of the year when you can only manage one day at a time?

Sometimes being nearsighted leads to consequences that we must deal with, whether it's going to the in-laws for Thanksgiving in the middle of the afternoon rather than midday, or a consequence with more severity.

Think about those times when we should work to correct our educational nearsightedness. When we're handling discipline issues with children, we must always ensure that we are not operating with nearsighted vision; otherwise, we may say something out of anger or disappointment that is hurtful to the relationship with the student. Perhaps you're having a rough patch with a colleague (it happens). Take a step back. Rather than focusing on the here and now, look further down the road and envision how you'd like the relationship to look in the future. It doesn't do anyone any good attempting to resolve a conflict in the heat of the moment. Your words matter. I don't know about you, but I tend to lose my filter when emotions are high. When I step back and allow a couple of minutes to pass (or more), I find that I am better able to depersonalize conflict and conduct myself in a more rational manner. Understanding that what I say directly impacts others, I realize that it is best practice to give myself, and the other party, time to calm down before continuing to discuss the topic at hand.

Farsighted

As with most things in life, going to extremes rarely leads to a positive outcome. With that in mind, we should also be wary of becoming too farsighted. Being farsighted in education is when we are so focused on the end game that we forget to live in the moment. For some people, that farsightedness might extend to a month, a semester, a year, or even farther. The farsightedness might directly coincide with a standardized assessment at the end of the semester or year.

Prepare yourself; this next sentence might not be well-received, but stay with me. Standardized tests are not the problem in education—the problem is how focused we are on those tests, how high-stakes they have become. The same can be said for any stand-alone activity that carries a disproportionate amount of weight. To set aside one day for students to show their knowledge and then use those results to determine if they pass or fail an entire year doesn't make any sense. We all have bad days. Imagine if your job came down to one lesson, one activity, one experience. Would you be stressed out? Very likely. Would you lose sleep? I would! Would you want someone else to state the obvious about how important that day is to your career? Absolutely not. Standardized tests give us a measurement of where an individual student's understanding lies in a sea of curriculum. They are important, but they should never be all we focus on. In twenty years, do you want your current students to be good test-takers or productive citizens?

I tell students at some point during the first week of school that there is an end-of-grade test and I will do everything in my power to help them learn the content that will be on that assessment. We will work hard, we will learn the curriculum, and most importantly, we will have fun doing it. Then I tell them that we won't speak of that test again until we begin our review, usually about two to four weeks before the test date. From that point on, we don't discuss it. They know the content on the assessment, but it's not about "the test"—it's about the learning.

I believe there are three main ways to achieve a balance between being nearsighted and farsighted in education:

1. Plan at least a week in advance.
2. Be present.
3. Make connections and maintain relevance.

Plan at Least a Week in Advance

Today is Friday. Before I go home, I will have next week's lessons planned and be prepared for whatever might come in the next five school days. My formative assessments are ready, reading groups and math stations are written on the board, and I have a plan B for when the technology fails. (Always have a Plan B when using technology; it can greatly reduce stress levels when something goes awry.) When I am thinking about work over the weekend (hey, we all do it), I am not worried about the week at hand. I'm thinking about the following week. I return to work on Monday with my ducks in a row. I remain flexible and fluid in my plans throughout the week, thinking about the next week. By Wednesday I have an idea of where my class will be in the content on Friday and begin finalizing the plans I have rolled around since the weekend. When I leave work on Friday, I am completely mapped out for the following week and the cycle begins again.

I have found that when I plan at least a week in advance, I free myself to think of more creative and engaging experiences for my students. I am more flexible during the week because I have already considered my back-up plans and have begun thinking about the next week's plans. Back when I planned for the upcoming week on the weekend before, I always felt rushed and ill-prepared on Monday. I would rush in the door to finalize my plans before my students walked in, which meant I was busy around the room rather than greeting students as they walked in the door.

Be Present

In *Teach Like a PIRATE*, Dave Burgess says, "At some point in your career you have to decide if you care more about teaching to tests or teaching kids. My decision was made a long time ago. I teach kids!" This quote has resonated with me since the moment I read it. Those words jumped off the page and implanted themselves in my soul that day. I, too, teach kids, and because I made that decision, I am present in my classroom. I made the decision to worry less about past and predicted scores and focus more on my students as they came to me. It is my job to teach the child who walks into my room every day, not the child who took a standardized test six months ago or the child some algorithm predicts will be present at the end of the school year. It is my responsibility to leave those children more socially, emotionally, and academically fulfilled at the end of the day than they were when they arrived that morning. How can I do that?

I can be present. Rather than finishing up last-minute plans on Monday morning, I can be at my door greeting students as they walk in. Rather than checking in and checking out books in the media center as students walk in the door, I can have the first activity displayed on our projector/television and tell students I'm happy to see them—and mean it. Those first two minutes set the tone for the next fifty-five minutes I have them. I can immediately tell which students will need a little extra grace and love that day and which students will knock it out of the park.

Because I have taken the time to plan ahead, I do not need to search the room for the book that has our excerpt for the day. It's right there within reach, and I can remain fully devoted to the story or experience the students and I are currently in together. I've had setbacks when I couldn't find our read-aloud book because I put it in an odd place the day before, or the folder I needed was left at home because I was finalizing something at the eleventh hour. I've learned from those setbacks and now make it a point to always place the book in the same spot, to keep myself prepared and organized. Nothing kills a teacher's capacity to be present and immersed in a classroom more than being unorganized.

Being present and immersed in your classroom is powerful. The learning happens *with* the students and not *to* the students when you, as the teacher, are involved and present. Having a hard time seeing the difference? Think of it as a game of catch in the backyard. When my oldest daughter and I are throwing the softball back and forth, we are throwing *with* one another. It is a give and take. If she didn't participate, there would be no point in continuing. If I were just throwing *to* her, it would be awfully boring for me, and I would get worn out pretty quickly because I'm doing all the work. Catching on? If the learning is happening *with* our students, it's a two-way street. We're both doing equal work. If learning is happening *to* them, they're likely bored, and we're exhausted. Be present and allow yourself to learn *with* your students.

But I'm the teacher. How do you expect me to learn with *them? I already know the content!* I'm so glad you bring that up! You might know the content, but can you do something to make it relevant from year to year? This brings us to the third strategy for achieving balance between nearsightedness and farsightedness.

Make Connections and Maintain Relevance

Captivating student interest with authentic learning is the best way to combat nearsightedness and farsightedness. In *Learner Centered Innovation*, Katie Martin writes:

> *The problem [with support programs like "response to intervention"] is that success was defined by the test scores, and, in some cases, this focus resulted in limiting (or eliminating) authentic learning experiences to make room for repeated exposure and practice on drill-and-kill test-prep questions.*

When we get caught up in what lies ahead, we neglect to create experiences that students will truly learn from. Our students aren't deeply learning and connecting to content when they're bubbling answers. Students build connections when they have high interest and see relevance in what they are learning. Katie goes on to say, "We will never achieve the results we want by focusing on performing well on a test." I couldn't agree more. I would never suggest ignoring standardized accountability; however, our focus should be on building real-world experiences and pulling in students' interests to inspire them to go above and beyond the standards set in place. The way I see it, if we exceed the given standards throughout the year, we will easily meet those standards at the end of the year.

Speaking of student interests: Fidget spinners. Pokémon Go. Mannequin Challenge. Bottle flipping. Have you tried teaching with these lately? I get eyerolls from middle schoolers when I bring these fads up now. It wasn't that long ago that these trends were popular among students (so popular, in fact, they were banned from many schoolhouses). Why? Because they drove most teachers crazy. Not this teacher! I was one of those teachers who took these ideas and tried to figure out how to bring them into the classroom. Fidget spinners? Instant inertia lesson. Pokémon Go? Statistics. Mannequin Challenge? Great way to get kids silently reading a book with expression on their face. Bottle flipping? (*Wait, is this educational? Sure is!*) What is the ideal amount of water in a bottle for optimum flipping? Measurement and fractions! I'm sure you have tons of other ways that you connected these instant wonders in your classroom too!

I will never forget September 11, 2001. I was a junior in high school, and on the day of the attacks, I was having my braces removed at the orthodontist. My mom took me to eat lunch afterward. (I got corn on the cob because I could. It was amazing.) The original plan was for me to return to school, but my mom and I picked up my younger brother from school and sat on the couch in the living room together, glued to the television. I also will never forget September 12, 2001, because that day, in my U.S. history class, my teacher completely stopped what we were doing mid-unit and said that we were going to stop *studying* U.S. history because we were *living* it. We started a daily section in our notes to update what was going on with the investigation and information as it became available. We speculated about the upcoming war and who was to blame for the attacks. Most of my notebooks from high school are long gone. My U.S. history notes from 2001, however, are currently housed on my Google Drive. Why did I save those and not anything else? It was relevant. I will never forget that class because the connections were authentic. They mattered.

Are we doing that for our students? When the Chilean miners were trapped for sixty-nine days in 2010, my students and I watched as they were rescued. When Michael Phelps broke all kinds of records in the 2008 Olympics in Beijing, our unit on decimals was all about swimming. When the presidential election came down to either our first African American president or our first female president, you'd better believe we took time to research the civil rights movement and women's suffrage, even though it "wasn't time" in our curriculum map to teach it. Think of the opportunities we have to make the learning relevant for our students. That worksheet you've used for the past five years? Toss it. You'll be better for it! I'm not saying you have to reinvent the wheel every year. I am saying, however, that if bottle flipping and fidget spinners aren't things you'd use to make learning relevant for students today, that five-year-old worksheet probably isn't doing much for them either.

CORRECTIVE MEASURES

- In what ways are you too nearsighted or too farsighted in education?

- How can you achieve a balance to correct your educational vision?

- What can you use tomorrow in your classroom that is relevant to your students today? What can you remove from your repertoire that is no longer relevant?

- What events can you use to connect learning to the real world for your students? How can you purposefully bring their world into the classroom?

- Share your thoughts using #EduEyeExam.

EDUCATIONAL HINDSIGHT

Observations

In my third year teaching, after a fly-by observation (the observer may have been in my classroom for five minutes), I was told to go observe a teacher in my school, Mrs. E., during her class's self-selected reading (SSR) time. I was told to watch for conferencing techniques and question stems and prepare a short reflection about what I observed, then share it with my professional learning community.

I was upset. Don't get me wrong, Mrs. E. was (and still is) a fantastic educator! But if I'm being asked to go observe her and write a reflection, then obviously I'm doing something wrong. Obviously, I'm inadequate in some area, and I need to figure out what that is, write about it, and share my failures with my PLC. Right?

What a horrible attitude I had! Why did someone not shake me and tell me to get over my own ego and take the opportunity to find something, even just one little thing, that I could replicate in my own classroom?!

Looking back, I realize there are some things you can't google (I don't recommend googling medical symptoms; you will always get the worst-case scenario from internet searches). There are some things you can't know just by reading about them. Some things just need to be experienced. That's why taking every opportunity to observe other teachers performing their craft is so valuable. I wish I had known that being asked to observe someone else doesn't mean that I'm inferior to them, and on the flip side, having someone come to observe me doesn't mean I'm superior either! It's about being in the trenches, experiencing someone else's mannerisms, witnessing their procedures, giving feedback, and learning from one another. We can tell others what we saw or we can read about it, but it will never compare to actually being there. That's why observations are so powerful.

There are so many movements in education that encourage observations. Learning walks, #ObserveMe, Open Door Policy, Pineapple Charts, and other observation protocols promote watching others teach, reflecting on it, and sharing with others. Hmmm . . . sounds a lot like the thing I had such a poor attitude about doing several years ago.

I've heard it said that the best professional development is the teacher down the hall. Every "teacher down the hall" is an expert at something! We all have strengths, so build on your struggles by learning from the strengths of others.

Now that I understand the true purpose behind observations, I am in classrooms as much as possible and invite others to come observe the learning in the media center as well. As an instructional coach, I am frequently co-teaching with educators in my building. My favorite thing to do is sit back and observe! I watch students' faces and body language, listen to tone of voice, and feel the vibe of the classroom. In order to understand what's going on at the heart of a school building, one must get into the classrooms.

Taking it a step further, I have expanded my own observations to include student shadowing. During this time, I am not focused on what the teachers are doing. Instead, I want to know what the student learning looks like. You can learn more about my student shadowing experiences at bit.ly/EduEyeExamShadow.

Whether you are observing another teacher (or student) or you are being observed by a peer, use that opportunity to depersonalize instruction and learn all you can during the time allowed. Be sure to leave meaningful, authentic, timely feedback to promote growth. Take the time to reflect on the experience, and get your next observation on the calendar.

Being asked to observe another teacher isn't a slap in the face; it's a pat on the back! It should be seen as an opportunity for growth and the most valuable way to gain pedagogical knowledge in our profession. Observations cannot be googled; they can only be experienced.

CHAPTER 10

Prescriptions

O nce the eye exams were complete and the diagnosis given, I was taken back to the lobby to make some decisions, and this was where the parallels between going to the eye doctor and school really hit home for me. I will never go to the eye doctor again without thinking about this!

Here's how it went down. I sat with an optician (the person who fits you with eyeglasses or contacts following a prescription) who asked if I would like contacts or glasses. Remember my major dislike of anything going near my eyes? Just the idea of putting in contacts made me cringe, so I told her that I'd like to purchase glasses. The optician then pulled my insurance information and shared with me what my insurance would cover for my frames and lenses. She directed me to the wall of frames and showed me where the men's, women's, and children's selections were located. She mentioned that the cheaper frames were on one side, while the name-brand frames were along the far side. She told me I could pick any frame I'd like and reminded me about the amount insurance would cover on my frames. She said she would be waiting at the desk when I was ready to order.

There were mirrors everywhere and probably upward of two hundred different frame options just in the women's section. I tried on pair after pair. Looking in the mirror (still blurry), I tried to find a shape that I liked, that looked right on my face, and that I could wear with most any outfit I owned. I thought about purchasing two frames so I could switch them out every so often but decided against it. Knowing how I liked my sunglasses to fit, I chose a few pairs of frames that looked very similar and took them to the desk where the optician was waiting.

We made some small talk, and after discussing the frames she thought looked best with my face shape (I had never done this before, so I wasn't really sure), I narrowed it down to two frames. One had the nose pads and the other did not. The frames with nose pads were lighter on my face and looked rather flimsy, while the other frames looked sturdier but were heavier on my face. I opted for the ones without nose pads (I broke my nose when I was younger and was concerned that the nose pads might not fit correctly).

After I selected my frames, we got down to business. The optician took several measurements of my eyes and keyed them into the computer. She checked the length from my eyes to my ears, the measurement of the bridge of my nose, and the distance between my pupils. She checked these measurements a couple of times before entering them into her computer.

She then moved on to the type of lenses I wanted. The optometrist suggested progressive lenses with non-glare coating, so I selected Eyezen lenses, which were anti-fatigue and known for reducing eye strain in people who spend a lot of time working at a computer. I also opted for transition lenses due to a sensitivity to sunlight. After finalizing my lenses and frame and running the order through insurance, the optician gave me my balance and informed me my new glasses would be delivered to the office in seven to ten business days.

Let's see how all of that parallels in our Educational "I" Exam!

Kindness

At the end of my exam, my optometrist could have told me to walk down the hall and take a right into the lobby where someone would be with me shortly, but she didn't. She personally walked me to the lobby, ensuring that I was in the care of an optician who would continue my eye care journey with me. Those little touches of kindness were so meaningful to me.

I encourage you to spread kindness everywhere in education. Be kind to other educators, be kind to parents, and be kind to students. Even if you don't receive kindness back, model the kindness that you wish to see from others. A smile goes a long way. That whole don't-smile-until-Christmas junk is ridiculous. Smile from day one. I encourage you to throw caution to the wind in this case and smile freely! Build relationships with those you serve! That can be the best "classroom management" available! There's no good reason to have a kindness deficit!

Choices

I was given choices. So many choices! There was literally a wall of choices! I was asked if I wanted glasses or contacts first. This was the first decision I had to make. This reminds me of pathways for students. Either option I chose would have cleared my vision, but only one was comfortable for me. Think of some of the objectives you are responsible for teaching within a unit. If you take the time to look, there are likely many opportunities to allow students to choose which one they want to learn first. This isn't always going to be feasible. Students need to learn how to add before they understand the concept of subtraction. Knowing how to multiply before finding equivalent fractions is helpful. Understanding the concept of a food chain could be considered a prerequisite to understanding a food web. Some things must be taught in a certain order.

There are other times, however, when you are teaching a concept that has multiple parts and can allow students the opportunity to choose which part they learn first, second, third, and so on, until they've mastered the whole. When I was a fifth-grade classroom teacher, my students were responsible for understanding three methods of heat transfer—conduction, convection, and radiation. I spent three years teaching them in a particular order, with absolutely no good reason for doing so! The years I allowed students to choose their own path were the years I had the highest proficiency for that unit of study on the end-of-grade test. I have no proof that there was causation, that the higher proficiency was the result of allowing the students to select which method they learned first, but there's enough correlation to make me feel as though I was on to something. Did it really matter if one student learned about conduction while another learned about radiation? Absolutely not! As long as they knew the three methods and how to compare and contrast them, the objective was met.

This approach would be perfect for those of you teaching human body systems. Allow students to choose any system in the human body from options you give them. Those options would be your standards, your objectives. In fifth grade in my state, that was skeletal, muscular, nervous, digestive, respiratory, and circulatory. When students show that they have mastered their first system, they can choose another from the list. After they master the second system, the students should share the similarities and differences they found, as well as how those systems interact and rely on one another to make the body work. When the students choose a third system, they will consider these same questions. Rinse and repeat until all six systems are covered. You will have various experiments going on at once, and it may get a little loud. You will have to prepare for all systems before beginning the unit. It's worth it. Do the work on the front end and watch the students amaze you when you give them more choice in the classroom.

Speaking of choice, did you notice how many frames were available? I was free to choose any frame! I was given parameters (insurance coverage, women's section, brand names, cost), but it was up to me to choose which frame I liked best.

When giving your students choices, it's best to include parameters. Start with tighter restrictions and allow them to expand their knowledge naturally. At the beginning of the year, I would show my students one option they might use for showing their mastery of a concept. This tool was simple and accessible to all. It might have been a poster on construction paper or a diagram. A few days later, I would show another mastery option. Maybe this time it was a technology tool like Google Drawings. Students could then choose between a poster or a Google Drawing. The following week, we'd learn about infographics. Now students can choose between a poster, a Google Drawing, or an infographic. Do you see how we started with restrictions and opened up the options one or two at a time, rather than overwhelming students with all the options in the world? Not only did this ensure that students were confident in the tool they selected, but it also gave me an opportunity to model expectations for each mastery project.

In the end, I took a couple of frames to the optician to get her opinion. She gave me tips about which shape would look better on my face, and we discussed whether or not I should have a frame with nose pads. I didn't know what I didn't know. If she hadn't shared frame shapes that complemented my face shape with me and told me nose pads could be of concern with a broken (read as crooked) nose, I might have ended up spending a lot of money on frames that I was utterly unhappy with. Let's not assume what our students do and do not know. Let's work with them, getting to know them and building a relationship so they feel comfortable sharing their strengths and struggles. Be the educator that students feel comfortable asking for help. "I don't know. Can you help me?" Those seven words are some of the most precious words a student can say to me. Why? Because it means I have succeeded in building a strong relationship, modeling humility, and creating a safe space for that student.

Measurements

The optician took the measurements she needed to properly fit my frames to my face. Was it before I even sat down? No. Was it as soon as I sat down? No. Was it while I was trying to find frames? No. She took the measurements she needed only after I was comfortable with the frames I had selected. She got to know me before she got to know my numbers.

Think about that. Let me repeat it for you.

She got to know *me* before she got to know my *numbers*.

Reflect with me about the moment you got your class list at the beginning of this year. Before meeting your students for the first time, did you go look at the cumulative folder to see test scores? Did you go to the teacher from last year to get the "inside scoop" on your students? Did you ask about their reputation from anyone else in the building? If you did any of these things, you got to know the numbers before you got to know the kid. Don't think I'm being hard on you or picking on you. I confess I did it too. Before even getting to know some of my students, I knew about their reputation, and I would dread meeting them that first day. Or I would be so excited to have them in my class because they had been labeled a "great student" by other teachers. Do you know who I did *not* ask about my students before I met them? Their parents. Open House, or Meet the Teacher Night, was about *them* meeting *me*. Let's flip that script! How about having a Meet the Parent Night instead? That night is a terrific time to get to know the parents/guardians/caregivers of our new group of students. Allow them to tell us about their child. Give them the opportunity to share their child's strengths, struggles, talents, and troubles. Let them share their hopes and dreams for their child. Ask them, "What's the one thing you want me to know about your child?" and have them write down the answer on a sheet of paper.

It is important—and a legality—to know if your students have Individualized Education Plans or other modifications and accommodations. It's a great idea to use the yearbook to look them up so you can call them by name the first time you meet them. (That's a relationship builder in itself!) It's imperative to learn as much as you can from their parents and guardians. At the same time, however, you must give every child a blank slate. I couldn't tell you the number of times a "troublemaker" has come into my class and been nothing but a joy! Or how many straight-A students ended up needing tutoring throughout the entire school year. If we have a preconceived notion about our students before they even walk through our doors, it has the power to become a self-fulfilling prophecy. Will your preconceived notion be positive or negative? Each year, our students deserve to have a teacher who is excited to embark on a journey with them. Give every child in your room the opportunity to start over new with you!

Personalized Learning

Every pair of prescription eye glasses is meant for one specific person, the wearer. My prescription is specific to my vision. This is amplified by the astigmatism. The measurements taken are from *my* face: my bridge width, the distance from my eye to my ear, and my pupillary distance. Let's make our classroom experiences like those glasses; make them fit the students in your class. Personalize the learning experiences your students have with you. This can be done through giving choice as mentioned above. It can be accomplished by finding out what your students are interested in through relationship building. Allowing students time for passion projects, incorporating project-based learning, encouraging students to set goals and crush them—these are all examples of providing personalized learning.

$$\boxed{\text{6∂}}$$

Now you see why this part of my visit to the eye doctor revealed a definite parallel to how I approach education. From this short time when the optometrist walked me to the optician until I left, I was hit with kindness, choice, personalized learning, and getting to know someone before getting to know their number, all of which are driving philosophies in my approach to education.

CORRECTIVE MEASURES

- 👁 Which philosophies above match your own? Which are different?

- 👁 What else can you pull from my experience at the optometrist that parallels with education?

- 👁 How can you provide choice through pathways in your role?

- 👁 How will you personalize learning experiences?

- 👁 Share your thoughts using the hashtag #EduEyeExam.

CHAPTER 11

Annual Check-Ups

I have joined the club—the annual eye exam club. I have to go every single year to have my vision re-evaluated for any changes. My prescription might need to be changed, or it might stay the same for a few years; either way, we should schedule regular check-ups with our eye care professional so we know when there are changes in our vision.

How do we do this in education? Fortunately for us, we don't need to wait a year to have a check-up. If our educational vision changes, we simply need to adjust our prescription, to update our lenses. There are many reasons our lenses might need to be changed. Perhaps they have a few scratches from normal wear and tear. Maybe the frame broke and is currently being held together with tape or super glue, barely making it a day at a time. Perhaps your lens looks like they've been run over by a school bus that backed up and hit them again, just for good measure. We've all been there. When you realize your vision has changed, how do you go about updating your lenses?

Connect with Others

Reaching out to colleagues is a great place to start when updating your lenses. This might mean connecting with your professional learning community or team (PLC/PLT) at your school or district, or it might be checking in with your professional learning network (PLN) on social media. Whatever platform you choose, it's important to be connected to other educators. This connection allows us to have check-ups anytime we want!

I've been on Twitter for several years and have used it for professional and educational purposes, with the occasional sports tweet mixed in. (I'm a huge football fan.) Social media, by its very nature, can be unpredictable and unwieldy. It can provide the best professional development you've ever had, and it can also become straight-up overwhelming. You hear about all these amazingly successful strategies, and you try some of them yourself, but when they don't turn out so great, you're left feeling frustrated and less effective than ever before.

It's important to remember that the trend on any social media platform isn't to post about all your setbacks or projects blowing up in your face; the trend is to highlight your triumphs and those moments when you struck gold in the classroom. Through the lens of Twitter, we often see only successes, and that can make us feel insufficient. It can make us feel as though we're not enough. I'm here to tell you, that's not the case! You are enough! Allyson Apsey says it best in her book, *The Path to Serendipity*: "All you need to do is move inch by inch toward the person you want to become; that is enough. You are enough."

If you're feeling social media pull you down, then change your lens. I've been there, and I've had to change my lens in my battle with self-doubt. There are several ways we can do this.

Interact with those who are posting their successes.

Ask them *about the process, how* they were successful. Find out the story behind that amazing tweet they posted. Not only does it validate what they've done, but it also gives you the opportunity to be a learner! Rather than walking away feeling inferior because they've done something incredible that you haven't thought of, you will have the tools and information to make it happen in your own classroom!

Engage in a community that embraces and celebrates one another's setbacks!

Setbacks are not failures. In *Rosie Revere, Engineer* by Andrea Beaty, Rosie Revere and her great-great aunt Rose say it best: "The only true failure can come if you quit." Take time to share the stumbling blocks and slap-your-head moments in your day-to-day activities. They happen. Anyone who says they don't is either lying or isn't doing anything that impressive anyway. We all have setbacks in our school setting. Share those. Celebrate that you now know one or two more ways that don't work! One of my favorite communities on Twitter is #waledchat run by Phil Strunk (@MrPStrunk), an educator in Virginia. This chat celebrates the *W*ins *A*nd *L*osses in *ED*ucation every Thursday night at 9:00 p.m. EST. Amazing educators from around the globe join together to discuss one win and how we celebrated, one loss (setback) and what we learned, and Phil always throws in a great last question to get us thinking and connecting. If you don't have a community that celebrates setbacks, come join this one on Twitter! I'll likely see you there!

Share your own story using your chosen platform.

Share the awesome things that are happening in your own space! Brag on teachers you work with and students you serve. Posting your own content on social media makes you a creator, and you know those times you've asked others about that super cool experience you saw them have with their students via social media? Now others will be asking you about your own super cool experience. It's like paying it forward.

Mute and unfollow.

These are some of my favorite current features of Twitter. I can simply mute those people I follow who are on a rant about something at the moment. Anytime something major happens in politics or a major sports event, there is a sudden influx of information on social media. There is inevitably an educator who is an avid sports fan (guilty!) who will blow up your social media feed with a play-by-play of the event. Mute them if you don't want it clogging up your feed. It's perfectly fine! Evaluate whether that person traditionally posts amazing things you don't want to miss on social media. If they do, go back and unmute them in a day or two. You might realize that you've not even missed their posts, and it's perfectly okay to unfollow them. I'm not suggesting a mass unfollow event; I wouldn't go "clean house." I'm simply reminding you that you have the power to remove negativity and unwanted content from your feed with a click of a button. If you're feeling negative vibes or aren't getting what you need from the content they are sharing, there is no good reason to let that keep you from all the other awesome opportunities that being active on social media as an educator can provide. Finally, if something is completely inappropriate, there is also the block feature on most social media platforms. They can't see you, and you can't see them. Problem solved. Lens changed.

If nothing else works, and you're still feeling inadequate when you view social media as an educator, that's a sign that it's time for a digital detox. Shut it down for a few days, weeks, however long it takes, and come back when you're ready. This will give you the space you need to revisit your own vision and come back stronger to the communities you have built for yourself!

What's really important is that we make sure we keep these frequent "appointments" with other educators, whether they're face-to-face or online, so we know when it's more than just a prescription update that needs to happen. Sometimes there are more serious conditions brewing just beneath the surface. The best forms of treatment are prevention and early detection. Maintaining annual check-ups gives you the benefit, in many cases, of early detection. In the next chapter, we'll discuss what happens when the problem is more serious than you initially thought.

CORRECTIVE MEASURES

- 👁 Share a moment that was successful with your PLC/PLT.

- 👁 Share about a time you experienced a setback but later found success. Use the hashtag #EduEyeExam.

- 👁 Do you need a check-up? Who can you connect with that will help you change your lens?

- 👁 Evaluate your social media connections, if needed.

CHAPTER 12

Diseased Vision

Just as our eyesight can become damaged or diseased, so too can our educational vision. Sometimes our educational vision deteriorates so slowly that we fail to recognize the change for quite a while. Other times it's immediately clear something is terribly wrong. Sometimes we can see the change happening but remain in denial because we are simply too scared or too stubborn to deal with the consequences. As with eye disorders, there are countless causes of deteriorating educational vision. Let's look at a few:

Negativity

Some of the best advice I've ever received, and some of the hardest advice to follow, is to surround yourself with positive people. Making this conscious effort can be tough, especially when we have already bonded with people who tend to be more negative. I have found that finding just one silver lining to every dark situation turns the conversation in a more positive direction, and positive conversations lead to more productive conversations. Rather than complaining about funding, absenteeism, colleagues, testing, and new initiatives, find something to praise! Find the open education resources available in your classroom and share them with your peers. Support that chronically absent student by calling her caregivers and asking how you can help.

Complaining about colleagues—an easy habit to fall into—is never conducive to collaboration and cooperation. Find something positive about that least favorite co-worker. You might have to dig deep, but it's there. Always. As for testing, it's not going away, but perhaps you can focus on teaching your students to be more prepared for the future that awaits them instead of dwelling on your frustration with how your school measures comprehension. When those new initiatives are driving you crazy, try changing your perspective to be thankful that new initiatives are being shared across your school district. It's an opportunity for growth.

I've heard it said that attitudes are contagious. Enthusiasm is contagious. Energy is contagious. So is positivity. Be the one who is spreading positivity everywhere you go. Not long ago, a student walked by the media center as I was standing in the halls during class change. I was not having the best of days, but I didn't want to spread the negativity. This student was looking down at his shoes and grumbling to himself. I spoke up and said hello with the biggest smile I could muster. He looked up and smiled back, walked a few paces, then turned around. He gave me a hug and said, "You know, Mrs. Ray, there are days that you just make me a happier person." We should want to spread that positivity for everyone. You will have bad days, but what good does it do to complain? Surround yourself with people who strive to be positive. Hold one another accountable. Negativity is a disease that will surely blind your educational sight, but it is 100 percent preventable.

Lack of Self-Care

During my #DBC50Summer, I read my first self-care book, *The Zen Teacher* by Dan Tricarico, and it was an eye-opener! (That pun happened completely on its own!) Before I started the book, I expressed my skepticism on my blog. While I was reading it, Dan helped me realize just how much my own self-care had declined. It made me realize I had to find my own Zen, a space that allowed me to just be me. As I worked through the activities at the end of the chapters, I tackled powerful questions: *Who am I if I strip away the titles of educator, mother, wife, sister, daughter? At my core, who am I?* After spending an uncomfortable amount of time on those thoughts, I realized that I truly didn't know. I had taken all this time to get to know others, my students, teachers, administrators, parents, and so on, but I had forgotten to get to know one of the most important people in my life—me! It sounds selfish to say that, but there's a reason the flight attendants tell you to strap on your own oxygen mask before helping others.

I followed that book with *The Path to Serendipity* and *Through the Lens of Serendipity* by Allyson Apsey, *Balance Like a Pirate* by Jessica Johnson, Jessica Cabeen, and Sarah Johnson, and *Sanctuaries* by Dan Tricarico. I could write for days about how to take care of yourself thanks to these brilliant minds, but I'd rather just encourage you to grab a copy of each of these five books and start reading them yourself. Complete the exercises. You'll be amazed by how much you learn about yourself. I'm talking about you as you, not you as Mr. So-and-so or Miss/Ms./Mrs. So-and-so or Coach So-and-so or Dr. So-and-so. There is only one you. If you don't stop to take care of yourself, your vision will surely become blurry again, and this time, it might take more than a simple prescription to repair it.

Trauma

Sometimes our eyesight is perfectly fine, and then we put a mascara stick in our eye. Or is that just me? Whatever. It hurts, trust me. It hurts bad! Trauma happens. It can be trauma that takes time to heal (or, let's be honest, hurt a little less) on its own or trauma that needs to be dealt with by a professional. The bright side to trauma (see the section above on overcoming negativity with positivity) is that we can usually pinpoint exactly where and when the trauma happened. We can look back and see *the moment* that everything changed.

Maybe it was "that student"—the one who made you want to pull out your hair. Maybe it's all of those students you worried about at the end of every school day. *Where will they sleep tonight? Will they eat supper tonight? Who is taking care of them tonight?* Maybe it's the students you felt you didn't quite reach or those you knew needed more of your time. Those girls and boys you embraced as soon as they walked in each morning, the ones looking tattered and torn and desperately in need of someone to believe in them. Maybe it was a poor decision made on a short fuse that caused the trauma, or maybe it was the result of something completely outside of education, perhaps an event in your personal life.

Seek help immediately. Talk to a trusted friend, counselor, or clergyman. The trauma and its aftermath can easily lead to diseased vision in education. Treat it now so you can not only be the best educator possible for those you serve but the best human being for those around you as well.

CORRECTIVE MEASURES

- 👁 How is your vision? What symptoms are you experiencing that are making it difficult to do your job?

- 👁 How do you respond to negativity? How can you be the one who spreads positivity everywhere you go?

- 👁 Do you know who you are? What can you do today to take care of yourself?

- 👁 Think of a trusted friend or professional you can talk to about a specific trauma or other concerns and list three things you might share with that person.

- 👁 Share your thoughts using the hashtag #EduEyeExam.

EDUCATIONAL HINDSIGHT

Look a Fool

My list of most embarrassing moments is extensive. When someone asks, "What's your most embarrassing moment?" most people try to think of a moment to share; I'm just trying to figure out *which* moment to share! I commonly find ways to humiliate myself.

I received my undergraduate degree from Appalachian State University in Boone, North Carolina. Boone is nestled atop the Blue Ridge Mountains with the most beautiful backdrop you can imagine for a college campus. I walked uphill both ways in the snow. No lie! School was rarely cancelled for winter weather, so I would leave my dorm room, walk down a hill, across the campus, and back up a hill to get to my math class. When it was over, I'd walk back down that hill, across campus, and back up the hill to get to my dorm room. I would do this all in snow and wind that made your eyes water when it hit your face.

One winter, after spending a pleasant evening at the campus cafeteria with a friend of mine, we said goodbye and headed back to our dorms. Hers was on the west side of campus and mine on the east. About that time, one of the men's intramural teams walked by, so I thought I'd put a little extra pep in my step. My pep forgot that I was heading back up a hill—in the mountains—after an ice storm. Do you see where this is going? I wiped out right in front of them! Not even a graceful wipeout either! Arms flailing, squealing (as if I wasn't bringing enough attention to myself), and landing on my bottom. Not my best moment.

I wish I had known when I started teaching that I would do much, much more embarrassing things for my students without being asked twice. In fact, I believe the best educators are ready and willing to do whatever it takes to get students pumped up and excited to learn. I love having fun with my students, and as educators, having fun sometimes means we embarrass ourselves a bit.

On spirit days, for example, we might wear pajamas, mismatched socks, wacky tacky outfits, or our favorite character costume during dinner with our own family because we didn't have time to change beforehand. Those are the easy days though! Here are some of the crazy things I've done in the past for students! Take a moment to visualize these and enjoy the laugh.

- Sumo Wrestling—in full, inflatable costume
- Sprinted a quarter of a mile and nearly passed out at the finish line—I am not a frequent runner
- Held a hissing cockroach and panicked a bit when it moved
- Lip synced to *Frozen*'s "Let It Go"—LIVE and in costume
- First dancer in a flash mob—at my daughter's school
- Dunking Booth—this one may have been my favorite though
- DJ Security—at every fifth-grade dance I chaperoned, I assumed the security detail of the DJ, sometimes in funky sunglasses
- Donut eating contest—without using hands we had to eat a donut dangling above our heads
- Lip synced to "Survivor" by Destiny's Child while throwing confetti (Bonus: the video lives on)
- Dressed as Cat in the Hat—the "official" costume
- Learned Zumba dance and performed for each of our three-minute stretch breaks in standardized testing (without music or talking, of course)

There are so, so many more, and I'm sure you've done many things that caused you to "look a fool" for your students! Share those moments with one another using #EduEyeExam!

CHAPTER 13

Glasses
Repair kit

My daughter Bailey has worn glasses since she was four years old. The summer she turned four, my husband and I noticed that she was crossing her eyes frequently. After watching her do it multiple times, we told her to stop. She replied that it made things look funny and giggled at us. It wasn't until her preschool vision screening that we realized that she meant crossing her eyes helped her see things more clearly. At her subsequent optometry appointment, Bailey struggled to describe the top line on the eye chart (which was a sailboat, by the way), and afterward the doctor prescribed glasses with a +6.75 correction and high-index lens. (Really thick glasses for really poor vision!) The optometrist told us that we would need to ensure that she wore them at all times, since many children will take them off when their parents aren't looking. We have *never* had that problem with Bailey. She worries all the time about breaking them because she knows that she really struggles to do basic functions without them.

Bailey is now ten years old and has never broken or lost a pair of glasses. How many adults can say that? Now "break" might mean various things, right? It's up to you if you want to consider scratching the lens a "break." How about when the nose pad breaks off? Have you ever had a frame break? Even if you don't wear glasses, you've likely worn sunglasses! What's the longest you've gone without breaking or losing them? Some of you are laughing right now because you have five or six different pairs stowed in various cars, purses, and backpacks! Some of you have only one pair and you just ran to be sure they're still in the last spot you left them. I was a member of the one-pair crew, and I protected those babies like a raw egg still in the shell!

For those of you who wear contacts—have you ever had one pop out, never to be seen again? My students will completely halt class because a contact popped out. It's a full-out, highly organized search party to find it. No one leaves the room until that contact is found!

What I'm getting at is that there's nothing worse than breaking your glasses or losing a contact lens. Insurance doesn't pay to replace those—at least mine doesn't—so you have two choices: either spend the money to purchase new ones or go without corrective eyewear.

In chapter 12 we talked about ways to prevent burnout and the importance of seeking help when trauma occurs. What happens when you've already reached the point of burnout? You can reverse it. You can conquer it. I am proof.

It was my second year of teaching. (I know, y'all—only my second year!) At the time, I was teaching math three times a day to fifth-grade classes as part of a three-teacher team. I was coming off what I considered to be a successful first year, and I was ready to take on anything—until I got my class list. Let's be honest—if you work at the "last stop," the highest grade-level of a school building, especially in a rural district with only a few hundred students in your school, you know the reputation of the students before they come to you. I *knew* the names on that list. I knew their reputations without seeking them out. I knew what I was up against. Even if I hadn't been aware, when the fourth-grade teachers came to see the lists, each one of them went wide-eyed, a bit pale, and mumbled something about praying for me as they patted me on the back and walked away with their heads down in my honor. That would have told me all I thought I needed to know. That particular grouping of kids had been separated in third grade and in fourth grade but had somehow ended up back in the same class together for fifth grade. My excitement for that year was knocked out of me like a balloon being popped.

After chatting with my incredible mentor, we created a plan to prevent poor behavior by setting high expectations. She convinced me I was up to the task and that if anyone could take on that class and be successful, it was me. It. Was. Not. True.

From day 1 of 180, the group was difficult to control. Not a single student was a "bad" kid, but the natural leaders of the room were not the best of influences, and the followers just fell in line. There were several extremely well-behaved kids, and to them and the rest of the class, I still apologize for how I handled things. I wish I had known then all the strategies for engagement and relationship building that I know now, but I didn't. I only knew what I knew as a second-year teacher. There were many days I was hoarse from yelling instructions. Most days I went home with a headache. I graded test after test with a big, fat F on the front. The paperwork I had to keep up with that year was unbelievable. Thirteen of the twenty-one or twenty-two (depending on the revolving door that brought students in and out throughout the year) were considered at-risk for one reason or another. All thirteen were to be monitored with individualized education plans (IEPs) or personalized education plans (PEPs). While IEPs were for students with special education designations or English as a second language plans, PEPs were for any other students with behavior problems, attendance issues, standardized test failures, or on standby to be tested by our educational services team.

I had students who threw pencils across the room as I watched and then swore they hadn't done it. Every time I picked them up from their special classes after my planning period (a.k.a., my reprieve), I received the same report, and it was never good. Recess was always filled with arguments and drama.

I had a student who told me daily that he hated me, announcing it proudly for the whole class to hear. He pushed every button I had, and yet I loved him. I didn't like him very much that year, but I can honestly say that I loved him. (There is a difference! Ever been in an argument with a significant other?) He would tell me to my face that he wasn't planning to do anything that day, and it would make me so angry. Whenever I mentioned the word *ring*, he would stand and sing his own improvisation of Johnny Cash's classic, "Ring of Fire," in the middle of class. It went something like this:

I fell down, down, down

Into a burning ring of fire.

And it burned, burned, burned . . .

It was at that point that I usually had to turn my back and compose myself. That student is just one example from my life that year. There were at least fifteen others I could tell similar stories about, but I'm trying really hard not to relive that year in my head right now.

This was also the year that I endured our second pregnancy loss after one of the hardest days I'd ever had. I cried more afternoons than I can even remember that year. My heart became stone that year. By the end of October, I had tried everything in my limited bag of tricks and dreaded every day more and more. I broke down during a tough conversation with my administrator. I was done. I never wanted to come back. All I wanted was to hand her the keys to my classroom, collect my belongings, and find a new career.

With the support of my team teachers, my mentor, and God's grace, I managed to make it to the end of the year, but I hated it. Every morning was a struggle to get out of bed, get dressed, and go to work. My test scores that year were atrocious. They pulled our school's performance down. I was the weakest link.

Some of you know exactly the kind of year I just described. You're the people who just nodded your head and felt your blood pressure rising a bit because you've been there. Why did I go back? It has taken me years to answer that question.

I spent a long summer reflecting on all I did wrong, all the times I should have asked for help, all the things I never should have said. I spent a lot of time in prayer, asking if I was truly in the right profession. How could something that felt so incredibly right go so terribly wrong? I believed education was my calling, so why was I feeling so beaten down?

I requested a change in teams that summer. It had nothing to do with my teammates; they were terrific. I felt as though I had let them down, and it was more to save face than anything. It gave me a chance to start over with a new teammate. This new team was only two teachers rather than three, so my roster would automatically decrease by a third. I would have to pick up another subject area, but I was okay with that.

I completely revamped many of my lessons. I ditched the workbooks and started doing more group work. I took time to really look within myself and examine my own attitude, and, oh boy, did my lens ever change then! When we stop and take a good look within ourselves, it's powerful. Many of us don't take the time to do that because, let's be honest, it can be scary. We fool ourselves into thinking we're something we're not, and when we pull the curtain back, the skeletons are dancing in our faces and we can't shut the curtain fast enough. The truth is, when we face those skeletons and have those conversations with ourselves, the potential for growth is exponential. I made the choice to change my lens by changing my perspective. Rather than it being the worst year I'd ever had, I decided that I'd learned 180 days' worth of hard lessons and was prepared for whatever the next year had in store. I'd try one more year and see how it went before making a decision.

If your glasses need to be repaired or replaced or your lens has popped out, you have several options. Give me an opportunity to outline just a few of them:

OPTION 1: REQUEST A CHANGE. Before you jump ship and throw this career out, change the scenery. Maybe that means you take on a new subject, a new grade level, or even a new school. Making the change from a three-teacher team to a teacher partner was instrumental in my staying in education. It gave me a fresh start and a place to exert all of my energy toward making positive change.

OPTION 2: REMAIN IN THE CLASSROOM, BUT GO BACK TO SCHOOL FOR ANOTHER CERTIFICATION OR TO ADVANCE YOUR CAREER IN EDUCATION. I had another tough year during my fourth year of teaching. It was in no way like my second year; it was a year of self-discovery. The best way to describe it is feeling unsettled. I knew I needed another challenge but wasn't sure where to go. I applied to graduate school and spent eighteen months earning a master's degree in instructional technology. It gave me the spark I needed; perhaps it will for you as well.

OPTION 3: BE MISERABLE. Not an option—see Option 4.

OPTION 4: IF YOU'VE TRIED TO STICK IT OUT AND EXHAUSTED ALL OF YOUR OPTIONS AND ARE TRULY DONE, AS IN D-O-N-E, THEN LET ME SAY THIS AS KINDLY AND WITH AS MUCH LOVE AS I CAN: GO FIND A NEW CAREER. Teaching is not a job for those content to simply clock in and clock out; teaching is for educators who are dedicated to ensuring that the next generation has the tools and optimism to make a positive difference in the world. If you are miserable, there's a really good chance those young people you're around every day are miserable too. This is doubly true if you are an administrator at any level. If you are miserable, then your teachers are likely miserable, which in turn makes their students miserable. Your legacy is too important. Your reach extends for generations. Because of educators, students can choose to love learning, embrace risk-taking, and feel encouraged and valued. Our career is one of intimidating levels of responsibility. It's not only that one student you are impacting; it's also their children, and their children's children. It's an entire community of learning that you touch, a culture of curiosity that you are responsible for fostering. So if you truly are miserable every day, and you see no hope of ever feeling differently, I lovingly ask on behalf of students and future generations, please leave.

By no means do I ever want to see effective, lively, inspirational teachers leave our field! With the same breath, I will also say that I never want my daughters to endure a teacher who hates coming to work every day, because it will suck the fun right out of their learning.

Now to the rest of my story.

Those students I had during my second year of teaching are now in their early twenties. They have finished high school and, like so many of my classes, have spread far and wide. Several of those students joined the military, some of them are starting families, and some are still in college, while many have graduated from college and are finding their niche in the world. My young Johnny Cash enthusiast? On the last day of school, he begrudgingly brought me a rock. A large river rock, flat and oval from being tossed and turned by the flow of the river. He found it outside of his house and all but threw it to me saying, "Here, this is for you." I insisted that he write his name on it so I'd never forget who it was from, and he did. Before the end of the day, he decided that the rock was to be called Rick. Rick the Rock has been with me in every classroom, media center, and school I've ever worked in. Rick reminds me when times are tough that I can do anything. Like the rock, I can survive the flow of the river. I can look at the pieces that fall off of me as lost opportunities, or I can see myself as clay that's molded by the potter, knowing that I will come out polished and smooth as I take the time to reflect and grow.

The student who gave me Rick the Rock called me during his junior year of high school to let me know that he would be singing the national anthem at the local high school basketball game. He said, "Mrs. Ray, can you be there?"

"Yes, yes, I can." That is how my glasses got repaired. The beauty and the tragedy of our career choice is that we likely won't know the impact we've made on young lives until much, much further down the road. Test scores don't define us as educators, just like they don't define our students. When that student called me to ask, after all those years, if I would attend his performance, I knew I had made an impact. I never gave up on him; I loved him, and he knew it. I am so thankful that I was able to fix my broken glasses, to replace my scratched lens. It is my sincere hope that you can do the same if you are feeling burned out.

CORRECTIVE MEASURES

- 👁 If you are feeling burned out, spend some time in reflection. This might be meditation, silence, prayer, whatever you choose. Determine if this noble profession is worth the effort for you, even on the worst of days. Consider the responsibility that comes with our career choice. Is it worth it to you to get those broken glasses repaired?

- 👁 If you are feeling strong and secure in your career choice, why not be there for others? Do you know any colleagues who might be dealing with burnout? Reach out to them. Share your own setbacks and offer love and encouragement. Who will you reach out to? Write their name down and make the commitment to talk to them before the week is over. They might need to hear from you right now.

- 👁 Share your thoughts using the hashtag #EduEyeExam.

CHAPTER 14

Your Vision

This space is for you to do as you wish regarding your vision for education! You might choose to write prose, poetry, or sketchnote, or to create graphic organizers. Whatever your preference, I've included a space here for it. I would recommend pencil, though, as it might very well change later. One thing about education that will never change is that education is always changing!

We have covered many topics, both through our Educational Eye Exam and through my personal moments of Hindsight. There are so many hot topics in education that will always be hot topics. Consider your philosophies about each of them. Aaron Tippin said it best in his 1991 country hit, "You've Got to Stand for Something," if we don't stand firm we'll fall for anything.

What do you stand for in education?

What is your *why*, your big "E"?

Do you believe it is important for students and teachers to integrate technology in the classroom? Why and how?

Is teaching a science or an art? Why do you believe that?

Are your lessons continually changing, or do you choose to reuse the same instruction because it works?

How will you share your work? Why is it important to share work? What are some of the benefits and drawbacks?

Two words: 1) Feedback; 2) Grading. Go!

Is it more important to perform well on a standardized test or to perform well in life? Be ready to defend this one to administration and to parents, no matter what your vision is.

Is it important for students to have choice and voice in their own education? Why? Should that choice and voice extend to all students?

Do you ask for help when you need it? How do you know when you need it? Who do you ask?

What is your vision of education? If you wrote the script and we played by your rules, what would be the nonnegotiables in your vision?

CHAPTER 15

See It Through

When I finished my eye exam and drove away from the optometry office, I felt much better. I felt as though a weight had been lifted from my shoulders. I knew I was struggling to see clearly, and I had taken action to improve my vision by facing my fears and visiting the optometrist! I had ordered my frames and lenses, and it was only a matter of time before I would be able to see much more clearly.

I was so proud of myself for overcoming my fears and addressing my issues head on, and if you've made it this far in the book, then I want to say "Congratulations!" to you for taking the necessary steps to experience your first educational "I" exam. If you've answered the questions at the end of each chapter and used the space provided in the previous chapter to outline your philosophy of education, then you have a much clearer vision of your own educational beliefs. One question remains: Now what are you going to do about it?

Creating your own educational philosophy is only half the battle. The most important part of this journey is determining what you will do with your new vision. Imagine if I had visited the optometrist, sat through the exam, ordered my glasses, and never gone back to pick them up. What would the point have been? There would be no point! It would be ridiculous to take the time for an appointment and not follow through. Similarly, there is no point in creating an educational philosophy if you don't do something with it. For most of us, I dare say that our practice needs to change so that it lines up with our vision. For the very few who believe you are already living your vision every day (did you really take the time to dig deep?), what will you do to inspire others to live their vision?

Remember what Dave Burgess said in *Teach Like a PIRATE*: "Inspiration without implementation is a waste." Just like I made a plan to implement something from every book in my #DBC50Summer, what will you implement now that you've established your educational beliefs? What actionable steps will you create from your vision? How will you live your vision in your classroom? How will your practice change?

I invite you to consider each of these areas in which your vision is paramount to the success of your learners. I've listed questions that I encourage you to take the time to answer.

In Your Classroom

This is the environment in which it is easiest to live out your vision. This is a shared space between you and your students. Sure, you likely have curriculum maps and pacing guides that come from someone else's vision; however, at the end of the day, you can literally or figuratively close your door and have the autonomy to choose *how* you teach. This is where you get to live out your vision and directly impact the lives of your learners!

You have created your vision for education. Write it here.

How will you share your philosophy with your students, their caregivers, and assistants/volunteers in your classroom?

What is one change you can make immediately to live out your vision?

What is one element of your classroom that already demonstrates your educational beliefs?

How will you advocate for your own vision to those who critique it?

In Your Professional Learning Community

I encourage you to take the time to share your vision with educators in your PLC! In the strong PLC that I mentioned previously, our visions were aligned. In my experience, strong PLCs result in high growth in our students. A retired administrator that I highly respect frequently stated that a year of learning should reflect at least a year of growth. PLCs that share a vision have the ability to make a year of learning equal much more than a year of growth.

How will you share your philosophy with your PLC?

What will you do if the philosophies of those in your PLC do not align with yours? How can you find common ground? What if you can't find common ground?

Can you create a single vision for your PLC? Try it!

In Your School

This is where having a unified vision truly becomes a game-changer. Imagine the powerful ripple effects moving through a community when a school has a shared vision. Imagine that every teacher in the school holds the same fundamental beliefs about education! It can happen! I've seen it!

How can you begin taking steps toward creating and implementing your school's vision?

What is the vision of your school? How long ago was it written? Should it be revisited?

Do you believe in your school's vision? What do you do if it doesn't align with your own vision?

How might you go about sharing an ideal school vision with all stakeholders?

How long would it take first-time visitors to determine the vision of your school? How do the actions of your school promote your school's vision?

How can you partner with administration to lead the way in implementing your school's vision?

Once the vision of your school is agreed upon, how can you support others in your school as they implement the vision?

In Your System/District

Now we're talking about some major scaling! A united vision throughout an entire district/school system is what separates the good from the great! When I think of some of the best schools in our nation, the vision is evident from every stakeholder! Some may worry that this has to be a top-down process, but I'm here to ease that concern. When you get to this level, a truly successful school district has organic roots. It cycles back to individual teachers in schools who are aware of their own vision and how it aligns with the vision of their PLC, their school, and their district. Take a few moments to consider your school system's vision.

What is the vision of your school district? How does your school's vision align with the district's vision? What about your own vision?

Is this vision shared mostly in words or through actions?

How can you promote your district's vision in your role?

In an Ideal Educational World

This is the fun part! Imagine with me that we live in an ideal educational world! We have unlimited funding, low emphasis on standardized testing, and our students' basic physical and social-emotional needs are met. You are tasked with determining the educational vision of a classroom, PLC, school, and district in this perfect world! With this idyllic environment in mind, write two sentences to describe the vision of each of these educational spaces.

Classroom Vision:

PLC Vision:

School Vision:

District Vision:

How do these visions of the ideal educational world differ from the realistic visions you listed above? How are they similar? What obstacles appear to be preventing this ideal vision from being your realistic vision? What can you do to remove those obstacles? Why would our realistic vision be any less optimistic than the vision we have for an ideal scenario?

CORRECTIVE MEASURES

- 👁 What are your actionable steps for implementing your educational beliefs?

- 👁 Get a group of colleagues together to discuss these visions. This is best done by beginning with your own vision and working your way to a larger scale.

- 👁 How can we empower students to create a vision for themselves?

- 👁 Do you believe it's important to have a unified vision for education? Why or why not?

- 👁 In your current role, at what level do you have influence over the vision? Stretch yourself and discuss the vision with someone who has influence at other levels.

- 👁 Share your thoughts using the hashtag #EduEyeExam.

CHAPTER 16

Scheduling Your Next
"I" Exam

A s I left the optometrist, they asked me if I wanted to schedule my next eye exam. For my daughter Bailey, it's every six months, but for me it's once a year. I like to go ahead and schedule them and immediately place them on my calendar, because otherwise I will forget to call and schedule my next eye exam until the last minute. They're usually booked solid for six to eight weeks by that point, which puts me on a waiting list and facing an appointment at a much less convenient time of year.

In this chapter, however, we aren't discussing your eyes; we are talking about scheduling your next "I" exam! How often and when should we stop and revisit our vision of education? If you're like me, perhaps you need to intentionally schedule it on your calendar. At the end of every year or every semester, you might feel that revisiting your vision is important. Perhaps it's after a couple of years. Maybe you are brand new to this journey and want to revisit it monthly or even weekly. It really doesn't matter how often you evaluate your educational vision—it just matters that you do. Determining my beliefs about education throughout the summer I read the first fifty Dave Burgess Consulting, Inc. books has been the most beneficial experience I have ever had. I had not even considered my personal thoughts about education since 2011 in a graduate school assignment. I was just repeating the thoughts of other educators I had uncovered through research and connections. Now I have my own beliefs. I expect that they will continue to evolve as I learn more and as education continually changes. This idea of developing your vision for education, your own educational philosophy, is evergreen. It will never go away and will constantly evolve due to the ever-changing landscape of education. It doesn't matter if you are an educator of thirty years at multiple levels in varying roles or if you are just entering your first college class in your education major—you need to have a set of educational convictions about which you can believe passionately and deeply. It's got to hit you at your core.

In every session I facilitate, every workshop I develop for educators, I ask for information from the participants before we begin. It gives me a quick glance at the people in the room. When educators come to my session, they typically see a projected slide with a URL that will lead them to a digital survey. I currently use Google Forms to collect the information.

On the survey, I share my name and ask for theirs. I share my social media information to get connected (and encourage others to become connected educators) and request details for how I can find them on social media. I share that I work in a middle school and ask which age group they work with on most days. I tell them about my role, ask for their role and subject area, and typically inquire about their experience level with whatever technology or topic it is that I will be covering that day. I ask what brought them to the session, what they hope to leave with, and then I ask one final question:

"I have been in education for <x> years. How many years have you been an educator?"

Their six choices are:

- Zero to three years
- Four to seven years
- Eight to ten years
- Eleven to fifteen years
- Sixteen to twenty-four years
- More than twenty-five years

These specific ranges didn't come about by accident. They are my own creation—the result of years of experience and observation. As a whole, they constitute a kind of growth chart of an educator's mindset. As you read on, please remember that these are my opinions. I am not calling you out, but if you feel convicted or start laughing, it's probably true for you too. Sometimes the truth hurts.

These are ranges and might differ from your experience by a year or two. They also might differ according to your state salary schedule and whether you are in the private or public sector of education. It is my guess, though, that these ranges do not specifically adhere to careers in education but are applicable to many occupations. Let's see what you think:

Zero to three years:

Welcome to the I-don't-need-this-PD-because-I-just-earned-a-college-degree phase. It can also be considered the my-mentor-says phase or even the eyeroll phase. During my first three years of teaching, I doodled my way through most of my professional development sessions because I felt I didn't need whatever the presenter was selling. I had just learned everything I needed to know about teaching from my university program. I figured if I encountered any problems, I would turn to my mentor, who would promptly give me a pep talk and a lesson plan, and I would be on my way.

Four to seven years:

I refer to these as the Oh-expletive-of-choice-I-have-no-idea-what-I'm-doing years. Yep! This is where reality hits. You no longer have an appointed mentor (if you even had one to begin with), and guess who is creating all of those lesson plans now? By this point you've seen a shift in education (because every few years something has cycled in and something else has cycled out), and you're wondering why you never heard about the new initiative in college. You vaguely remember doing something similar when you were in school. It's okay. It happens to all of us. These years are the years of the most growth. These teachers have enough humility to share that they don't have it all together quite as much as they thought when they started.

Eight to ten years:

This is the honeymoon of teaching! After all that hard work and all those nights of creating spectacular experiences and grading papers, you finally have some systems that work. What's beautiful about this time period is that you've fallen under the radar. You aren't a beginning teacher anymore, and you are mostly left alone to do what you do with students, which for many of us means taking risks. This can also be a great time to begin new initiatives and professional development of your own outside of what your school or district offers. This is when I really began branching out. I discovered *Teach Like a PIRATE* my eighth year! This phase might come on quickly, sometimes appearing as early as the sixth year.

Eleven to fifteen years:

I'm currently in this stage of education. I have left the classroom and spend a lot of time wondering if I should go back. (The grass is always greener, right?) I feel confident enough in my practice to share with others, but I know that I don't know everything! I can readily and often admit that I am a learner just as much as I am a teacher, if not more so. At this point, some of the risks in the previous years will have paid off, and you will find yourself leading initiatives in your school and district. You likely have a full calendar leading workshops, PLC, School Improvement Team meetings, and the like.

Sixteen to twenty-four years:

I have not experienced this stage personally, but from observation, it appears to be a major turning point for educators. This is the halfway point! It's when many of us start looking at retirement statements and wondering if we can make it another five to fifteen years. Those things that cycled in during the first years have already cycled out, and you've experience at least one new curriculum overhaul. This is a time for real soul-searching. Are you still on fire for teaching others? These symptoms might not last long. You might even return to the honeymoon stage when your soul-searching is complete and determine that you are still on fire!

More than twenty-five years:

In my state, at the time this book was published, educators do not make a single penny more at thirty years of experience than at twenty-six years of experience. Is it worth it financially to stay the course for the final few years? You have to ask yourself if you are in it for the income or for the outcome? Education looks completely different from how it looked during your first year, and you are teaching the children of kids you taught years ago. You hear a lot of "Remember me, Mrs. So-and-so? I had you when I was in third grade. This is my son. He's in your class this year."

I truly believe that there is value in all experience levels of education, whether it is the "shiny and new" of the first year or the "tried and true" that only years upon years of experience can bring. What breaks my heart is the divide that society places on us in regard to years of experience. I believe it is due to the generational differences and the expedition of educational revolution made possible through the use and accessibility of technology. If I could say anything to the masses of educators out there, it would be this: Lean on one another regardless of how many years of experience you each have.

Beginning teachers, go to the veteran teachers before jumping on Pinterest or Teachers Pay Teachers! I enjoy visiting these websites just as much as the next educator, but these sites don't know the stories of the young girl's family who grew up down the road from the veteran teacher next door. If you have one student who is singing Johnny Cash in your room, then they've had five similar stories! Pinterest doesn't prepare you for that! There are tried and true practices in education because they work! Pick the brain of someone who can help you figure out where the obstacles may lie. Beginning teachers, go to experienced teachers for your "I" exam!

Experienced teachers, when you aren't sure how this new initiative will go over in your classroom, step out of your classroom to chat with those first-year and second-year teachers two doors down! They likely just learned about it, in depth, and have notebooks and research papers that share the method behind what appears to be madness. When you need that unbridled enthusiasm and freshness to get you through the day, find those beginning teachers and pick their brains! Experienced teachers, go to beginning teachers for your "I" exam!

Tween teachers, you aren't getting out of this one! You are the glue. You see both sides of the coin. Go grab a beginning teacher, walk across the hall to the veteran teacher's classroom, and plan an incredible experience together for your students, one that showcases all the best that education has to offer. Mix in the tried and true practices with the innovative ideas, and pull in curriculum to ensure that all students succeed.

It is so important to value one another's educational philosophies. We will differ. It's like I tell my students—you might not agree, but you will be respectful. The tragically ironic part of the whole thing is that each of us has what the other needs. None of us is "right" about our philosophies. Philosophies might include research-based practices and factual data, but a philosophy by nature is simply a theory! It is what we believe to be true until we are shown otherwise! You just need to schedule your next "I" exam and discover it, then rediscover it again and again. Revisit your vision, your philosophy, to be certain you still believe in what you're selling.

CORRECTIVE MEASURES

- What range of experience do you currently identify with? What would you add or remove from these descriptions?

- Who will you schedule your next "I" exam with?

- Go ahead and get it on the calendar! Be sure to chat with someone in a different experience range! They will have a different view and likely challenge your own. This will either make you reconsider your belief or will make it more concrete. Neither is wrong!

Crystal-Clear Vision

f Johnny Nash were singing about vision for education when he sang, "I can see clearly now the rain is gone. I can see all obstacles in my way," I would suspect he was feeling a bit overconfident. There's no way we can see all obstacles in the future of education. What we can do is have a crystal-clear vision of what we believe is best for our students and the field of education. I have shared with you what constitutes my vision for education. It's drawn from my personal experiences from childhood, college, career, and relationships. Having had a front-row seat to my brother's struggles in education, I knew I wanted to change the game. I wanted to flip the script for kids like him everywhere. I wanted to change the lens through which we see the children in our classrooms and in our schools.

Bill Nye was exactly right when he said, "Every person you will ever meet knows something that you don't." I don't believe for even a second that I know more about the field of education than any other educator out there. If we remain silent about our beliefs and our vision for education, however, we are doing our students and our own future a disservice. We might not agree on the vision we have after examining these topics, but as educators, we will do as we require of our students: we will be respectful and empathetic. The best way to teach empathy, kindness, and respectfulness is to model it. While we share our philosophies publicly, we must remember that everyone has a story that has molded that portion of their vision. Any philosophy is up for discussion, and no one has it completely right or completely wrong. No one knows the future of education, so we ought to be able to discuss and respectfully debate our different philosophies as these visions come to light.

My educational philosophy is ever-changing. Some parts of my vision, however, are unwavering and truly quite simple.

I believe that our calling as educators is to tap into the minds of students and create connections from what they already know to what they need and desire to know.

I believe students are innately creative and that if we put fewer parameters on outcomes, there will be more joy in the journey, which will equate to more learning in life. I believe education as we know it is changing at a rapid pace, and our students should be in charge of that change.

I believe students should have choice in what they learn and the opportunity to choose their own pathways in life. As an educator, it is my chief responsibility to facilitate opportunities for my students to make connections to content, information, and other people.

I believe that the best is yet to come and that educators hold the key to the future. Those keys are in our classrooms every day, which means we have the most horrifyingly consequential jobs in the world. We cannot and must not let them down.

I thank you from the bottom of my heart for taking this journey with me. Thank you for trusting me, and, most importantly, thank you for questioning my own vision. If at any point in reading this book you didn't agree with something I wrote, you are already beginning to live out your own vision, and I love that! I invite friendly discussion on any piece of my vision. As I mentioned earlier, there are only two outcomes that will result from those discussions: I will either question my own vision and schedule another "I" exam, or my vision will become clearer after I share it with others.

Remember to share your own vision for education that you have created on your journey with me using the hashtag #EduEyeExam.

Until we meet again for your next "I" exam, thank you for stopping by. Be sure to "grab a card" as you head out. See you soon!

BIBLIOGRAPHY

Chapter 2

- Burgess, Dave. *Teach Like a PIRATE: Increase Student Engagement, Boost Your Creativity, and Transform Your Life as an Educator*. San Diego: Dave Burgess Consulting Inc., 2012.
- Rollins, Quinn. *Play Like a PIRATE: Engage Students with Toys, Games, and Comics*. San Diego: Dave Burgess Consulting Inc., 2016.
- Wyborney, Steve. *The Writing on the Classroom Wall: How Posting Your Most Passionate Beliefs about Education Can Empower Your Students, Propel Your Growth, and Lead to a Lifetime of Learning*. San Diego: Dave Burgess Consulting Inc., 2016.
- Spencer, John, and A.J. Juliani. *LAUNCH: Using Design Thinking to Boost Creativity and Bring Out the Maker in Every Student*. San Diego: Dave Burgess Consulting Inc., 2016.

Chapter 5

- Wettrick, Don. *Pure Genius: Building a Culture of Innovation and Taking 20% Time to the Next Level*. San Diego: Dave Burgess Consulting Inc., 2014.

Chapter 6

- Ashcraft, Mike, and Rachel Olsen. *My One Word: Change Your Life With Just One Word*. Grand Rapids: Zondervan, 2012.

Chapter 9

- Burgess, Dave. *Teach Like a PIRATE*. San Diego. Dave Burgess Consulting Inc., 2012.
- Martin, Katie. *Learner-Centered Innovation*. San Diego, California: IMPress, 2018.

Chapter 11

- Apsey, Allyson. *The Path to Serendipity: Discover the Gifts along Life's Journey*. San Diego: Dave Burgess Consulting Inc., 2018.
- Beaty, Andrea. *Rosie Revere, Engineer*. New York: Abrams Books, 2013.

Chapter 12

- Tricarico, Dan. *The Zen Teacher: Creating Focus, Simplicity, and Tranquility in the Classroom*. San Diego: Dave Burgess Consulting Inc., 2015.
- Apsey, Allyson. *The Path to Serendipity: Discover the Gifts along Life's Journey*. San Diego: Dave Burgess Consulting Inc., 2018.
- Cabeen, Jessica, Jessica Johnson, and Sarah Johnson. *Balance Like a Pirate: Going Beyond Work-Life Balance to Ignite Passion and Thrive as an Educator*. San Diego: Dave Burgess Consulting Inc., 2018.
- Tricarico, Dan. *Sanctuaries: Self-Care Secrets for Stressed-Out Teachers*. San Diego: Dave Burgess Consulting Inc., 2018.

Chapter 13

- Cash, Johnny, vocalist. "Ring of Fire," by June Carter Cash and Merle Kilgore. Recorded on March 25, 1963. Track 1 on *Ring of Fire: The Best of Johnny Cash*. Columbia, 1963, compact disc.

Chapter 15

- Burgess, Dave. *Teach Like a PIRATE: Increase Student Engagement, Boost Your Creativity, and Transform Your Life as an Educator*. San Diego: Dave Burgess Consulting Inc., 2012.

Conclusion

- Nash, Johnny, vocalist. "I Can See Clearly Now." I Can See Clearly Now. Epic, 1972.

Schedule Your Educational Eye Exam with Alicia Ray

Alicia's workshops and keynote presentations encourage educators to create their own vision of education. Through high-energy interaction and passionate storytelling, Alicia addresses current trends and best practices in education. Invite Alicia to your school and district events! Common speaking topics include:

- 👁 Educational Eye Exam
- 👁 Creating a Unified Vision
- 👁 Rediscovering Your "Big E": How Your *Why* Impacts Your Profession
- 👁 Dilating Your Eyes: Trends in Technology
- 👁 Fighting against Tunnel Vision
- 👁 A Go-To Glasses Repair Kit: How to Re-Energize and Avoid Burnout
- 👁 Seeing the World through Your PLN
- 👁 Hindsight in Education
- 👁 Using Augmented Reality and Virtual Reality to See the Impossible
- 👁 Building and Sustaining Relationships
- 👁 Seeing the Future of Education through a New Lens

Connect with Alicia

Alicia Ray
Educational Eye Exams

Twitter & Instagram: @iluveducating
#EduEyeExam #HindsightEDU
iluveducating@gmail.com
aliciaray.com

ACKNOWLEDGMENTS

To Chris, Bailey and Sophie: Thank you for allowing me to make my dream of being an author come true! Your support and encouragement mean more to me than you will ever know. You three are my world, and I love you to the moon and the stars.

To Mom and Dad: I love you both!

To Jacob: Thanks for making our childhood fun by being my living room dance-off, car windows down and radio up too loud, "Voila in reverse," "Mamma No," *Fresh Prince of Bel-Air*-watching, amazing little brother. My best memories include you! I'm so proud of you! Thank you for letting me share your story; it's such a big part of mine! Love you, kiddo!

To all of my family: Thank you for helping make this happen! Whether it was babysitting the girls, texting encouragement, or giving me time and space to share my thoughts, you inspired me to chase my dreams. I love you all!

To my optometry office: You have a new patient for life! Thank you!

To my mentors, colleagues, and PLN: Each of you has made me better today than I was yesterday and will continue to make me better tomorrow than I am today. I am forever grateful for everything I've learned from you and look forward to learning even more! We're never done growing!

To my students: My best days are the days I get to spend with you. Thank you for going on this journey with me! I love you and believe you will change the world!

To Dave and Shelley Burgess: I am forever grateful for you two! Your belief in me has astounded me from the very beginning. The world is better because you are in it. Thank you for amplifying the voices of so many incredible educators so I could learn from them, and for believing my voice was worth amplifying. I can't wait to see what you do next!

To each of the DBC, Inc authors: You have helped shape my educational philosophy into what it is today through your words. I admire and respect each of you and am so grateful you took this same journey, writing your manifesto and sharing your story with the world. I am a better educator and a better person because of each of you. You have been supportive beyond words! Thank you for welcoming me into this Pirate family with open arms! It is an honor to join you!

To Tara, Wendy, Erin (and team), and Genesis: From the very beginning, you blew me away! Thank you for your advice and encouragement and for helping me see that Hindsight was just a small piece of my story. Thank you for your amazing editing skills and magnificent cover. I am astounded by the final product; it is my story, my message, my manifesto, and you were able to create something beautiful from my typo-infused manuscript created in the middle of many nights.

To everyone who supported, encouraged, motivated, and believed in me: Thank you!

MORE FROM

Since 2012, DBCI has been publishing books that inspire and equip educators to be their best. For more information on our DBCI titles or to purchase bulk orders for your school, district, or book study, visit DaveBurgessConsulting.com/DBCIbooks.

More from *Like a PIRATE*™ Series

Teach Like a PIRATE by Dave Burgess
eXPlore Like a Pirate by Michael Matera
Learn Like a Pirate by Paul Solarz
Play Like a Pirate by Quinn Rollins
Run Like a Pirate by Adam Welcome

Lead Like a PIRATE™ Series

Lead Like a PIRATE by Shelley Burgess and Beth Houf
Balance Like a Pirate by Jessica Cabeen, Jessica Johnson, and Sarah Johnson
Lead beyond Your Title by Nili Bartley
Lead with Culture by Jay Billy
Lead with Literacy by Mandy Ellis

Leadership & School Culture

Culturize by Jimmy Casas

Escaping the School Leader's Dunk Tank by Rebecca Coda and Rick Jetter

From Teacher to Leader by Starr Sackstein

The Innovator's Mindset by George Couros

Kids Deserve It! by Todd Nesloney and Adam Welcome

Let Them Speak by Rebecca Coda and Rick Jetter

The Limitless School by Abe Hege and Adam Dovico

The Pepper Effect by Sean Gaillard

The Principled Principal by Jeffrey Zoul and Anthony McConnell

Relentless by Hamish Brewer

The Secret Solution by Todd Whitaker, Sam Miller, and Ryan Donlan

Start. Right. Now. by Todd Whitaker, Jeffrey Zoul, and Jimmy Casas

Stop. Right. Now. by Jimmy Casas and Jeffrey Zoul

They Call Me "Mr. De" by Frank DeAngelis

Unmapped Potential by Julie Hasson and Missy Lennard

Word Shift by Joy Kirr

Your School Rocks by Ryan McLane and Eric Lowe

Technology & Tools

50 Things You Can Do with Google Classroom by Alice Keeler and Libbi Miller

50 Things to Go Further with Google Classroom by Alice Keeler and Libbi Miller

140 Twitter Tips for Educators by Brad Currie, Billy Krakower, and Scott Rocco

Block Breaker by Brian Aspinall

Code Breaker by Brian Aspinall

Google Apps for Littles by Christine Pinto and Alice Keeler

Master the Media by Julie Smith

Shake Up Learning by Kasey Bell

Social LEADia by Jennifer Casa-Todd

Teaching Math with Google Apps by Alice Keeler and Diana Herrington

Teachingland by Amanda Fox and Mary Ellen Weeks

Teaching Methods & Materials

All 4s and 5s by Andrew Sharos

Boredom Busters by Katie Powell

The Classroom Chef by John Stevens and Matt Vaudrey

Ditch That Homework by Matt Miller and Alice Keeler

Ditch That Textbook by Matt Miller

Don't Ditch That Tech by Matt Miller, Nate Ridgway, and Angelia Ridgway

EDrenaline Rush by John Meehan

Educated by Design by Michael Cohen, The Tech Rabbi

The EduProtocol Field Guide by Marlena Hebern and Jon Corippo

The EduProtocol Field Guide: Book 2 by Marlena Hebern and Jon Corippo

Instant Relevance by Denis Sheeran

LAUNCH by John Spencer and A.J. Juliani

Make Learning MAGICAL by Tisha Richmond

Pure Genius by Don Wettrick

The Revolution by Darren Ellwein and Derek McCoy

Shift This! by Joy Kirr

Spark Learning by Ramsey Musallam

Sparks in the Dark by Travis Crowder and Todd Nesloney

Table Talk Math by John Stevens

The Wild Card by Hope and Wade King

The Writing on the Classroom Wall by Steve Wyborney

Inspiration, Professional Growth & Personal Development

Be REAL by Tara Martin

Be the One for Kids by Ryan Sheehy

Creatively Productive by Lisa Johnson

The EduNinja Mindset by Jennifer Burdis

Empower Our Girls by Lynmara Colón and Adam Welcome

The Four O'Clock Faculty by Rich Czyz

How Much Water Do We Have? by Pete and Kris Nunweiler

P Is for Pirate by Dave and Shelley Burgess

A Passion for Kindness by Tamara Letter

The Path to Serendipity by Allyson Apsey

Sanctuaries by Dan Tricarico

Shattering the Perfect Teacher Myth by Aaron Hogan

Stories from Webb by Todd Nesloney

Talk to Me by Kim Bearden

Teach Me, Teacher by Jacob Chastain

TeamMakers by Laura Robb and Evan Robb

Through the Lens of Serendipity by Allyson Apsey

The Zen Teacher by Dan Tricarico

Children's Books

Beyond Us by Aaron Polansky

Cannonball In by Tara Martin

Dolphins in Trees by Aaron Polansky

I Want to Be a Lot by Ashley Savage

The Princes of Serendip by Allyson Apsey

Zom-Be a Design Thinker by Amanda Fox

ABOUT THE AUTHOR

ALICIA RAY is a veteran educator of thirteen years from North Carolina. She has taught PreK—eighth-grade students and currently serves as a digital learning coach and media coordinator in a STEM magnet middle school. She earned a Bachelor of Science in Elementary Education from Appalachian State University, a Master of Arts in Education in Instructional Technology, and a Master of Library Science from East Carolina University.

Alicia is passionate about being a catalyst for change and lifelong learning, and about inspiring others to be better today than they were yesterday. She believes every event in life contains a lesson and seeks to discover those lessons (sometimes learning them the hard way). Alicia enjoys seamlessly and effectively infusing technology into the classroom. She firmly believes that relationships with students and stakeholders are everything. Alicia uses virtual reality, blended learning environments, gamification, and game-based learning to engage and empower students while coaching teachers through co-planning and co-teaching. She encourages teachers to take risks by giving them a safe place to fail during these co-teaching experiences.

She began a journey of true introspection and implementation during the summer of 2018 through reading and blogging about the first fifty books published under the Dave Burgess Consulting, Inc. label, a journey she called #DBC50Summer. Never wanting to become stagnant again, she continues sharing her reflections and implementations using the hashtag #DBCBookBlogs.

She blogs frequently about #DBCBookBlogs and education at aliciaray.com and is active on Twitter as @iluveducating. She and her husband, Chris, have two intelligent, spunky, beautiful daughters, Bailey and Sophie.